Edexcel AS English Literature

Sue Dymoke   Ian McMechan   Mike Royston   Jennifer Smith

STUDENT BOOK

Contributors: Unit 1 Exploring Prose
Barbara Bleiman and Lucy Webster of the English and Media Centre

Consultant: Jen Greatrex

Skills Coverage Map

Skill/specification coverage	UNIT 1	UNIT 2
Defining poetry, narrative and drama	8-9, 50-51	
Building on your experience of poetry, prose and drama	10, 50, 83, 89, 99	119
Exploring the various types (genres) of poems and narratives	11-12, 52-3	
Understanding common poetic forms	12-19	
Understanding the structural devices used in poems, narratives and drama	20-24, 92	142-51
Understanding rhyme and rhythm in poems, and verse forms in drama	24-30	139-41
Analysing the choice of language (style) in poetry, narrative and drama	31-4, 71-4, 87, 92	139-41, 143-6, 148-50
Exploring imagery, symbols and motifs in poetry and narrative	34-7, 69-70, 81	
Exploring different kinds of narrative voice in poetry and prose	38-41, 56-60, 87	
Understanding tone and mood in poems	42-8	
Exploring openings and endings	53-5	131-4, 146-51
Understanding the difference between narrative voice and point of view	58-9	
Analysing how writers use dialogue in narrative	61-3	
Analysing the use of time and tense in narrative	64-8	
Understanding methods of characterisation in narrative and drama	75-6	135-8
Understanding plot, story and theme in narrative and drama	77-8, 92	142-5
Understanding different perspectives on drama (audiences', actors', directors', critics')		119-30
Analysing reviews		124-30, 171-2
Using the language, style and structure of different forms of writing, depending on context and purpose	72	121, 129, 179-82
Making connections and comparisons between selected texts	17-19, 24, 29-30, 32, 63, 68, 70, 91-101, 103-6	128-9, 153-6, 174
Relating texts to their context	75	122-3, 156-62, 164-6
Exploring readers' reactions to and interpretations of texts	47, 60, 85, 90, 96-8, 100-101, 111-13	151, 160, 163-72
Communicating clearly your responses to texts	29, 34, 74, 76, 81, 93, 105, 115-16	173-82
Constructing critical arguments about texts	107-9	175

Contents

Introduction   4

Unit 1: Explorations in Prose and Poetry   6

Introduction   6

Part 1: Exploring poetry   7
1. What is poetry?   8
2. Type   11
3. Form and structure   12
4. Rhyme   24
5. Rhythm   27
6. Language   31
7. Imagery   34
8. Voice   38
9. Tone and mood   42

Part 2: Exploring prose   49
1. Introduction: what is a narrative?   50
2. Different types of narrative: genre   51
3. Exploring narrative openings   53
4. Modes of telling: narrative voice and point of view   55
5. Dialogue and voices   61
6. Narrative structure   64
7. Symbols and motifs   69
8. Prose style   71
9. Methods of characterisation   75
10. Presentation of themes   77

Part 3: Preparing for the exam   79
1. Section A: unseen poetry   80
2. Section A: unseen prose   86
3. Section B: poetry   91
4. Section C: prose   103

Unit 2: Explorations in Drama   117

Introduction   117

Section A: Responding to drama   119
1. Introduction   119
2. Viewing drama: the audience's perspective   119
3. Performing drama: the actor's and director's
   perspective   122
4. Reviewing drama: the critic's perspective   124
5. Commenting on drama: voices from inside and
   outside the theatre   127

Section B: Analysing key elements of drama   131
1. Introduction   131
2. How dramatists set the scene   131

3. How dramatists develop the characters   135
4. How dramatists use language and verse form   139
5. How dramatists advance the plot   142
6. How dramatists construct an ending   146

Section C: Comparing plays in their context   152
1. Introduction   152
2. Exemplar assignments for the explorative study   152
3. Spotting links, finding connections: how to
   get started   153
4. Making a plan   153
5. Developing connections and comparisons   155
6. Identifying contexts for your plays   156
7. Relating your plays to their context: an example   157
8. Building material on context into your
   explorative study   159
9. Writing about context   160
10. The history of English drama, 1300–1800   161

Section D: Exploring others' reactions to plays   163
1. Introduction   163
2. The range of critical reception: an example   163
3. Researching the critical reception of your plays   167
4. Including critical reception in your explorative
   study   168
5. Using critical reception by theatre professionals
   in your explorative study   169
6. Summing up this section   172

Section E: Writing your explorative study   173
1. Meeting the Assessment objectives   173
2. Making sure you compare: some strategies   174
3. Making sure you argue: some strategies   175
4. Making sure you quote: some strategies   176
5. Making sure you express yourself well: some
   strategies   177
6. Getting it right   178

Section F: Writing your creative critical response   179
1. Choosing your topic   179
2. Choosing your format   180
3. Planning and drafting   180
4. Writing appropriately   181

Glossary   183

GCE AS English Literature

Introduction

Welcome to English Literature at Advanced level. From your previous study of literature you will already be familiar with the genres of poetry, prose and drama.

Now you will have the opportunity to explore new texts in these categories in new ways.

How can I make English Literature most rewarding?

- Enjoy reading – even when the text may seem unfamiliar and strange. The more you stick with it, the more you will learn and be able to say about it.
- Try to read more widely than just the texts for the course – if you find a poet or a playwright or a writer whose work interests you then search out something else written by that person. Look them up on websites or in sound archives too.
- Find out what other people, including the writers themselves, have said about the texts you are studying.
- Practise writing about your texts. During the course you will need to do this sometimes concisely by providing short answer responses, sometimes in essays and sometimes creatively.

What texts will I explore?

Unit 1 – Explorations in Prose and Poetry: These texts cover the period from 1800 to 1945. You will study poetry and prose. You will learn about ways to analyse poems and how narrative works in novels. You will also develop your skills of comparison and argument. By argument we mean the ability to take an essay title and develop a written response which allows the reader to understand what you think and what you have found in the texts you have studied to prove your points. There is one further explanation that will help you. When literary students are asked to develop their *critical reading and supply a critical response or critical appreciation* this does not mean that they are expected to write negatively about what they have read, but that they are using the agreed literary approaches and methods to bring their responses to the reader.

Unit 2 – Explorations in Drama: The drama texts must include a play by Shakespeare as well as wider reading about the factors that influence writers. You will also be expected to prove that you know how other people have responded to the texts. Your teacher or tutor will help you to gain access to these aspects but you can help yourself by reading critical reviews in newspapers and magazines, watching review programmes on TV and taking an interest in news stories about literary events such as prize awards and festivals. If you have the chance to go to a live performance try to take the opportunity. Thousands of people all over the world regularly put literature at the heart of their free time and many choose it as a means to earn a living.

Both Units build on the skills you developed at GCSE in studying literature and develop your understanding of new literary terms so you can write successfully about different aspects of your texts. There's a whole world of texts out there – not counting the ones yet to be written.

We wish you success as you build your confidence and skills in reading them, responding to them, and enjoying them.

Jen Greatrex, Edexcel

How to use this book

This **Student Book** is divided into Unit 1 and Unit 2:

- **Unit 1** supports your work for the AS exam on poetry and prose.
- **Unit 2** supports your work for the AS coursework on drama.

The **Teaching and Assessment CD-ROM** provides additional support for the poetry and prose texts you will study for the exam. It can be used alongside this book.

Unit 1   Explorations in Prose and Poetry: an outline

Unit 1 in this **Student Book** is divided into three parts. They can be used in the order they are printed, or you can move between them. They are:

Part 1: Exploring Poetry (pages 7–48). This part helps you develop your skills in reading and analysing poems for Sections A and B of the exam. You are given an in-depth understanding of the key features of poetry and the techniques poets use.

Part 2: Exploring Prose (pages 49–78). This part helps you develop your skills in reading and analysing prose for Sections A and C of the exam. You are given an in-depth understanding of the key features of prose and the techniques prose writers use.

Part 3: Preparing for the exam (pages 79–116). This part helps you prepare in detail for the three Sections of the exam. It gives you step-by-step guidance on how to do what the examiners expect.

> **In the exam**
>
> Section A asks you questions on unseen poetry *or* prose. Section B asks you for an essay on poetry. Section C asks you for an essay on prose.

Unit 2   Explorations in Drama: an outline

Unit 2 in this **Student Book** is divided into three paired sections. They can be used in the order they are printed or you can move between them. They are:

Sections A and B (pages 119–151). These sections provide you with a foundation for your coursework. They help you develop your skills in reading and commenting on plays.

Sections C and D (pages 152–172). These sections help you plan and prepare your main piece of coursework – the Explorative Study on two plays from 1300–1800.

Sections E and F (pages 173–182). These sections help you write both of your coursework pieces – the Explorative Study and the Creative Critical Response.

Unit 1

Explorations in prose and poetry

What you will do in the course

In Unit 1 of Edexcel AS English Literature, you will:

- analyse unprepared (or 'unseen') poetry and prose
- study a group of poems on a common theme
- study one nineteenth or twentieth-century novel and relate it to a second text.

In your work on poetry, you will learn:

- how writers make use of the conventions of poetry
- how to identify and comment on the key features of poetry
- how to apply your knowledge of poetry to unseen and prescribed texts.

In your work on prose, you will learn:

- how writers make use of narrative
- how to identify and comment on the key features of narrative
- how to apply your knowledge of narrative to unseen and prescribed texts.

How you will be examined

- There is one exam of 2 hours 15 minutes.
- In Section A you will provide three short responses on an unprepared poem OR prose extract. (20 marks: a) 5 marks b) 5 marks c) 10 marks)
- In Section B you will answer an essay question comparing prescribed poems. (40 marks)
- In Section C you will answer an essay question linking together the core and the second text. (40 marks)

What the examiners are looking for

Examiners use three Assessment objectives (AOs) to mark your answers.

Assessment objective		What this means in practice
AO1	Articulate creative, informed and relevant responses to literary texts, using appropriate terminology and concepts, and coherent, accurate written expression	You should use: • ideas from literary study • suitable literary terms • a clear and fluent style.
AO2	Demonstrate detailed critical understanding in analysing the ways in which structure, form and language shape meanings in literary texts	You should show: • an understanding of how language conveys meaning • an understanding of how form and structure convey meaning • an understanding of how language, form and structure combine to convey meaning.
AO3	Explore connections and comparisons between different literary texts, informed by interpretations of other readers	You should show: • an awareness of how texts compare • an awareness of how texts can be interpreted differently.

Part 1 Exploring poetry

This part of the book explores the techniques and key features of poetry that poets use in their craft. Understanding these key genre features of poetry, as listed in the Literature specification, will inform your responses to Section A (if you choose Unseen Poetry) and Section B (the essay on your prescribed poems) in your exam.

Introduction

In **Section A** you can choose to answer questions on a poem or on a prose passage. You will not have seen the poem or the prose passage before.

In **Section B** of the exam you have to write an essay that compares and contrasts at least two poems on a common topic, from a selection of poems you have studied.

Contents

This part of the book helps you develop your skills in reading and analysing poems for Sections A and B of the exam. The sub-sections below cover the aspects of poetry study listed in the Specification. These are:

1 What is poetry?   8
2 Type   11
3 Form and structure   12
4 Rhyme   24
5 Rhythm   27
6 Language   31
7 Imagery   34
8 Voice   38
9 Tone and mood   42

Additional support

The **Teaching and Assessment CD-ROM** provides detailed material for studying all the prescribed poetry groupings in Section B. It is designed to be used with this part of the book.

1 What is poetry?

The word poetry originates from the Greek word 'poiesis' meaning 'a making' or 'a creating' and from a time when poetry was predominantly an oral form of carefully crafted, patterned language which was recited to listeners and then passed on to others through the medium of speech. Spoken poetry is with us all from birth, in the rhythms of words we babble when we are babies, and the word-play and rhymes we enjoy as children long before we have learned to read. Poetry of course comes in many written forms too and can serve a variety of functions in people's lives, such as to help them make sense of their grief or their joy, or to capture a key moment or experience.

Over the centuries, many people have attempted to define poetry. You have only to look in a dictionary or carry out an internet search to find that every definition has a slightly different take on what poetry is. Many of these definitions do share a sense that poetry contains language which has been crafted in some way. In this section you will discover more about the different aspects of this craft – for example how poets choose and use types and forms of poetry, how they make rhythmic and rhyming patterns with language, how they create images, tones, moods and a variety of voices to express what they wish to say. Poetry provokes many different reactions from its audiences and you will all have your own personal responses to the poems you are studying. This section will help you to develop an in-depth understanding of the different features of the craft and to express your views with confidence.

Activity 1

Think about the following comments. How easy would it be to replace the words 'poetry' or 'poet' with the words 'prose' or 'prose writer'? What do the comments reveal to you about the nature of poetry?

> They said he was the last poet of the grass court era.

> Look at his movement on the pitch! Sheer poetry!

> The way that car purred along the open road was poetry in motion.

> She's a poet and she doesn't know it!

The comments reveal something of the special nature of poetry and, at the same time, the way it is rooted within our consciousness and the rhythms of everyday life. It is interesting to see how sports journalists often use the word 'poetry' in their accounts of notable sporting performances. The poet Tom Leonard writes that 'if you dribble past five defenders it isn't called sheer prose'. What do you think he is saying about poetry in making this comment?

Activity 2

1   Read the following descriptions of poetry and the comments on the impact that poetry has on its readers. They were written by poets, critics and those involved in English teaching.

What is poetry?

'a verbal contraption'
W.H. Auden

'Like a microscope'
Richard Andrews

'a tough old bird'
David Horner

'The best words in the best order'
Samuel Taylor Coleridge

'a jigsaw puzzle'
Michael Baldwin

'a knit of words'
George Steiner

poetry demands of its readership
'a new effort of attention'
D.H. Lawrence

'Poetry can tell us what human beings are. It can tell us why we stumble and fall and how, miraculously, we can stand up.'
Maya Angelou

'Prose is like TV and poetry is like radio.'
Simon Armitage

'Poetry is … speech with song in it, the song made by words made to dance.'
Robert Nye

Poems are 'objects crafted in a medium of riddling wordplay, yielding a range of meanings.'
Michael Benton and Geoff Fox

'Poetry is a concise way of participating in others' experience.'
Jay Rogoff

'Poetry cannot be defined, only experienced.'
Christopher Logue

'Poetry springs from a level below meaning; it is a molecular thing, a pattern of sound and image.'
Nuala Ní Dhomhnaill

'What is good poetry if not language awake to its own powers?'
Jane Hirshfield

2   Sort the descriptions into different groups (for example, you could group those that focus on the content or the language of poetry). You will find that some will fit into a number of different groups.

3   With a partner, discuss how you have grouped them. Explore together what you have found. What aspects of poetry do the descriptions highlight as being significant? Which groups and individual descriptions do you find most interesting? Which reflect your own views on poetry? Do the descriptions reveal any of the pleasures or difficulties with poetry that you have experienced so far?

4   Share your ideas with the rest of your group.

Take it further

Discuss whether you think there are any aspects of poetry that are not covered by the descriptions in Activity 2. If you think something is missing, try to write your own description and share it with the rest of your group.

Your previous experiences of poetry

In completing Activity 2 you have begun to explore some of your own views about poetry. In your discussions you may have touched on some of your previous experiences of reading, listening to and/or studying poetry.

We are now going to focus more fully on these previous experiences in order to highlight some of the skills and knowledge you need to develop further during your preparation for the exam.

Activity 3

1   With a partner or in a small group, briefly discuss the following:

   a any poetry you have read or studied before and how you responded to it. Talk about specific poems that impressed you in one way or another, poems you found most challenging and poems you disliked at first, but then changed your view on

   b the different ways in which your poetry study was assessed (eg as a coursework essay, writing your own poems in the style of another poet and providing a commentary, short answer questions in an exam, as part of a speaking and listening assessment)

   c the methods of assessment you found the most difficult, the easiest, the most rewarding, and why.

2   Individually, read the statements in the chart and on a copy, tick the one box on each row which you think applies to your level of experience at this stage.

Poetry experiences				
Statement	A lot	Some	A little	None
a I can identify different types of poems (eg **sonnet**, **ballad**, **lyric**, **free verse**).				
b I have experience of talking and writing about rhyme and rhythm in poetry.				
c I have experience of talking and writing about forms and structures of poems and why they have been chosen.				
d I have experience of talking and writing about voice in poetry.				
e I have experience of talking and writing about a poet's use of **imagery**.				
f I have experience of talking about tone and mood in poetry.				
g I have experience of talking and writing about language choices made by poets and the impact that these have on audiences.				
h I have experience of writing poems.				
i I have experience of reading poems aloud and sharing my ideas in class and small group discussion.				
j I have experience of exploring different readers' interpretations of poems.				
k I have experience of comparing and contrasting poems.				
l I have experience of writing a comparative exam essay about several poems.				
m I have experience of writing about unseen poems in an exam (poems not previously read or studied).				
n I have experience of using a 'clean' copy of a poetry anthology (ie one without my notes) in an exam.				
o I am familiar with and can use technical terminology when I am analysing poems (eg metaphor, caesura, onomatopoeia, personification).				

3   With a partner or with your teacher:

   a explore your answers and identify which aspects of poetry (a–g in the chart) and which experiences or features of the way poetry is assessed in Unit 1 (h–o) you feel most confident about at this stage

   b focus on the points you need to gain more experience of for your exam. Talk about the boxes you ticked with specific reference to poems, classroom activities and assessments that you have previously completed. You may wish to colour code or shade in areas of particular strength or weakness and/or to add brief notes to your copy of the chart to remind you.

4 Keep your completed chart so you can revisit it later in the light of your developing experience.

In the rest of this section you will learn more about various poetic features (a–g in the chart above). You will also explore poems in different ways and begin to focus on how these areas will be assessed (h–o).

2 Type

When we talk, hear or read about a type of poetry, the word 'type' is being used to convey the general form, structure or distinguishing characteristics of a poem. Not all poems will conform to a 'type' but many do and there are many different types of poems. For example, one type is lyric poetry. This is poetry that expresses feeling and emotion rather than telling a story. It is the most commonly found type of poetry. Lyric poems are usually quite short and have a song-like quality due to their use of rhyming and rhythmical structures. 'O, My Love is like a Red, Red Rose' by Robert Burns and 'Down by the Salley Gardens' by W.B. Yeats are examples of lyric poetry.

Look at the chart below for some other different types.

Type of poetry	Examples
Metaphysical poetry	'The Definition of Love' by Andrew Marvell
	'The Flea' by John Donne
Romantic poetry	'Ode to a Nightingale' by John Keats
	'She Walks in Beauty' by Lord Byron
First World War poetry	'Dulce et Decorum Est' by Wilfred Owen
	'Glory of Women' by Siegfried Sassoon
Protest poetry	'The Rights of Woman' by Anna Letitia Barbauld
	'The Mask of Anarchy' by Percy Bysshe Shelley
Beat poetry	'Howl' by Allen Ginsberg
	'Constantly Risking Absurdity' by Lawrence Ferlinghetti
Bush poetry	'The Man from Snowy River' by A.B. 'Banjo' Patterson
	'My Country' by Dorothea Mackellar

The types above are all associated with particular philosophical movements, historical periods, events or (as with Australian Bush poetry) geographical locations. The poems contain distinctive features of **form**, **structure**, **rhythm**, **rhyme**, language or imagery. They are often concerned with particular topics or themes that were of significance to the time when and/or the place where they were written, although many speak at least as directly to twenty-first-century readers as they did to the people of their own time.

Here are some more different types of poetry.

Type of poetry	Examples
Performance poetry – written to be performed to a listening audience, it has a distinctive rhythm and can be about a wide range of topics.	'Dis Poetry' by Benjamin Zephaniah
	'R.A.W.' by Patience Agabi
Kinetic, **shape** or **concrete poetry** – with a distinctive shape or pattern on the page, which reflects the topic, kinetic poems seem to make words move in lively ways and need to be seen to be fully appreciated.	'The Honey Pot' by Alan Riddell (page 23)
	'Quiet Secret' by Robert Froman
Found poetry – written by selecting words and phrases from a found object such as an advert, road sign, newspaper article or recipe. No other words are added and, in strict found poetry, the words have to be used in the same order as the original.	'My Greenhouse' and 'Found Poem: Glasgow' by Edwin Morgan

Key terms

sonnet
ballad
lyric
free verse
imagery
form
structure
rhythm
rhyme
performance poetry
kinetic, shape or
  concrete poetry
found poetry

Activity 4

1 As a group, each find a copy of a different poem from those listed in either of the charts on page 11. Make a list of the distinctive features that suggest the poem belongs to a particular type.

2 Use your school, college or local library or the internet to locate at least one other example of the same type of poem for yourself and identify any of the same distinctive features you have already listed in 1.

3 Present your findings to your group and agree on a list of distinctive features for each of the types of poetry you have investigated.

Take it further

What other types of poetry can you discover and what distinctive features do they have? Search for other types (e.g. syllabic, pastoral, Georgian, satirical or love poetry). Use your school, college or local library or the internet to help you in your search. Make notes on their distinctive features for future reference and report back on your findings.

Independent research

When researching, look in a library for poetry anthologies that feature poems from specific periods or on particular themes. The websites listed below also provide some useful starting points. Make sure that you always cross check information gleaned from internet sites and acknowledge your sources.

- www.thepoetryhouse.org/Petryrooms/rooms.html
- www.poets.org/
- www.poetryarchive.org
- http://en.wikipedia.org/wiki/List_of_poetry_groups_and_movements
- www.bushverse.com/

Further research will help you to consolidate your understanding. You will find that the type a poem falls into is often closely (but not exclusively) linked to a particular form or structure, and distinctive use of language, rhythm or rhyme. However, not all poems conform to any particular type at all and others can be considered to belong to more than one type. For example, a kinetic poem such as 'Easter Wings' by George Herbert is also seen as a Metaphysical poem. Poets borrow ideas and develop their writing from many different influences and you need to be alert to the ways poems conform to any particular type or how they might break the mould through their use of language and form.

This section has introduced you to the idea of types of poems. In the following sections you will have the chance to develop your understanding of the specific features of poetry that contribute to the overall effects and meanings created.

3 Form and structure

Form is the shape of the poem on the page. As you will probably already know from your experiences of reading and writing of poetry in KS3 and at GCSE, poetry can be written in many different forms. Traditional forms with a set number of lines or syllables, like sonnets or haikus, can be very tightly structured. Alternatively poets can adapt these forms and use them in a looser way or choose to write in free verse.

As you will see in Activity 5, poets have very different views about form. They might begin writing spontaneously and shape the poem into a particular form at a later stage, or they might make a very conscious choice about the poem's form early on during the drafting process – even before they have written a word. The finished form is always an important factor in terms of the poem's meaning and impact on the reader.

Poets on form

Activity 5

1 Read the comments about form below, written by five very different poets.

2 From your analysis of each comment, what can you conclude about each poet's views on the importance of form? Or about the connection between poetic form and a poem's subject matter? Add your key points to a copy of the table below.

Comment	What views on the place and importance of form in poetry are expressed?	What views on the relationship between poetic form and a poem's subject matter are expressed?
A		
B		

A 'I believe content determines form, and yet that content is discovered only *in* form. Like everything living, it is a mystery. The revelation of form itself can be a deep joy; yet I think form *as means* should never obtrude, whether from intention or carelessness, between the reader and the essential force of the poem, it must be so fused with that force.' (Denise Levertov, an English poet who emigrated to the US and wrote tightly structured, clearly expressed free verse)

B 'Form is a straitjacket in the way that a straitjacket was a straitjacket for Houdini.' (Paul Muldoon, an Irish writer, a professor of poetry and long-term resident in the US)

C 'You can't write a poem until you have a form. It's like … trying to play an untuned instrument.' (Les Murray, a prize-winning Australian poet)

D 'I think there is a 'fluid' as well as a 'solid' content, that some poems may have form as a tree has form, some as water poured into a vase. That most symmetrical forms have certain uses. That a vast number of subjects cannot be precisely, and therefore, not properly rendered in symmetrical forms.' (Ezra Pound, a controversial and highly influential American writer who emigrated to London in 1909 with a mission to reinvent poetry in a form which, in his view, was truer to the rhythms of everyday life and experience; he made a significant contribution to the development of Modernism in poetry)

E 'I like to write in a patterned arrangement, with rhymes; stanza as it follows stanza being identical in number of syllables and rhyme-plan, with the first stanza… I have a liking for the long syllable followed by three (or more) short syllables , – 'lying on the air there is a bird,' and for the inconspicuous or light rhyme, – 'let' in flageolet … I feel that form is the outward equivalent of a determining inner conviction, and that the rhythm is the person.' (Marianne Moore, an American poet who frequently used complicated syllabic forms)

For some poets, form is their first consideration as soon as they start to draft a poem, whereas for others the form becomes increasingly apparent as they begin to shape their words on the page. Some poets choose to adopt a form in the way it has been used traditionally. Others might use the spirit of the form, but adapt elements of its structure to suit their own purposes (eg unrhymed sonnets or **haikus** with 20 rather than 17 syllables). All poets' choices of form will be closely allied to the effects they want to create in their poems and the meanings they wish to convey to their readers.

Key term

haiku

Poetic forms

There are many forms a poem can take. Those listed in the next activity are the most common ones you will encounter, but there are others too.

Activity 6

1   Which forms do you recognise from the descriptions below? First, match the poetic forms you recognise with their jumbled descriptions. You can use a photocopy of the two lists and cut out the elements like cards so that you can match them easily and make a collage as a record for future reference.

2   Discuss the unknown forms as a class and decide on the correct descriptions.

Haiku	**A** A poem, written as a lament in memory of a person, place or even a way of life, that has a melancholy tone, but does not follow any set metrical pattern.
Limerick	**B** A five-lined poem, which usually tells the story of a character from a particular place, and has a distinctive rhythm and an *aabba* **rhyme scheme**.
Ballad	**C** A poem that addresses an object, event or element of landscape or a person, sometimes in an elevated style; modern versions of the form can be witty or even irreverent.
Sonnet	**D** A 19-line poem with an *aba* rhyme scheme, and five three-lined and one four-lined **stanzas**, in which lines from the first stanza are picked up and repeated in the rest of the poem.
Ode	**E** A 39-lined poem with six stanzas and a final three-lined **envoi** (summary), in which the six words in each stanza are repeated in a set pattern but a changing order.
Sestina	**F** Originally a Japanese form, a three-lined poem of 17 syllables often capturing a tiny moment in time.
Villanelle	**G** A 14-lined poem in iambic pentameter, usually following either a Shakespearean or Petrarchan form.
Ghazal	**H** Rhyming pairs of lines usually in iambic pentameter with ten alternately stressed syllables and a rhyme scheme progressing *aa bb cc* and so on; the strong rhyme scheme and very regular beat made it a popular choice for satirical or epigrammatic poetry in the seventeenth and eighteenth centuries.
Elegy	**I** A poem that tells a story or describes a series of events.
Free verse	**J** A narrative poem, often written in **quatrains**, with a tight rhyme scheme and a memorable rhythm, which usually tells a dramatic story (eg Broadside poetry, Literary and Folk ballads are all variations of this form).
Epigram	**K** A lengthy narrative poem that is heroic and written in an elevated style.
Blank verse	**L** A unrhymed poem written in **iambic pentameter**, said to mirror the rhythms of everyday speech.
Narrative poem	**M** A popular verse form in Urdu, which is increasingly used in English, consisting of at least five couplets; the first couplet has an *aa* structure with subsequent couplets *ba*, *ca*, *da*, etc; the final couplet traditionally includes a reference to the poet's real or literary name.
Epic	**N** Poetry that does not use traditional rhyme schemes or metrical arrangements.
Heroic couplets	**O** A short witty saying usually about an event or a person and written in very compressed language.

Forms can be governed or shaped by metrics, syllables, rhyme, the pattern to be created on the page or combinations of several of these factors.

Activity 7

1 Read the following poems, taking particular note of the form of each one and the effect this form has on the impact of the poem.

2 With a partner, discuss the following questions:

a What form do you think is being used in each case?

b The choice of form is integral to the meaning and the effects the poet wishes to create. Why do you think the poet chose the particular form?

Rain

On this bleak hut, and solitude, and me
Remembering again that I shall die
And neither hear the rain nor give it thanks
For washing me cleaner than I have been
5 Since I was born in this solitude.
Blessed are the dead that the rain rains upon:
But here I pray that none whom once I loved
Is dying tonight or lying still awake
Solitary, listening to the rain,
10 Either in pain or thus in sympathy
Helpless among the living and the dead,
Like a cold water among broken reeds,
Myriads of broken reeds all still and stiff,
Like me who have no love which this wild rain
15 Has not dissolved except the love of death,
If love it be for what is perfect and
Cannot, the tempest tells me, disappoint.

Edward Thomas

Oh, oh, you will be sorry for that word!

Oh, oh, you will be sorry for that word!
Give back my book and take my kiss instead.
Was it my enemy or my friend I heard,
'What a big book for such a little head!'
5 Come, I will show you now my newest hat,
And you may watch me purse my mouth and prink!
Oh, I shall love you still, and all of that.
I never again shall tell you what I think.
I shall be sweet and crafty, soft and sly;
10 You will not catch me reading any more:
I shall be called a wife to pattern by;
And some day when you knock and push the door,
Some sane day, not too bright and not too stormy,
I shall be gone, and you may whistle for me.

Edna St. Vincent Millay

In the village pond

In the village pond
the full moon is shaken by
the first falling leaf.

James Kirkup

Hoard

What kind of figure did he cut
huddled in the dusk, gut wound
packed with sphagnum,
as he sank into the bog
5 his offering of weaponry,
blades courteously broken,
his killed cherished swords?

Kathleen Jamie

The Sisters

We were two daughters of one race;
She was the fairest in the face.
    The wind is blowing in turret and tree.
They were together, and she fell;
5 Therefore revenge became me well.
    O, the earl was fair to see!

She died; she went to burning flame;
She mix'd her ancient blood with shame.
    The wind is howling in turret and tree.
10 Whole weeks and months, and early and late,
To win his love I lay in wait.
    O, the earl was fair to see!

I made a feast; I bade him come;
I won his love, I brought him home,
15   The wind is roaring in turret and tree.
And after supper on a bed,
Upon my lap he laid his head.
    O, the earl was fair to see!

20 I kiss'd his eyelids into rest,
His ruddy cheeks upon my breast.
    The wind is raging in turret and tree.
I hated him with the hate of hell,
But I loved his beauty passing well.
    O, the earl was fair to see!

25 I rose up in the silent night;
I made my dagger sharp and bright.
    The wind is raving in turret and tree.
As half-asleep his breath he drew,
Three time I stabb'd him thro' and thro'.
30   O, the earl was fair to see!

I curl'd and comb'd his comely head,
He looked so grand when he was dead.
    The wind is blowing in turret and tree.
I wrapt his body in the sheet,
35 And laid him at his mother's feet.
    O, the earl was fair to see!

Alfred, Lord Tennyson

Preparing for the exam (Section B)

- The ability to compare poems is a key skill you need to use in the exam. You may already have gained some experience at GCSE. Activity 9 will help you to develop your skills further.

- Make sure that you can identify the form of each of your chosen poems, and can comment on how the form impacts on its meaning.

3 Once you have explored the overall form and outer shape of each poem, reread them and look out for other distinctive features. Discuss the following questions with your partner.

a Is there a noticeable rhyming pattern? If so, what effect does this have? If the poet has chosen not to rhyme, what does this enable the writer to do with lines and line ending?

b How would you describe the rhythm of each poem? How does it work to drive the poem along?

c What can you say about any other structural elements of each poem? Listen to the way the lines break up, stop, move and link together. What effect do they have on you and on the meanings conveyed?

d What other patterns or aspects of language do you notice?

Key term

Limerick	Epic
Ode	Heroic couplets
Sestina	rhyme scheme
Villanelle	stanza
Ghazal	envoi
Elegy	quatrain
Narrative poem	

Sonnets

Now let's look in more detail at the different ways poets use the sonnet form. The two most common forms – Shakespearian and Petrarchan – are outlined here, although you will also come across **Miltonic** and **Spenserian sonnets** as well as other unnamed variations on the form.

Key terms

Miltonic sonnet
Spenserian sonnet
volta

Shakespearian sonnets

Edna St. Vincent Millay's poem 'Oh, oh, you will be sorry for that word!' (page 15) is an example of a sonnet, in the form so expertly crafted by Shakespeare. Shakespearean sonnets have distinctive features:

- they consist of 14 lines
- each line is in iambic pentameter (a sequence of five soft and five hard stresses)
- they contain three quatrains which rhyme *abab cdcd efef*
- they contain a **volta**, a turn of thought in the poem which often occurs after the first two quatrains
- they end with a rhyming couplet: *gg*.

Activity 8

1   Reread 'Oh, oh, you will be sorry for that word!' and revisit what you have already discovered about its overall shape.

2   Now discuss other aspects of this poem with a partner. Use the following questions to help you:

   a   What effect does use of iambic pentameter have on how you hear the speaker's voice in the poem?

   b   How does the poet use the 'volta' in the poem to mark a change in mood?

   c   What impact does the final rhyming couplet have?

3   Write a short statement explaining how you think Millay has used the sonnet form.

4   Compare your statement with your partner's.

Activity 9

Now compare Millay's sonnet on page 15 with Shakespeare's 'Sonnet 138', below.

1   First identify the features of the Shakespearean sonnet (as listed above), annotating a copy of each poem.

When my love swears that she is made of truth,
I do believe her though I know she lies,
That she might think me some untutored youth,
Unlearned in the world's false subtleties.
5   Thus vainly thinking that she thinks me young,
Although she knows my days are past the best,
Simply I credit her false-speaking tongue:
On both sides this is simple truth suppressed.
But wherefore says she not she is unjust?
10   And, wherefore say not I that I am old?
O love's best habit is in seeming trust,
And age in love loves not to have years told.
      Therefore I lie with her, and she with me,
      And in our faults by lies we flattered be.

William Shakespeare

William Shakespeare

2 Now think about how Shakespeare uses the sonnet form. Consider the following questions to help you.

    a How does the speaker in the poem present the relationship between the two lovers?

    b What final statement is made about the relationship in the concluding couplet?

3 How does the presentation of the relationship in Shakespeare's sonnet compare with the way the partnership in Millay's sonnet is portrayed? Write a short paragraph explaining how each relationship seems to be presented and drawing at least one comparison between them.

4 Which sonnet did you personally find most difficult and which the most thought-provoking to read? Jot down a list of reasons for your preferences and discuss them in your group.

Petrarchan sonnet

Another widely used sonnet form is the Petrarchan, so called because it was first used by a fourteenth-century Italian poet named Petrarch who wrote a sonnet sequence for his beloved Laura. Petrarchan sonnets also have distinctive features:

- they consist of 14 lines
- they are written in **iambic pentameter**
- they are divided into two distinct parts: the first eight lines are an **octet** (eight lines of two quatrains, rhyming *abba abba*) and the final six are a **sestet** (rhyming *cdcdcd*)
- they include a 'turn' after the octet with the sestet offering a kind of resolution or answer to the problem or idea explored in the octet.

Activity 10

1 Read the example of a Petrarchan sonnet below.

2 Annotate the distinctive features of Petrarchan sonnets on a copy of the poem.

> **Composed Upon Westminster Bridge**
> **September 3rd, 1802**
>
> Earth has not anything to show more fair;
> Dull would he be of soul who could pass by
> A sight so touching in its majesty;
> This city now doth, like a garment, wear
> 5 The beauty of the morning; silent, bare,
> Ships, towers, domes, theatres, and temples lie
> Open unto the fields, and to the sky;
> All bright and glittering in the smokeless air.
> Never did sun more beautifully steep
> 10 In his first splendour, valley, rock, or hill;
> Ne'er saw I, never felt, a calm so deep!
> The river glideth at his own sweet will:
> Dear God! the very houses seem asleep;
> And all that mighty heart is lying still!
>
> *William Wordsworth*

Activity 11

1   Now read the following selection of four sonnets. Try to read each poem at least twice. Hear it in your head and also listen to it read aloud.

Grandfather

They brought him in on a stretcher from the world,
Wounded but humorous; and he soon recovered.
Boiler-rooms, rows upon rows of gantries rolled
Away to reveal a landscape of a childhood
5   Only he could recapture. Even on cold
Mornings he is up at six with a block of wood
Or a box of nails, discreetly up to no good
Or banging round the house like a four-year-old –

Never there when you call. But after dark
10   You hear his great boots thumping in the hall
And in he comes, as cute as they come. Each night
His shrewd eyes bolt the door and set the clock
Against the future, then his light goes out.
Nothing escapes him; he escapes us all.

Derek Mahon

Sonnets from the Portuguese
XIV

If thou must love me, let it be for nought
Except for love's sake only. Do not say,
'I love her for her smile … her look … her way
Of speaking gently, … for a trick of thought
5   That falls in well with mine, and certes brought
A sense of pleasant ease on such a day' –
For these things in themselves, Beloved, may
Be changed, or change for thee, – and love, so wrought,
May be unwrought so. Neither love me for
10   Thine own dear pity's wiping my cheeks dry, -
A creature might forget to weep, who bore
They comfort long, and lose they love thereby!
But love me for love's sake, that evermore
Thou mayst love on, through love's eternity.

Elizabeth Barrett Browning

Ozymandias

I met a traveller from an antique land
Who said: Two vast and trunkless legs of stone
Stand in the desert … Near them, on the sand,
Half sunk, a shattered visage lies, whose frown,
5   And wrinkled lip, and sneer of cold command,
Tell that its sculptor well those passions read
Which yet survive, stamped on these lifeless things,
The hand that mocked them, and the heart that fed:
And on the pedestal these words appear:
10   'My name is Ozymandias, king of kings:
Look on my works, ye Mighty, and despair!'
Nothing beside remains. Round the decay
Of that colossal wreck, boundless and bare
The lone and level sands stretch far away.

Percy Bysshe Shelley

Poem

And if it snowed and snow covered the drive
he took a spade and tossed it to one side.
And always tucked his daughter up at night.
And slippered her the one time that she lied.

5   And every week he tipped up half his wage.
And what he did not spend each week he saved.
And praised his wife for every meal she made.
And once, for laughing, punched her in the face.

And for his mum he hired a private nurse.
10   And every Sunday taxied her to church.
And he blubbed when she went from bad to worse.
And twice he lifted ten quid from her purse.

Here's how they rated him when they looked back:
sometimes he did this, sometimes he did that.

Simon Armitage

2   After reading, write a short statement answering each of these questions:

   a Which sonnets follow either the Shakespearean or the Petrarchan forms in a strict fashion?

   b Which other rhyming patterns and verse structures can you find?

3   Add an example from one of the poems as evidence to support each of your statements.

4   Think about the effects that the strict sonnet form and the other patterns and structures have on what is expressed. Add your analysis or conclusion to each statement.

5   Add a sentence or two, drawing some conclusions about the way the sonnet form is used by the different poets. The following questions may help you.

   • Why do you think each poet has written about the chosen subject matter in the form of a sonnet?

   • What conclusions can you come to about the way poets use sonnet forms to explore ideas, emotions and experiences?

Structural features: the inner workings of the poem

We cannot really say a certain sort of car has been well made or would be a good vehicle to drive just by taking a casual glance at it on a garage forecourt. We need to look under the bonnet at the mechanics, the engine. In addition, if we want to understand what it would be like to drive a car or whether it would be comfortable, relaxing, safe or thrilling to be a passenger in it, we have to experience the car on the road, take it for a test drive to hear and feel it in action. In the same way, to understand a poem's form and the effect it has on us, the readers, we need to do much more than look at the form that the poet has used. We need to hear how the words sound and knit together to make the poem perform in a certain way. We need to soak up its atmosphere and experience how its elements work together (or perhaps in opposition) to create this effect.

In the previous sub-sections on type and form, you have already begun to piece together key elements of a poem's make up and to understand how these work. In the rest of this section you will focus even further on the inner workings of the poem. But remember that these should not be written about in isolation from what has gone before.

You may already be familiar with some of the technical terms in the next sub-section. If you are, then take a moment just to refresh your memory and try to recall how and where you have seen and heard each term being used previously.

End-stopped lines

The punctuation at the end of **end-stopped lines** of poetry demarcates a short or long pause.

Activity 12

Look back at Simon Armitage's 'Poem' on page 19. Every line in this poem is end-stopped.

1   How does this make the poem sound when you read it aloud? Which of the following descriptions seem appropriate?

clipped	hesitant	sarcastic	matter of a fact	vague
negative	doubtful	positive	questioning	bleak

2   Write a short paragraph on how the poet's use of end-stopped lines influences your understanding of the poem.

Enjambement

Enjambement is used when a poet wants a line to run on to the next line rather than complete a line to create a particular effect, as in these lines from 'Hunting Snake' by Judith Wright:

> Cold, dark and splendid he was gone
> into the grass that hid his prey.

This technique can be used to create a number of different effects. It can help to place emphasis on key words and can add variety to the sound of the poem by breaking up the lines and mirroring speech patterns. Enjambement can also be used to reflect the thought processes of the narrator or the movement of an object (in this case, the disappearance of the snake).

Activity 13

1   Reread aloud the first six lines of 'Rain' by Edward Thomas on page 15.

   a These lines are all one sentence. What do you notice about how the poem's narrator seems to be speaking to you?

   b What impact do you think the full stop at the end of line 6 has?

2   Now imagine that Thomas had decided to end-stop some of these lines, as shown below. Read them aloud.

> Rain, midnight rain nothing but the wild rain,
> On this bleak hut, and solitude, and me,
> Remembering again that I shall die,
> And neither hear the rain nor give it thanks
> 5 For washing me cleaner than I have been,
> Since I was born in this solitude.

   a How different does this end-stopped version sound from your reading of the published version with enjambement?

   b How does it change the way the narrator is talking to you?

3   Now look again at the rest of 'Rain'. Thomas uses enjambement extensively in this poem, but he has made a deliberate decision to use end-stopped lines at certain points in the poem. Write a commentary identifying the end-stopped lines and saying why you think Thomas has made the decision to use them in each case.

Activity 14

1   Reread Kathleen Jamie's poem 'Hoard' on page 15. Notice how she has used enjambement at very specific points in the poem.

2   What do you notice about the positioning of the words 'cut' and 'wound', 'huddled' and 'packed' in the opening three lines?

> What kind of figure did he cut
> huddled in the dusk, gut wound
> packed with sphagnum,

With a partner, discuss how the positioning of these words could link with the poem's subject.

3   Write a short statement describing the effect of the enjambement on you and the way you might read the poem.

4   Compare your statement with your partner's.

Independent research

If you want to find out more about different poetic forms, refer to: *The Poet's Craft: A Handbook of Rhyme, Metre and Verse* by Sandy Brownjohn, *The Making of a Poem* by Mark Strand and Eavan Boland or the detailed glossary at www.poetryarchive.org.

Take it further

Read poems written in as many different forms and structures as possible and experiment with writing poetry in different forms yourself.

Activity 15

Enjambement is a very valuable technique in a poet's toolkit. Read the next two poems – one very light-hearted, the other much more serious in tone. They are both about people and make extensive use of enjambement, but to create very different effects.

Discuss the use of enjambement in the two poems. What conclusions can you come to about why poets might choose to use enjambement and end-stopping?

Uncle Jed

Uncle Jed
Durham bred
raised pigeons
for money.

5   He died
a poor man
however

as the pigeons
were invariably
10   too quick for him.

Roger McGough

Evans

Evans? Yes, many a time
I came down his bare flight
Of stairs into the gaunt kitchen
With its wood fire, where the crickets sang
5   Accompaniment to the black kettle's
Whine and so into the cold
Dark to smother in the thick tide
Of night that drifted about the walls
Of his stark farm on the hill ridge.

10   It was not the dark filling my eyes
And mouth appalled me; not even the drip
Of rain like blood from the one tree
Weather-tortured. It was the dark
Silting the veins of that sick man
15   I left stranded upon the vast
And lonely shore of his bleak bed.

R.S. Thomas

Key term

caesura

Caesura

A **caesura** is a slight pause that occurs approximately in the middle of a line of metrical verse (like a sonnet or heroic couplet). Sometimes the pause occurs naturally after a word, but on other occasions the line will be punctuated to dramatic effect and break up the rhythm. For example, the first line of Louis MacNeice's poem 'Prayer before Birth' is:

> I am not yet born; O hear me.

The semi-colon in this line seems to stop the reader in their tracks and make them think about who is speaking, when and why.

Activity 16

Read the opening lines from 'My Last Duchess' by Robert Browning, a much-anthologised and terrific dramatic monologue, which uses the heroic couplet form to tell a very disturbing tale. (You can read the rest of the poem on page 40.)

What do you think is the impact of the pauses shown in bold? Jot down your ideas and compare them with a partner's.

> That's my last duchess painted on the wall,
> Looking as if she were alive. I call
> That piece a wonder, now: Frà Pandolf's hands
> Worked busily a day, and there she stands.
> 5   'Will't please you sit and look at her? I said

Line length and use of white space

All poets make decisions about the length of the lines they use, whether they are adhering to particular metrical or syllabic forms or choosing to use a seemingly looser structure. Within free verse poetry especially, poets have the freedom to make use of space in a line and on the page as a whole in a variety of ways.

Activity 17

Read the following three contrasting poems.

The Red Wheelbarrow

so much depends
upon

a red wheel
barrow

5   glazed with rain
water

beside the white
chickens.

William Carlos Williams

Opening the Cage

14 variations on 14 words
I have nothing to say and I am saying it and that is poetry

John Cage

I have to say poetry and is that nothing and am I saying it
I am and I have poetry to say and is that nothing saying it
I am nothing and I have poetry to say and that is saying it
I that am saying poetry have nothing and it is I and to say
5   And I say that I am to have poetry and saying it is nothing
I am poetry and nothing and saying it is to say that I have
To have nothing is poetry and I am saying that and I say it
Poetry is saying I have nothing and I am to say that and it
Saying nothing I am poetry and I have to say that and it is
10   It is and I am and I have poetry saying say that to nothing
It is saying poetry to nothing and I say I have and am that
Poetry is saying I have it and I am nothing and to say that
And that nothing is poetry I am saying and I have to say it
Saying poetry is nothing and to that I say I am and have it

Edwin Morgan

The Honey Pot

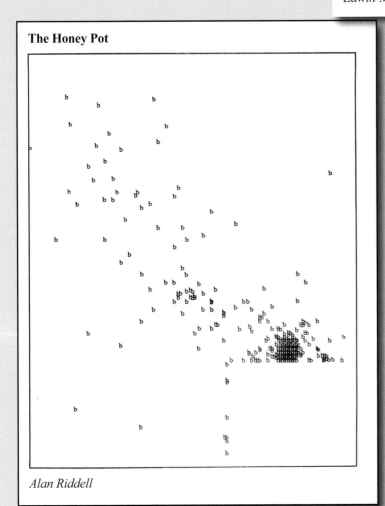

Alan Riddell

With a partner, discuss the following questions.

a   What can you say about how the poets have used line lengths and spaces?

b   What is your view of these poems?

c   Are they poems? If you think so, what makes them poems? You might want to refer back to the section 'What is Poetry?' on page 8 to help you.

Playing with form and structure

Activity 18

1   To conclude this section on form and structure, first read the following short text.

> **Midsummer, Tobago**
>
> Broad sun stoned beaches. White heat.
> A green river. A bridge, scorched yellow
> palms from the summer sleeping house
> drowsing through August. Days I have held,
> 5   days I have lost, days that outgrow, like
> daughters, my harbouring arms.

2   Now experiment with different ways of using form and line structure by turning the prose text into lines of poetry.

3   Read your draft aloud to a partner or to the rest of your group.

4   Compare your draft with other people's.

5   Discuss how and why you have made your decisions about form and structure and explore the different effects you have created.

6   Once you have shared your ideas, turn to page 32 and compare your poem with the original. Write a short statement or prepare a short presentation for the rest of your group in which you describe the differences and similarities, and explain why you think the poet has chosen to structure his words in this way.

4 Rhyme

Rhyme is when one sound is echoed by another sound exactly the same or very similar. It is a fundamental element of much of the language around us. It is important to remember that it is not exclusive to poetry: it is an essential part of the word play in many types of texts like adverts, slogans, sayings and football chants. In poetry, rhyme can be found in many different forms and is used for many different purposes and to create a variety of effects.

Different types of rhyme

Full rhyme

Full rhyme, or **perfect rhyme**, is where the vowel sounds at the end of lines echo each other exactly (eg 'sash/cash', 'imply/defy'). The rhyming words can be in different patterns such as in rhyming couplets, alternate lines or any of the more elaborate rhyme schemes found in sonnets, sestinas, villanelles, etc. For example:

> **Dreams**
> Here we are all, by day; by night we're hurl'd
> By dreams, each one into a several world.
> *Robert Herrick*

> **Pedigree**
> The Pedigree of Honey
> Does not concern the Bee;
> A Clover, any time to him
> Is Aristocracy.
> *Emily Dickinson*

Preparing for the exam (Sections A and B)

When you are writing about rhymes at the ends of lines or the rhyme scheme in a poem, you should use the common notation system. This is where you code each new rhyming word with a new letter of the alphabet. For example, if you look at the poems on the right, Herrick's poem would be annotated as *aa* and Dickinson's poem would be *abcb*.

Take it further

Invent a rhyme scheme of your own and then challenge yourself to write a poem using it. Annotate your finished poem to show the effects of the rhyme scheme.

Activity 19

1 Look at a small selection of other rhyming poems in this book or in your examination collection. Work out their rhyme schemes and think about why the poets might have chosen to use these schemes.

2 Discuss your findings with a partner and agree on your conclusions.

3 As a class or in a group, share your ideas for future reference.

Half rhymes

Half rhymes, or **para-rhymes**, usually occur where the consonant sounds at the end of lines match, rather than the vowel sounds (eg 'flesh/ flash', 'yours/years'). However, you will also hear this term used more broadly to refer to vowel sounds that sound similar, but are not an exact match (eg 'mask/pass' or 'sense/meant').

Sight rhymes

Sight rhymes are half rhymes that look on the page like they should be a full rhyme, but the words actually sound differently when spoken (eg 'now/know', 'plough/tough').

> **Key terms**
> full rhyme
> perfect rhyme
> half rhyme
> para-rhyme
> sight rhyme

Activity 20

Who in your class can come up with the longest list of potential half rhymes and sight rhymes? Individually, list as many as you can in two minutes. Compare your lists as a class and see who has got the longest list. Take a vote on the best and worst examples!

Activity 21

The First World War poet Wilfred Owen makes very assured use of full, half and sight rhymes in his work.

1 Read his poem 'Arms and the Boy' and, on a copy, highlight the different types of rhyme you have identified in different colours.

2 Say the half rhymes aloud and listen to their sounds.

3 Consider how you would write about them.

   a How would you describe the sound of each pair of half rhymes? What differences are there in the sounds they make? For example, read the first stanza again. Listen to the difference between 'flash' and 'flesh' here. Both begin with the same 'fl' sound, but you might think that one seems to have an open expansive, lingering 'ash' sound whereas the 'esh' sound seems softer or quieter.

   b Now think about the effect of the half rhymes. Why do you think Owen made these deliberate choices? In your view, how, if at all, do the sounds contribute to the overall meaning/effects of the poem? Is Owen perhaps wanting to say something about the nature of life and death, innocence and the grim reality of war, or something else through his use of these sounds?

4 Write a short commentary about Owen's choice of half rhymes and their effectiveness in the poem.

Arms and the Boy

Let the boy try along this bayonet-blade
How cold steel is, and keen with the hunger of blood;
Blue, with all malice, like a madman's flash;
And thinly drawn with famishing for flesh.

5 Lend him to stroke these blind, blunt bullet-leads
Which long to nuzzle in the hearts of lads,
Or give him cartridges of fine zinc teeth,
Sharp with the sharpness of grief and death.

For his teeth seem for laughing round an apple.
10 There lurk no claws behind his fingers supple;
And God will grow no talons at his heel,
Nor antlers through the thickness of his curls.

Wilfred Owen

Independent research

Refer to other poems by Owen in your exam collection for further examples of skilful rhyming. To consolidate your understanding, you might also want to investigate poems by Emily Dickinson, Elizabeth Jennings, Philip Larkin or W. B. Yeats, to explore how other poets use full and half rhymes to create different effect.

Internal rhymes

Words that rhyme within a line or adjacent lines (rather than at the end) are called **internal rhymes**. This technique can help a poet to create a particular mood in a poem. Examples of internal rhyme being used for comic effect can be seen in this extract from 'The Cliché Kid' by Carol Ann Duffy.

> Distraught in autumn, kneeling under the chestnut trees,
> seeing childhood in the conkers through my tears.
> Bonkers. And me so butch in my boots down the macho bars …

Duffy is a poet who uses internal rhyme quite frequently in her writing, although not always in a comic way. Read her poems 'Disgrace' and 'Mean Time' on pages 37 and 48 to explore further how she uses this technique.

Other rhyme terms

When writing about rhyme, you will also want to use other terms that describe how rhyming lines are arranged into groups:

> Couplet: a pair of lines
>
> Quatrain: a group of four lines
>
> Sestet: a group of six lines
>
> Octave: a group of eight lines
>
> Stanza: any unit of rhyme and/or metre used in a repeated pattern in a poem.

For example, Owen's poem 'Arms and the Boy' has three stanzas, all quatrains. Stanzas in a poem can consist of lines of the same or different lengths. They work separately, but also cumulatively to build the sense of the poem. Mark Strand and Eavan Boland have written a very helpful description of the stanza:

> the word stanza in Italian means 'room'. In a simple, practical way, the stanza has that figurative purpose. It is as self-contained as any chamber or room. And yet to be in it is to have the consciousness at all times that it also leads somewhere.

Why use rhyme?

Sometimes rhyme can be almost unnoticeable in a poem, whereas on other occasions it contributes to the harmonious feel of the poem and helps it to move along. Sometimes a poet can over use a rhyme or a particular rhyming sound either for deliberate effect or unintentionally. Alternatively a poet might choose a word just because it rhymes rather than because it really contributes anything original to a poem.

In conclusion

Preparing for the exam (Sections A and B)

Always remember to use the term 'stanza', rather than 'verse', when discussing or writing about poetry. It is a much more precise term.

Take it further

- Look back at some of the poems in this section in the light of this room metaphor. What kind of building do you think the stanzas or rooms combine to create in each case?

- Next time you are listening to music, see if you can identify song lyrics that seem to make effective use of rhyme as well as those where a rhyming word seems to be out of place or just chosen for the sake of it.

Activity 22

1 Read the following poem by Jackie Kay, preferably two or three times and aloud at least once.

2 Share your ideas on these discussion points, making notes for later use.

  a What different types of rhymes can you find in this poem?

  b Do any of the rhymes have associations for you?

  c What do you hear and notice in the lines where Jackie Kay has used rhyme and in those where she has chosen not to use it?

  d How and what do you think the use of rhyme contributes to the mood of the poem?

e What else do you want to say about the way this poem is written? You might want to consider the words Kay has chosen, the repetitions, the rhythms of the lines or her reasons for writing the poem.

3 Use your notes to help you write about Kay's use of rhyme and its effectiveness in the poem. Remember to describe the types of rhyme she uses, giving examples from the poem. You should explain how you have responded to the examples and analyse what effect they have.

Childhood, Still

The sun is out and so is childhood – remember
How the summer droned its song forever.

Three small girls tumble down the steep hill.
Grass skip, gust makes their skirts frill.

5 A wee boy scoots towards the big blue loch.
His fishing net bigger than his baw face.

It's hot; there's a breeze like a small caught breath.
This is it; these are the days that never stop.

Childhood ticks, tocks, ticks. Metronome.
10 *Speaking clock. Sand glass. Time bomb.*

A boy kicks a ball through a window, smashes
a gaping hole, but this is childhood still

where big things grow small; small as a petal
or a freckle, on a face, a speckle

15 on a egg, or as small as a tadpole,
small as the space where the ball missed the goal,

as dot to dot, as a crumb of Mrs Jack's cake,
small as the silver locket around her neck.

The long grass whines in the high wind.
20 Away in the distance, the church bells chime.

Childhood ticks, tocks, ticks. Metronome.
Speaking clock. Sand glass. Time bomb.

Suddenly: the clatter of boots in the street.
The sob of a white van speeding away.

25 The cries of a small boy alone in a stairwell.
This is childhood; this is childhood as well.

The policeman caught by the Candyman.
A town's sleep murdered by the Sandman.

There goes the janitor, the teacher, the priest,
30 Clergyworker, childminder, careworker. *Wheesht.*

The auntie, the uncle, the father, the mother;
opening and closing and opening the door.

Childhood ticks, tocks, ticks. Metronome.
Speaking clock. Sand glass. Time bomb.

35 *Oh There she goes.*
Oh There she goes.
Peerie heels and pointed toes.
Look at her feet. She thinks she's neat.
Black stockings and dirty feet.

40 Remember the toadstool, the promise of a chrysalis,
the taste of lemon bonbons, the taste of liquorice.

The past keeps calling the children back.
Number six: pick up sticks. Tick tack. Tick tack.

The clock hands crawl, August's slow talk.
45 Autumn comes: the snap and crackle of amber leaves.

There's a brand new friend waiting in the school,
a gleam in her eye, ready for Tig or marbles.

Skip, skop to the barber's shop, Keepie-Uppie, Kerbie.
Be Baw Babbity, Following Wee Jeannie.

50 Green peas and Barley. Okey Kokey. My mummy told me.
Stotty. Peever. Thread the needle. The Big Ship sails.

This is childhood, let it be childhood still.
Jackie Kay

5 Rhythm

Key term
metre

Poets can make many choices about the way they want their poems to sound. One of the major decisions they make is about the rhythm – the flow and beat of the sounds within the poem and the way these are grouped together to create an effect – just as musicians arrange patterns of sounds to make music.

The rhythm of a poem is what drives it along. Philip Hobsbaum describes rhythm as 'the working machinery of poetry as its metre is its ground plan or blueprint'. The number of times a dominant rhythm occurs in a line of poetry gives it its **metre**, governed by the number of stresses or strong syllables in a line and the pattern that they form. The metre is just one element of the rhythm of a poem. Think of it as being the framework or skeleton that supports it.

Iambic pentameter

The most common form of metre in English poetry is iambic pentameter. This is a pattern of one weak or lightly stressed syllable followed by one strongly stressed syllable. Each **iamb** (the pattern of soft <u>hard</u>) forms one **foot**. Iambic *penta*meter therefore has five feet, which sets up the familiar pattern:

di Dum	/di Dum	/di Dum	/di Dum	/di Dum
soft <u>hard</u>	/soft <u>hard</u>	/soft <u>hard</u>	/soft <u>hard</u>	/soft <u>hard</u>

You can see iambic pentameters at work in the following extracts from 'Sonnet 130' by William Shakespeare and 'The General Prologue to the Canterbury Tales' by Geoffrey Chaucer, where the stressed syllables have been underlined:

> My <u>mistress'</u> <u>eyes</u> are <u>nothing</u> <u>like</u> the <u>sun</u> ('Sonnet 130')
>
> Ful <u>big</u> he <u>was</u> of <u>braun</u>, and <u>eek</u> of <u>bones</u> ('The General Prologue')

Iambic pentameter is the metre used in **blank verse** and in the rhymed forms, the villanelle and the sestina. (For more on blank verse, see Unit 2, pages 139–141.)

Iambic tetrameter

Iambic tetrameter is the metre used in most ballad forms.

Independent research

Find copies of the four poems referred to on this page (they are all widely available). Read them aloud and listen to the way their rhythms work.

Activity 23

1 Look at the following example from Andrew Marvell's 'To His Coy Mistress'. How many iambic feet does it have? What effect does the rhythm have?

> Had <u>we</u> but <u>world</u> <u>enough</u>, and <u>time</u>
> This <u>coyness</u>, <u>lady</u>, <u>were</u> no <u>crime</u>.

2 Find a copy of the poem. Read it aloud and listen to the rhythm. What effect does it have on the subject of the poem?

3 The first and third lines of most traditional ballads will have four stresses. The second and fourth will have three stresses (**iambic trimeter**). Here is an example from the ballad 'Sir Patrick Spens' (Anon) which should help to confirm for you how many iambic feet there are in each line:

> They had not sailed a league, a league,
> A league but barely three,
> Came wind and weet and snow and sleet
> And gurly grew the sea.

gurly – rough

Other patterns

It can be helpful to identify other patterns of stresses in poetry, although the iamb is the most important type of metre for your exam. Other patterns found in feet are:

- **Trochee** – two syllables: one stressed followed by one unstressed syllable
- **Spondee** – two stressed syllables in succession
- **Anapaest** – three syllables: two unstressed followed by one stressed syllable
- **Dactyl** – three syllables: one stressed followed by two unstressed syllables
- **Amphibrach** – three syllables: one unstressed followed by one stressed and rounded off with one unstressed syllable.

Metre is just one element of a poem. Poets play around with it to create different effects and emphases, but a lot more than its metre goes into creating a poem's movement (eg also think about the use of enjambement (page 20) and caesuras (page 22) to link together or to break up lines).

(page 20) ... (page 22)

Key terms

iamb
foot
iambic tetrameter
trochee
spondee
anapaest
dactyl
amphibrach
blank verse
iambic trimeter

Take it further

- Look at the following words and say them aloud. Which are iambs, trochees, anapaests, dactyls or amphibrachs?

understand	fingers	impound
mobile	confetti	builder
aloud	argument	mesmerise
backward	orange	incline

  Now suggest another word as an example in each category.

- Write a brief description of rhythm and metre explaining these two poetic features in simpler term, eg for a course guide for GCSE students.

Preparing for the exam (Sections A and B)

When you are writing about the rhythm of a poem, you need to be able to comment on the impact that it has on you as the reader. How do the words work together to create the rhythm? What effect does this have on the tone and mood of the poem, and on its overall meaning? You will need to read poems aloud to hear this at first. Even though you will not be able to do this in the exam, it is a good habit to get into before discussing any of the poems in this section.

Activity 24

1   Read the following poems aloud to a partner or in a small group. If you are in a group, you could practise reading them together as a chorus or by using different volumes and combinations of voices, and by varying your pitch and tone so that you bring the poems off the page and can hear their rhythms.

simple tings
(for Miss Adlyn and Aunt Vida)

de simple tings of life, mi dear
de simple tings of life

she rocked the rhythms in her chair
brushed a hand across her hair
miles of travel in her stare   5

    de simple tings of life

ah hoe mi corn
an de backache gone
plant mi peas
arthritis ease   10

    de simple tings of life

leaning back
she wiped an eye
read the rain signs
in the sky   15
evening's ashes
in a fireside

    de simple tings of life

Jean 'Binta' Breeze

Men Talk (Rap)

Women
Rabbit rabbit rabbit women
Tattle and titter
Women prattle
5 Women waffle and witter

Men Talk. Men Talk.

Women into Girl Talk
About Women's Trouble
Trivia 'n' Small Talk
10 They yap and they babble

Men Talk. Men Talk.

Women gossip Women giggle
Women niggle-niggle-niggle
Men Talk.

15 Women yatter
Women chatter
Women chew the fat, women spill the beans
Women aint been takin'
The oh-so Good Advice in them
20 Women's Magazines.

A Man Likes A Good Listener.
Oh yeah

I like A Woman
Who likes me enough
25 Not to nitpick
Not to nag and
Not to interrupt 'cause I call that treason
A woman with the Good Grace
To be struck dumb
30 By me Sweet Reason. Yes –

A Man Likes a Good Listener
A Real
Man
Likes a Real Good Listener

35 Women yap yap yap
Verbal Diarrhoea is a Female Disease
Women she spread she rumours round she
Like Philadelphia Cream Cheese.
Oh
40 Bossy Women Gossip
Girlish Women Giggle
Women natter, women nag
Women niggle niggle niggle

Men talk.

45 Men
Think First, Speak later
Men Talk.

Liz Lochhead

2 Discuss what you have noticed about the way the words work. Make notes or annotate copies of the poems as you discuss them. Start with the following questions and then broaden your discussion to include other aspects you have noticed.

- How does Breeze convey a rocking rhythm in her poem through her choice of words and the way she has constructed the lines?
- How does Lochhead create the different sounds of the women's and men's speech through her language?

3 Discuss how the punctuation and/or the line breaks help to shape meaning, again making notes or annotating copies. The following questions may help to get you started.

- Why do you think Breeze uses so few punctuation marks in the whole of her poem?
- How does Lochhead use the caesura in the penultimate line?
- How is she representing her view of the way men speak?
- How does this contrast with her lines about women's speech?

4 Discuss the effects any repetitions have on the way you read and understand each poem. Record your thoughts as before.

5 Write three short paragraphs in response to the poems, comparing the effects that the words, punctuation and line breaks, and repetition have on their rhythm. For each feature, make a point about how it is used in one of the poems, giving an example. Then compare the use of the same feature in the other poem, giving another example. Draw a conclusion about the effectiveness of the feature, before moving on to the next one.

6 Language

When you discuss or write about a poet's choice and use of language, you are exploring the essence of a text: without the words (and the spaces between them), there would be no poem.

Looking closely at diction

Activity 25

1   With a partner, investigate the bank of words in the box below by answering the following questions. You might like to use coding or highlighting on a photocopy or even to cut out the individual words to help you. Make notes on your findings.

    a What do the words reveal to you about the choices the poet made?

    b What conclusions can you come to about the language used? Are there, for example, particular types of words? Could you group them in different ways? Do certain words occur very frequently?

    c Does the poet perhaps seem preoccupied with a theme or subject?

Words from 'Children's Song' (including the title)

A	adult	all	amused	an	analytic	and	and	And	and	And
asleep	blue	cannot	centre	Children's	closed	cupped	dance			
eavesdrop	eggs	enter	Even	eye	faded	find	flower	For	hands	
heaven	in	in	is	is	knees	life	live	look	mock	nest	Of	Of
on	our	our	own	play	probe	pry	remoter	shell	small	smooth
Song	still	stoop	subterfuge	Talk	that	That	The	the	the	the
the	the	though	to	too	Under	Under	We	we	we	Where
where	Where	With	With	world	world	you	you	You	your	

---

2   Present your ideas to the rest of your group.

3   Either individually or with a partner, use the words in the box to draft your own poem entitled 'Children's Song'. You can organise the words in any way you wish and add any punctuation you require.

4   Share your draft poem with another reader. Ask them to read it aloud to you. Discuss how you have ordered the words and why, including:

- the effects you were striving for
- which lines or phrases you are most happy with
- which lines need further development
- which words you found most challenging to include and why
- if you were tempted to add other words, why and what they were.

Activity 26

1   Now read the original poem 'Children's Song' by R.S. Thomas.

2   Make notes on how the poet has ordered the words, punctuated them and structured the poem. Add your ideas on what effects and/or meanings have been created.

3   Now compare the effects and meanings of Thomas' poem with those of your own draft. How has Thomas used the words in his poem? Write one sentence about each point you want to make about Thomas' poem, adding evidence from the poem to support your point. Now look at your own draft. What effects have you created through your use of language? How does your version compare with the original? You may have used the words very differently! Make a separate comment on each effect you have created and then, where possible, make a comparison between the two poems, before moving on to your next point.

4   How do you think the activities in this section (your word bank investigation, the drafting of your own poem and the comparison of two versions) have helped you to develop your understanding of the language of poetry more fully?

5   There is another poem on the subject of childhood by Jackie Kay on page 27. Compare it with 'Children's Song'. Which do you prefer? Which do you think uses language in the most interesting ways? Write a commentary, comparing the two poems.

Children's Song

We live in our own world,
A world that is too small
For you to stoop and enter
Even on hands and knees,
The adult subterfuge.   5
And though you probe and pry
With analytic eye,
And eavesdrop all our talk
With an amused look,
You cannot find the centre   10
Where we dance, where we play,
Where life is still asleep
Under the closed flower,
Under the smooth shell
Of eggs in the cupped nest   15
That mock the faded blue
Of your remoter heaven.

R.S. Thomas

Many of you will already be familiar with much of the terminology you need to use in discussing and writing about the language used in poetry. Indeed, many of the terms are not used just to talk about poetry texts. You should aim to use them confidently in all aspects of textual study.

Midsummer, Tobago

Broad sun stoned beaches.

White heat.
A green river.

A bridge,
scorched yellow palms   5

from the summer sleeping house
drowsing through August.

Days I have held,
days I have lost,

days that outgrow, like daughters,   10
my harbouring arms.
Derek Walcott

Solution to
Activity 18, page 24.

Activity 27

Working in a small group, decide which of the following definitions most accurately describe each technical term. Be careful – in some cases two of the three answers are correct.

Terms	Definitions
Alliteration	• repetition of consonant sounds • repetition of hyphenated words • repetition of 'lit' sounds
Assonance	• repetition of consonant sounds • repetition of vowel sounds • repetition of 'a' sounds
Diction	• the correct use of English • the choice of words made by a writer • a synonym for the word 'vocabulary'
Ellipsis	• a phrase or sentence where words are missed out but can be inferred from the surrounding context • three dots to show words are missed out or to indicate suspense • the repetition of 'el' sounds
Irony	• language that says one thing but means another • language that lacks emotion • language that is flat and uninspiring
Onomatopoeia	• words that make a booming sound • words that make an echoing sound • words that replicate or mimic the sound they are making
Oxymoron	• a contrasting word or phrase that contains two elements with opposite meanings • a phrase that makes something difficult seem easy • a phrase used by someone to show their anger
Sibilance	• the sound of snakes • repetition of 's' sounds • the use of sinister sounds in poetry

If you are uncertain about any of the terms, refer to the glossary and discuss them with your teacher. If you are already confident about these terms, ensure that you use them in class discussion as well as in your writing about poetry.

> **Preparing for the exam (Section B)**
>
> Find examples of the techniques listed in Activity 27 in use in the poems in this section or in your exam collection. Write a short commentary on the effects created through their use.

Language toolkit for writing in the exam

When you talk about the language of a poem, you should be able to focus on a number of different aspects, many of which are interlinked. You should be concerned with:

- the choice of words a poet makes and why they have chosen particular words rather than others
- the **syntax** of the poem (the way the words are arranged into phrases, questions, statements, commands, dialogue, sentences, lines, stanzas and whole poems)
- how the language is punctuated (or not)
- the patterning of words (eg whether words are repeated, contrasted with one another or juxtaposed)
- the sounds of the words (the way they rhyme, create a particular tone and mood, might echo other words in the poem, introduce, repeat or reinforce specific sounds)

> **Key terms**
>
> diction
> ellipsis
> irony
> onomatopoeia
> oxymoron
> sibilance
> syntax
> simile
> metaphor
> personification

- whether the vocabulary and/or the phrasing are associated with a particular time, place, situation, person, group of people (and/or whether it is being used to deliberately evoke such things)
- who (or what) is speaking the words and how their language addresses the reader
- what may be left unsaid but can be inferred from the language that is present
- the types of lexical and grammatical words used (eg verbs and/or adjectives extensively or rarely used).

Activity 28

Now use the toolkit above as a checklist to help you to explore the language of at least one of the poems in the form and structure pages (12–24) of this section. Choose one poem, reread it several times and write at least two sentences for each of the bullet points in the toolkit.

7 Imagery

Imagery is the creation of pictures in language, which help us to visualise something or appeal to our senses so that we can hear, feel or see an idea or subject for ourselves. The best images help us to view or experience the idea afresh or in a different way. A lot of poetry is rich in imagery and some critics have argued that contemporary English poetry is essentially poetry of the eye, whereas poets from other nations (or those writing in other times) can be more concerned with writing for the ear.

Simile and metaphor

You should already be familiar with the terms **'simile'**, **'metaphor'** and **'personification'**, which are essential when writing about imagery in poetry. We will look at simile and metaphor in more detail here, and personification on page 36. A simile is a comparison between two things that are not usually compared and uses the words 'as' or 'like' (eg in the poem 'Wind', Ted Hughes describes the movement of the wind as 'flexing like the lens of a mad eye'). Metaphor is a comparison between seemingly unrelated things. Metaphors create a much stronger, more definite image than a simile because one object is transformed into the other, eg ' she was my rock'. The use of the verb 'to be' in some form or tense can be an indicator that there is a metaphor in a poem.

Preparing for the exam (Sections A and B)

- English Literature AS students will not be expected to comment on this technical aspect of language as fully as those studying English Language and Literature. Nevertheless, the more confidently you can discuss language, the more you will be able to explore how poets create their effects.
- Whenever you are writing about any aspect of language or literature you must do more than simply identify the features used. To write a successful AS level answer you should explore *how* and *why* a poet uses language. What is the purpose? Why has the choice been made? How do the effects that the poet creates impact on you, the reader?

Activity 29

1   Read the poem 'Praise Song for My Mother' by Grace Nichols at least twice and note her use of powerful metaphorical language to praise her mother.

2   Reread the poem and identify the metaphors in it. What can you say about the metaphors Nichols has created? What might they reveal about her feelings for her mother or about the context of their relationship?

3   The metaphors are interspersed throughout the poem in each stanza apart from the last. What impact does this seem to have on:
   - the rhythm of the poem
   - the overall effects and meanings created?

Praise Song for My Mother

You were
water to me
deep and bold and fathoming

You were
moon's eye to me
pull and grained and mantling

You were
sunrise to me
rise and warm and streaming

You were
the fishes red gill to me
the flame tree's spread to me
the crab's leg/the fried plantain smell

   replenishing, replenishing
Go to your wide futures, you said

Grace Nichols

Activity 30

1 Another poet whose early work is particularly rich in metaphorical imagery is Craig Raine. Read his poem below.

2 After this poem was published, some critics said Raine belonged to the Martian school of poetry because of his particular use of metaphor which enabled readers to look at the world through different eyes.

   a In a sequence of metaphors in this poem, Raine is describing aspects of everyday life. List the everyday aspects or objects he includes.

   b Write a sentence or two about each object, explaining how Raine's use of metaphor makes you think about it differently.

3 If this poem had been written in the twenty-first century, it may well have included other everyday items. Choose two or three from the list on the left and draft some additional stanzas for the poem. Try to imitate Raine's style (including his use of metaphor) as closely as you can.

4 Now share your metaphors with other readers. Which are the most successful?

ipod or Mp3 player

microwave oven

pot noodle

hair straighteners

electric razor

internet

play station or gameboy

sun bed

mobile phone

digital camera

pda

A Martian Sends a Postcard Home

Caxtons are mechanical birds with many wings
and some are treasured for their markings –

they cause the eyes to melt
or the body to shriek without pain.

5 I have never seen one fly, but
sometimes they perch on the hand.

Mist is when the sky is tired of flight
and rests its soft machine on the ground:

then the world is dim and bookish
10 like engravings under tissue paper.

Rain is when the earth is television.
It has the property of making colour darker.

Model T is a room with the lock inside –
a key is turned to free the world

15 for movement, so quick there is a film
to watch for anything missed.

But time is tied to the wrist
or kept in a box ticking with impatience.

In homes, a haunted apparatus sleeps,
20 that snores when you pick it up.

If the ghost cries, they carry it
to their lips and soothe it to sleep

with sounds. And yet, they wake it up
deliberately, by tickling with a finger.

25 Only the young are allowed to suffer
openly. Adults go to a punishment room

with water but nothing to eat.
They lock the door and suffer the noises

alone. No one is exempt
30 and everyone's pain has a different smell.

At night, when all the colours die,
they hide in pairs

and read about themselves –
in colour, with their eyelids shut.

Craig Raine

The term **'extended metaphor'** might be new to you. This is when the metaphor, the comparison between two objects, is developed throughout the poem, rather than in just a line or two, in order to explore it more fully.

Activity 31

1 Read William Blake's poem below. See if you can identify the extended metaphor within it, which explores an aspect of human nature.

William Blake

> **A Poison Tree**
>
> I was angry with my friend;
> I told my wrath – my wrath did end.
> I was angry with my foe;
> I told it not – my wrath did grow.
>
> 5 And I watered it in fears,
> Night and morning with my tears,
> And I sunned it with my smiles.
> And with soft deceitful wiles.
>
> And it grew both day and night,
> 10 Till it bore an apple bright,
> And my foe beheld it shine,
> And he knew that it was mine,
>
> And into my garden stole
> When the night had veiled the pole.
> 15 In the morning glad I see
> My foe outstretched beneath the tree.
>
> *William Blake*

2 Write a short statement to explain how you think Blake has used the extended metaphor to explore an abstract human emotion. To begin to answer this question you will need to:

a look at how he has used and developed the metaphor in each stanza in order to focus on different aspects of the emotion he is representing;

b think about why he might have chosen a natural image to represent this human feeling.

Take it further

The literary critic I. A. Richards suggests the following three part model for analysing metaphor (his system is not agreed on by everyone, however):

- Tenor – the thing which the metaphor is describing or characterising – its first term;
- Vehicle – the thing which is being used to describe or characterise the tenor – its second term;
- Ground – the quality which the tenor and vehicle share which makes the metaphor 'work'.

For example, in the metaphor 'No man is an island, entire of itself', the tenor is 'man', the vehicle 'an island' and the ground could be said to be 'separateness' or 'isolation'.

Look again at some of the poems you have been exploring. What does thinking about metaphors in this way add to your understanding of the ways in which imagery is used?

Preparing for the exam (Section B)

Imagery is a prominent feature of many poems in Section B and in your exam collection. It contributes to the richness of poetry and enables us to experience ideas and events differently through language. Explore how other images have been created in the poems in your collection. Why have the poets chosen them and what effects they have created?

Personification

Writers and poets use personification when they present an inanimate object or an idea as having human qualities and feelings.

Activity 32

1 Read the following poem by Carol Ann Duffy several times.

Disgrace

But one day we woke to disgrace; our house
a coldness of rooms, each nursing
a thickening cyst of dust and gloom.
We had not been home in our hearts for months.

5 And how our words changed. Dead flies in a web.
How they stiffened and blackened. Cherished italics
suddenly sour on our tongues, obscenities
spraying themselves on the wall in my head.

10 Woke to your clothes like a corpse on the floor,
the small deaths of lightbulbs pining all day
in my ears, their echoes audible tears;
nothing we would not do to make it worse

and worse. Into the night with the wrong language,
15 waving and pointing, the shadows of hands
huge in the bedroom. Dreamed of a naked crawl
from a dead place over the other; both of us. Woke.

Woke to the absence of grace; the still-life
of a meal, untouched, wine-bottle, empty, ashtray,
20 full. In our sullen kitchen, the fridge
hardened its cool heart, selfish as art, hummed.

To a bowl of apples rotten to the core. Lame shoes
empty in the hall where our voices asked
for a message after the tone, the telephone
pressing its ear to distant, invisible lips.

25 And our garden bowing its head, vulnerable flowers
unseen in the dusk as we shouted in silhouette.
Woke to the screaming alarm, the banging door,
the house-plants trembling in their brittle soil. Total

disgrace. Up in the dark to stand at the window,
30 counting the years to arrive there, faithless,
unpenitent. Woke to the meaningless stars, you
and me both, lost. Inconsolable vowels from the next room.

Carol Ann Duffy

2 Write a response to this poem, identifying where and how Carol Ann Duffy has used personification and, most importantly, why you think she has used this technique. Remember to use evidence from the poem to support your views. The following questions may help you.

- What inanimate objects and concepts have been given human attributes and feelings?
- How has Duffy used the personification of these things to explore the breakdown of a relationship?
- What else do you notice about Duffy's use of imagery in this poem?
- What are your views about the poem's title?

8 Voice

Key term

voice

The term 'voice' is often used in relation to poetry and refers to the speaker or thinker who is expressing a view, the person who is talking to you, the reader. The voices used in poetry can be many and varied. Be careful not to assume, when reading a poem for the first time, that the poet is speaking in their own voice and that everything they express directly reflects their own feelings or experiences. To some extent, all writers draw on their own lives in their writing, but remember that poems are constructed creations and the voices a poet chooses to use are part of this construction.

Decisions about voice are not made in isolation: in creating a voice for a poem, a poet draws on all the other aspects that we have explored so far. A poet chooses the voices that are most appropriate for what they want to express and select the form, language, imagery, etc. that best fits each voice.

Creating a voice

There are no taboos in terms of what poetry can give voice to. Poets can give all kinds of objects, concepts and people voices in their poems.

Activity 33

1 Choose one of the voices and situations in the box below. With a partner, and jotting down significant words and phrases as you talk, discuss:

   a how the voice might speak in this context

   b how it might view the world

   c what concerns it might have about past or future events

   d how it would express these views and concerns.

> A traffic cone in motorway roadworks.
>
> A young horse taking part in the Grand National.
>
> A single coathanger in an empty wardrobe.
>
> A father who is holding his child for the first time.
>
> A grandmother thinking back to her childhood.
>
> A fox on the prowl in a city.
>
> A fire fighter entering a burning building.
>
> A ten pence piece down the back of a sofa.
>
> A student waiting outside the head teacher's office.
>
> A pond filled with frogspawn.
>
> Someone preparing to claim asylum in an airport terminal.
>
> An identical twin on his or her 18th birthday.
>
> A parachutist waiting to jump.
>
> A tree about to be chopped down.

2 Shape your words and phrases into the rough draft of a poem. File your draft safely while you read and discuss the following poems. They should give you some ideas about how different voices can be brought to life on the page, so that you can revise and finish your poem later.

Activity 34

1 Working in a small group, read the six very different poems that follow and then choose one for your group to work on in more detail.

A Fish-Hook

You have put a fish-hook in my chest behind the
breast bone,

and one barb is around my gullet, and one around my
wind-pipe and the third is embedded in the root of
5 the aorta.

There is a cord attached, of tantalum-hardened steel,
marvellously supple,

and the least movement you make, that cord tightens,
the tip of each barb jerks deeper, the blood eddies
10 around the metal.

You have the other end of that cord, you have hidden it,
inside your skull or at the base of your spine,
and though your hands are empty, you are winding it in,

and my mouth is dry as I flounder towards you.

Gael Turnbull

Mirror

I am silver and exact. I have no preconceptions.
Whatever I see I swallow immediately
Just as it is, unmisted by love or dislike.
I am not cruel, only truthful –
5 The eye of a little god, four-cornered.
Most of the time I meditate on the opposite wall.
It is pink, with speckles. I have looked at it so long
I think it is a part of my heart. But it flickers
Faces and darkness separate us over and over.

10 Now I am a lake. A woman bends over me,
Searching my reaches for what she really is.
Then she turns back to those liars, the candles or the moon.
I see her back, and reflect it faithfully.
She rewards me with tears and an agitation of hands.
15 I am important to her. She comes and goes.
Each morning it is her face that replaces the darkness.
In me she has drowned a young girl, and in me an old woman
Rises toward her day after day, like a terrible fish.

Sylvia Plath

The Self-Unseeing

Here is the ancient floor,
Footworn and hollowed and thin,
Here was the former door
Where the dead feet walked in.

5 She sat here in her chair,
Smiling into the fire;
He who played stood there,
Bowing it higher and higher.

Child-like, I danced in a dream;
10 Blazings emblazoned that day;
Everything glowed with a gleam;
Yet we were looking away!

Thomas Hardy

My Last Duchess

That's my last duchess painted on the wall,
Looking as if she were alive. I call
That piece a wonder, now: Frà Pandolf's hands
Worked busily a day, and there she stands.
Will't please you sit and look at her? I said
'Frà Pandolf' by design, for never read
Strangers like you that pictured countenance,
The depth and passion of its earnest glance,
But to myself they turned (since none puts by
The curtain I have drawn for you, but I)
And seemed as they would ask me, if they durst,
How such a glance came there; so, not the first
Are you to turn and ask thus. Sir, 'twas not
Her husband's presence only, called that spot
Of joy into the Duchess' cheek: perhaps
Frà Pandolf chanced to say 'Her mantle laps
Over my lady's wrist too much,' or 'Paint
Must never hope to reproduce the faint
Half-flush that dies along her throat': such stuff
Was courtesy, she thought, and cause enough
For calling up that spot of joy. She had
A heart – how shall I say? – too soon made glad,
Too easily impressed; she liked whate'er
She looked on, and her looks went everywhere.
Sir, 'twas all one! My favour at her breast,
The dropping of the daylight in the West,
The bough of cherries some officious fool
Broke in the orchard for her, the white mule
She rode with round the terrace – all and each
Would draw from her alike the approving speech,
Or blush, at least. She thanked men – good! but thanked
Somehow – I know not how – as if she ranked
My gift of a nine-hundred-years-old name
With anybody's gift. Who'd stoop to blame
This sort of trifling? Even had you skill
In speech – which I have not – to make your will
Quite clear to such an one, and say, 'Just this
Or that in you disgusts me; here you miss,
Or there exceed the mark' – and if she let
Herself be lessoned so, nor plainly set
Her wits to yours, forsooth, and make excuse,
– E'en then would be some stooping; and I choose
Never to stoop. Oh sir, she smiled, no doubt,
Whene'er I passed her; but who passed without
Much the same smile? This grew; I gave commands;
Then all smiles stopped together. There she stands
As if alive. Will't please you rise? We'll meet
The company below, then. I repeat,
The Count your master's known munificence
Is ample warrant that no just pretence
Of mine for dowry will be disallowed;
Though his fair daughter's self, as I avowed
At starting, is my object. Nay we'll go
Together down, sir. Notice Neptune, though,
Taming a sea-horse, thought a rarity,
Which Claus of Innsbruck cast in bronze for me!

Robert Browning

Arrival

Finally we arrived at the city of silence,
enormous, high-walled, its furious traffic lights
signalling in panic. The streets were covered over
In thick rugs. It was a place without doors, a series
5 of moving mouths.

                       Their eyes of course, spoke volumes,
vast encyclopaedias. There was little light reading.
Their white gloves fluttered before them
with grotesquely dancing fingers.

10 It was written that all this should be as it was.
Their thought-crimes, hand-crimes, and heart-crimes
were listed in long numbered chapters.
Policemen pulled faces or pointed at notices.
The civic authorities were sleeping in the park.
15 DO NOT DISTURB, said the signs.
ASK NO AWKWARD QUESTIONS.

The rest went on feeding and breeding.
They were planting tongues in the cemetery,
thick flowering shrubs of silence.

George Szirtes

Epigram Engraved on the Collar of a Dog Which I Gave to His Royal Highness

I am his Highness' dog at Kew;
Pray tell me, sir, whose dog are you?
Alexander Pope

---

2 Discuss the following points in preparation for presenting your findings as a poster or in a chart.

- Who is speaking in each poem and why?
- To whom do you think they are speaking?
- What might be the situation or context within each poem?
- What can you say about the language and form with which each of the poets has chosen to create their voices?
- What might be their purposes in writing the poems?
- What else would you like to know about each poet?

3 Now prepare your poster and chart, and be prepared to explain your decisions to the rest of the class.

Activity 35

Return to the own draft poem you started in Activity 33 and work on it further. Read the draft aloud again and, if appropriate, redraft it, paying close attention especially to how you shape the voice and the way it speaks to the reader.

In the next section you will move on to look at tone and mood. Before you do that, consider the diction and structure of the poems in Activity 34. How do you think these features help to convey the tone of the voices created in poems?

Preparing for the exam (Sections A and B)

When writing about the voice of a poem, whether an unseen poem or one in your collection, go beyond simply identifying what the voice is. It is more important to comment on how the voice conveys the poet's attitude to the topic.

9 Tone and mood

Tone and **mood** are the aspects of a text that some students find most challenging to write about. The activities on the following pages should confirm that you do already know something about these terms and will help to develop your understanding of them.

Activity 36

Let's start by thinking about tone. Individually or with a partner, think about or discuss the following points.

- If someone says to you 'Don't speak to me in that tone of voice!', what do you think they are implying about the *way* you have spoken to them? Read the sentence aloud. Does that give you any further clues?
- How do you think the speaker has arrived at that view of your tone? Is it because of your choice of words? Is it because of how you have spoken to them? Is it as a result of something else?
- What do you think they mean by the word 'tone'?

Activity 37

1   Working in a small group, take it in turns to say the sentence 'Please, will you help me?' aloud in different tones from the box below and others you can think of. Note that some of the tones have very subtle differences (eg sinister and mysterious). Don't tell the rest of the group what tone you are using – let them guess.

desperate	sarcastic	uncertain	resigned	puzzled
hopeful	angry	romantic	bored	grieving
casual	sinister	mysterious	confident	enigmatic

2   Discuss:
- how your voices changed when you adopted different tones
- how you used the punctuation in the sentence
- what different emphases you placed on the words depending on the tone you chose.

Key term

tone
mood

In real life, when we adopt different tones, they reveal different facets of our personality in different situations. In literary texts, writers use a variety of tones to help to convey the complexity of the voice(s) or situations as well as the mood in an individual work (whether it is a poem, play or any other form).

Definitions

The *New Shorter Oxford English Dictionary* defines tone as 'a characteristic sound made by a voice, instrument etc …; a sound having a definite pitch or character …; the quality or luminosity of colour, a shade, a tint …; a style of speech or writing regarded as reflecting a person's mood, attitude or personality; a mood or attitude conveyed by an author's style'.

Mood is defined as 'the atmosphere or pervading tone of a place, event, composition, etc; one inducing a certain state of mind or emotion'.

The words 'tone' and 'mood' are often used interchangeably. However, the definitions above show that the mood of a poem or the overriding feeling it invokes is created *through* a writer's use of tone. Therefore, tone encompasses sound, word choices and the many other features of language that contribute to the writer's style.

When you are looking and listening for tone in a poem, pay close attention to the following aspects, which all make a contribution. The questions will help you analyse each aspect.

Looking and listening for tone

Voice
(also refer to the section on voice on pages 38–41)

- How does the speaker talk to you, the reader?
- Is the speaker speaking directly or are they recalling what someone else has said?
- Can you trust what you are hearing?
- Do you sympathise with the speaker?
- Do they make you feel uncomfortable?

Rhythm
(also refer to the sections on rhyme on pages 24–27 and rhythm on pages 27–30)

- What can you say about the rhythm of the lines? What impact do they have?
- Are there frequent pauses or end-stopped lines that break up the lines?
- Does the poet use enjambement so that the lines, images or arguments flow coherently together?
- How else does the punctuation seem to contribute to the rhythm and tone of the piece?

Diction

- What can you say about the words used (eg are they simple, ordinary, unusual, old-fashioned, hard to understand, official sounding, conversational, child-like, contemporary)?
- How do the words combine together? What impact do they have?

Sound
(also refer to the sections on rhyme on pages 24–27 and rhythm on pages 27–30)

- What can you say about the sounds of the words used? Listen to the consonants and vowels. Does the poet use assonance or alliteration in any way? Are there soft or hard sounds in the poem? Are there repetitions of sounds, words or phrases? Is the sound quickly over or are there moments when a sound lingers?
- Does the poem have a rhyme scheme? If so, what effect does this have on the tone?

Structure
(also refer to the section on form and structure on pages 12–24)

- How are the words laid out on the page?
- Is the poem arranged in stanzas? Do these indicate changes in tone?

Content

- What does the poem seem to be about? Are there things you seem to be told?
- Does the poet use imagery? How does this contribute to tone?
- Does the poem leave you with questions?
- How does it make you feel?

Once you have identified the tone a poet is using, you are well on your way to developing a clearer understanding of the piece as a whole. Tone can be very obvious or very elusive. Sometimes it will take you several readings to be clear about what you have heard. Hearing the poem read aloud by different people and reading the poem aloud yourself will help you to recognise how tone works in a poem.

Independent research

If you would like to hear a wide range of modern and contemporary poets reading their work aloud, go to www.poetryarchive.org

Activity 38

If possible, listen to the four poems in Activities 39 and 40 being read by their poets at www.poetryarchive.org. Refer to the word bank of tones in the box below and to the 'Looking and listening for tone' box on page 43 to help you describe the tone of each poem. (These tone words are only suggestions to help you. You can add other ideas of your own.)

desperate	bored	grieving	careworn	casual
sinister	sarcastic	triumphant	mysterious	confident
enigmatic	distracted	uncertain	resigned	puzzled
hopeful	proud	angry	smug	argumentative
passionate	defiant	nostalgic	satirical	bleak
happy	ironic	indifferent	optimistic	edgy
sad	conspiratorial			

Activity 39

1 Read the following poem by Owen Sheers, and if possible, listen to him reading it on www.poetryarchive.org.

2 What do you notice about the different tones he uses to convey his father's feelings first when visiting the fort with his son and then on returning years later to scatter someone's ashes?

3 How would you describe these tones?

The Hill Fort (Y Gaer)

On a clear day he'd bring him here,
his young son, charging the hill
as wild as the long-maned ponies

who'd watch a moment
before dropping their heads to graze again.   5
When he finally got him still

he'd crouch so their eyes were level,
one hand at the small of his back
the other tracing the horizon,

pointing out all the places lived in   10
by the fathers and sons before them:
Tretower, Raglan, Bredwardine …

And what he meant by this but never said, was
'Look, Look over this land and see how long
the line is before you – how in these generations   15

we're no more than scattered grains;
that from here in this view, 1, 19 or 90 years
are much the same;

that it isn't the number of steps
that will matter,   20
but the depth of their impression.'

And that's why he's come back again,
to tip these ashes onto the tongue of the wind
and watch them spindrift into the night.

Not just to make the circle complete,   25
to heal or mend,
but because he knows these walls,

sunk however low,
still hold him in as well as out:
protect as much as they defend.   30

Owen Sheers

Activity 40

1 Now read the following three contrasting poems, again listening to the poets reading them on www.poetryarchive.org, if possible.

Haunts

Don't be afraid, old son, it's only me,
though not as I've appeared before,
on the battlements of your signature,
or margin of a book you can't throw out,
5   or darkened shop front where your face
first shocks itself into a mask of mine,
but here, alive, one Christmas long ago
when you were three, upstairs, asleep,
and haunting *me* because I conjured you
10 the way that child you were would cry out
waking in the dark, and when you spoke
in no child's voice but out of radio silence,
the hall clock ticking like a radar blip,
a bottle breaking faintly streets away,
15 you said, as I say now, *Don't be afraid.*

Michael Donaghy

George Square

My seventy seven year old father
Put his reading glasses on
To help my mother do the buttons
On the back of her dress.
5   'What a pair the two of us are!'
my mother said, 'Me with my sore wrist,
you with your bad eyes, your soft thumbs!'

And off they went, my two parents
To march against the war in Iraq,
10 Him with his plastic hips, her with her arthritis
To congregate at George Square where the banners
Waved at each other like old friends, flapping,
Where'd they'd met for so many marches over their years,
For peace on earth, for pity's sake, for peace, for peace.

Jackie Kay

Jean 'Binta' Breeze

earth cries

she doesn't cry for water
she runs rivers deep
she doesn't cry for food
she has suckled trees
5 she doesn't cry for clothing
she weaves all that she wears
she doesn't cry for shelter
she grows thatch everywhere
she doesn't cry for children
10 she's got more than she can bear
she doesn't cry for heaven
she knows it's always there
you don't know why she's crying
when she's got everything
15 how could you know she's crying
for just one humane being

Jean 'Binta' Breeze

2 'Haunts' also features a father (perhaps two fathers).

   a Write a sentence to describe the tone of the poem.

   b Write a short paragraph, comparing the tone of 'Haunts' with that of 'The Hill Fort (Y Gaer)'.

3 In 'George Square' Jackie Kay focuses on both a father and a mother.

   a Write a sentence to describe the tone.

   b Write a short paragraph, explaining how you think the poem's narrator feels about her parents and the march they are going to participate in. Comment on how the tone helps you to arrive at your views.

4 'Earth Cries' is very different in subject matter and tone from the other three poems. Write a short paragraph to describe it. Make sure you explore the effectiveness of the poet's use of patterns and repetition in the poem as a whole.

If a poem includes speech, or a number of different voices, this can help with identification of tone. For example, Philip Larkin's 'Mr Bleaney' contains contrasting tones, which contribute to the overriding mood of the poem.

Activity 41

1 Read Philip Larkin's poem below and, if possible, listen to him reading it at www.poetryarchive.org.

Mr Bleaney

'This was Mr Bleaney's room. He stayed
The whole time he was at the Bodies, till
They moved him.' Flowered curtains, thin and frayed,
Fall to within five inches of the sill,

5 Whose window shows a strip of building land.
Tussocky, littered. 'Mr Bleaney took
My bit of garden properly in hand.'
Bed, upright chair, sixty-watt bulb, no hook

Behind the door, no room for books or bags –
10 'I'll take it.' So it happens that I lie
Where Mr Bleaney lay, and stub my fags
On the same saucer-souvenir, and try

Stuffing my ears with cotton-wool, to drown
The jabbering set he egged her on to buy.
15 I know his habits – what time he came down,
His preference for sauce to gravy, why

He kept on plugging at the four aways –
Likewise their yearly frame: the Frinton folk
Who put him up for summer holidays,
20 And Christmas at his sister's house in Stoke.

But if he stood and watched the frigid wind
Tousling the clouds, lay on the fusty bed
Telling himself that this was home, and grinned,
And shivered, without shaking off the dread

25 That how we live measures our own nature,
And at his age having no more to show
Than one hired box should make him pretty sure
He warranted no better, I don't know.

Philip Larkin

2 Now read this possible response to the different tones (underlined) that might be detected in the poem. Do you agree with these points of view or do you have a different interpretation?

> You can hear the <u>optimistic</u> landlady, who is keen to rent out Mr Bleaney's old room and tell her visitor about how well he fitted into her establishment. However, the <u>cynical</u> narrator first casts his eye around his new lodgings, conveying his <u>irritation</u> for the ingratiating landlady. Then, there is a change in tone as he finds himself almost <u>resigned</u> to a solitary, grim life and questions if Mr Bleaney felt this way too.

3 Now look again at the words in the poem. On a copy and using different colours, highlight the parts that indicate contrasting tones.

  a Why do you think Larkin has included the landlady's words?

  b How do you think they contrast with the rest of the poem?

4 How else does Larkin appear to use language to show what the narrator thinks of the landlady and of his new situation?

5 What do you think the mood of the poem is? How does the language contribute to this?

6 Look at the sample response again. What essential elements are missing? Write your own commentary about the tone and mood of the poem, ensuring that you refer to evidence to support your ideas.

7 Share your commentary and discuss your ideas with a partner or the rest of your group.

Activity 42

For one final look at tone and mood in poetry, it is helpful to turn to the work of two other poets who both demonstrate real mastery of these elements: Thomas Hardy and Carol Ann Duffy.

1 Read the poems once and then reread them, preferably aloud to someone else.

Neutral Tones

We stood by a pond that winter day,
And the sun was white, as though chidden of God,
And a few leaves lay on the starving sod;
– They had fallen from an ash, and were gray.

5   Your eyes on me were as eyes that rove
Over tedious riddles solved years ago;
And some words played between us to and fro –
On which lost the more by our love.

The smile on your mouth was the deadest thing
10 Alive enough to have strength to die;
And a grin of bitterness swept thereby
Like an ominous bird a-wing …

Since then, keen lessons that love deceives,
And wrings with wrong, have shaped to me
15 Your face, and the God-curst sun, and a tree,
And a pond edged with grayish leaves.

Thomas Hardy

Mean Time

The clocks slid back an hour
and stole light from my life
as I walked through the wrong part of town,
mourning our love.

5 And, of course, unmendable rain
fell to the bleak streets
where I felt my heart gnaw
at all our mistakes.

If the darkening sky could lift
10 more than one hour from this day
there are words I would never have said
nor have heard you say.

But we will be dead, as we know,
beyond all light.
15 These are the shortened days
and the endless nights.

Carol Ann Duffy

2   Jot down your initial impressions of the tone and mood of each poem. How would you describe each poem?

3   Now imagine you have a card of paint colours in front of you and an mp3 player.

  a   Which broad colour group might you pick for each poem? Why?

  b   What broad type of music might you pick to reflect the mood of each poem? Why?

4   What do the poems have in common in terms of tone and mood? Write notes in answer to each of the questions below. You could also refer to the 'Looking and listening for tone' box on page 43 for further ideas.

  a   How do Hardy and Duffy use the settings in their poems (the pond in a winter landscape and the wet streets on the wrong side of town) to contribute to tone and mood?

  b   Both poems are written in stanzas. How do these structures, the rhythms and other patterns within each poem create a pervading atmosphere or mood? What impact do the poets' word choices have on us?

5   Now look again at your initial impressions. Listen to the poems again inside your head. Can you be more precise about the distinctive tones of each poem? What do the tones created by the poets contribute to the overall moods in each poem?

  a   What specific shade would you choose within the broad colour group? Are there subtle differences in tone or nuances you hadn't noticed before? Is, for example, one poem vermillion and the other scarlet? Is one azure and the other turquoise?

  b   What specific piece of music would you choose for each? How have you arrived at these choices?

6   What do the tones created by the poets contribute to the overall moods in each poem? Write a comparison of the tone and mood of the two poems. Remember to use evidence from the poems to support each of your points and follow this with further analysis or exploration.

Preparing for the exam (Section B)

For each of your chosen poems, think about how the following features help to create a particular tone:

- voice
- rhythm
- diction
- sound
- structure
- content.

How does the tone created contribute to the overall mood of the poem?

In conclusion

Throughout the 'Exploring poetry' section you have explored the different choices poets make when they write poetry and the effects these choices can have both on the poems they create and on the readers, performers or listeners who engage with them.

Return to the Poetry experiences grid you completed in Activity 3. Reflect on your progress with a partner or your teacher. Which aspects do you feel more confident about now? Which do you feel are your current areas of strength? Which areas do you think you need further work on?

Part 2 Exploring prose

This part of the book explores the techniques and key features of prose that writers use in their craft. Understanding these key genre features of prose, as listed in the Literature specification, will inform your responses to Section A (if you choose Unseen Prose) and Section C (the essay on your prescribed novels) in your exam.

Introduction

In **Section A** you can choose to answer questions on a prose passage or on a poem. You will not have seen the prose passage or the poem before.

In **Section C** of the exam you have to write an essay discussing two prose texts – your core novel and a second text. Your novels will be related in theme, style or structure.

Content

This part of the book helps you develop your skills in reading and analysing prose for Sections A and C of the exam. The sub-sections below cover the aspects of prose study listed in the specification. These are:

1	Introduction: What is a narrative?	50
2	Different types of narrative: genre	51
3	Exploring narrative openings	53
4	Modes of telling: narrative voice and point of view	55
5	Dialogue and voices	61
6	Narrative structure	64
7	Symbols and motifs	69
8	Prose style	71
9	Methods of characterisation	75
10	The presentation of themes	77

Additional support

The **Teaching and Assessment CD-ROM** provides detailed material for studying all the prescribed novel groupings in Section C. You will find it useful as you work on this part of the book.

1 Introduction: what is a narrative?

The following sections develop your understanding of the main features of **narrative** and the techniques that writers of narratives use to tell their stories.

We hear and tell **stories** all the time, in all aspects of our lives, from dreams and jokes to anecdotes and novels. Stories help us to see and interpret the world.

In everyday use, the two terms 'story' and 'narrative' are usually used interchangeably, but some critics define them slightly differently. They say that:

- a story is what happens and who it happens to (plot and character)
- a narrative is the story plus the *telling* of it – all the things that go into bringing the story to life for a listener or reader.

Studying narrative means studying not only what happens and to whom, but also all the ways in which the teller (in the case of this unit, the writer rather than a speaker) creates the story and the reader responds to it.

The critic Roland Barthes has said:

> ... narrative is present in myth, legend, fable, tale, novella, epic, history, tragedy, drama, comedy, mime, painting ... stained-glass windows, cinema, comics, news items, conversation. Moreover, under this almost infinite diversity of forms, narrative is present in every age, in every place, in every society; it begins with the very history of mankind and there nowhere is nor has been a people without narrative.

> **Key terms**
> narrative
> story

Activity 1

1 Write down four or five examples of stories you have read, heard or watched over the past 24 hours.

2 Annotate each of your examples with anything you can say about how it was told, by whom and in what context.

3 Share your list with someone else and compare your findings about the range of stories you come across or tell in a typical day, and the ways they are told.

Activity 2

1 What makes a narrative a narrative? Here are four short texts. For each one decide:

   a whether you think it is or is not part of a narrative

   b what it is about the extract that helped you to decide.

Text A:

Earl Ober was between jobs as a salesman. But Doreen his wife, had gone to work nights as a waitress at a twenty-four-hour coffee shop at the edge of town. One night, when he was drinking, Earl decided to stop by the coffee shop and have something to eat.

Text B:

And so I'm like, 'How could you do that to him?' and she's like, 'Well he did the same to me, so he deserved everything he got,' and I'm like, 'Well no wonder he decided to leave you.' And we haven't talked to each other since.

Text C:

Humpty Dumpty sat on a wall,

Humpty Dumpty had a great fall,

All the king's horses and all the king's men

Couldn't put Humpty together again.

Text D:

I wouldn't go today if I were you. The sales are on, there'll be masses of people and the car parks'll be full. I'd leave it till a bit later in the week when it's less crowded. I'm sure there'll still be some good bargains.

2 Using the texts above to help you, talk about which of the following ingredients you think are essential in a narrative (E); which are sometimes found in narratives, but are not essential (S); and which are never found in a narrative (N). Against each ingredient, put a label (E), (S) or (N).

  a a teller

  b more than one event

  c one thing leading to another (cause and effect)

  d a moral or message

  e people

  f things taking place in time (a sense of time passing)

  g description of places

  h everything is told in the past tense

  i events are seen through one person's eyes

  j a beginning, a middle and an end

3 Is there any other ingredient, not on the list, which you think can also be essential or typical of a narrative? If so, add it to the list and mark it with E or S.

4 Come back to this list after working on narratives for a while to see if your views have changed at all.

Take it further

Choose three or four tiny fragments of your own from fiction or non-fiction texts. Do any of your non-fiction examples show narrative features? What does this tell you about how non-fiction writers can use narrative techniques to engage the reader? Present your examples to other people in your class, describing and analysing the features of narrative that you have identified.

2 Different types of narrative: genre

A **genre** is a type of writing. Within the big genre that we call narrative, there are sub-sets such as the novel or the short story, which are also called genres. Within these sub-sets, there are further kinds of writing that, perhaps unhelpfully, are also called genres (eg horror or romance) and even within these, there are further divisions. For instance, there are several different genres of detective fiction (country house, hard-boiled and so on). Below is a chart showing just some of the sub-genres within the big genre of narrative.

What makes a genre?

Key terms

genre

conventions

sub-genre

generic features

Each genre has its own **conventions**, in other words typical features. Each **sub-genre** has its own conventions too. A reader either knows in advance what genre they are reading or listening to, or works this out while reading, by recognising the conventions. A reader has expectations about what the narrative in a particular genre will be like. The writer can choose to:

- fulfil these expectations
- extend these expectations by developing and changing the conventions
- challenge these expectations by rejecting the conventions
- mix up genre conventions and **generic features,** in a playful or experimental way.

Activity 3

1 Read these two lists of generic features and see if you can match each one to a genre.

A	B
• a very short story • generalised characters or types, often without a name (eg a young girl, an old man, an animal) • generalised, often rural setting (eg an unnamed village, a forest) • language that is not everyday, but has a more 'noble' flavour • a strong metaphorical element • ends with a strong moral, often made absolutely explicit in the last sentence (eg 'And so …')	• a woman is in search of love • a possible object of her desire appears (not always obviously suitable) • an obstacle is placed in the way (misunderstandings, a competitor or another problem) • the obstacle persists and becomes more complicated • it looks as if it is all going to end badly • finally the obstacle is overcome

2 From your own knowledge, make a list of the conventions of one of the other written genres in the diagram above. (Depending on the genre, you could use your knowledge of film to help you, since some of the generic features are the same in books and films of the same genre.)

3 Share ideas with other students looking at the same genre and debate the conventions. Create a final, clear list of what you consider to be the most important conventions of that genre.

Identifying genres

Activity 4

The text on page 53 follows many of the conventions of its genre.

1 Read the text and identify the genre.

2 Explore what made you come to your decision by talking about the features you noticed.

3 Compare your decisions with those of other students.

Below the grill there was an iron knocker. I hammered on it.
Nothing happened. I pushed the bell at the side of the door and heard it ring inside not very far off and waited and nothing happened. I worked on the knocker again. Still
5 nothing. I went back up the walk and along to the garage and lifted the door far enough to see the car with white side-walled tyres was inside. I went back to the front door.
A neat black Cadillac coupé came out of the garage across the way, backed, turned and came along past
10 Lavery's house, slowed, and a thin man in dark glasses looked at me sharply, as if I hadn't any business to be there. I gave him my steely glare and he went on his way.
I went down Lavery's walk again and did some more hammering on his knocker. This time I got results. The
15 judas window opened and I was looking at a handsome bright-eyed number through the bars of the grill.
'You make a hell of a lot of noise,' a voice said.

'Mr Lavery?'
He said he was Mr Lavery and what about it. I poked
20 a card through the grill. A large brown hand took the card. The bright brown eyes came back and the voice said: 'So sorry. Not needing any detectives today please.'
'I'm working for Derace Kingsley.'
'The hell with both of you,' he said, and banged the
25 judas window.
I leaned on the bell beside the door and got a cigarette out with my free hand and had just struck the match on the woodwork beside the door when it was yanked open and a big guy in bathing trunks, beach sandals and a white
30 terrycloth bathing robe started to come out at me.
I took my thumb off the bell and grinned at him.
'What's the matter?' I asked him. 'Scared?'
'Ring that bell again,' he said, 'and I'll throw you clear across the street.'

Take it further

Choose one genre of narrative that interests you. Find three or four examples of texts in that genre. (Some bookshops or libraries organise their books in terms of genre.) Read just the opening pages of each one and note down how your expectations of the genre are fulfilled, extended or challenged. You could do this individually or as a small group activity and present your findings to the rest of the class.

Preparing for the exam (Section C)

Can you define the genre of your core text? Does the writer of your further text draw on a range of genres, use generic conventions, challenge them or deliberately play with your expectations? Does your reading of the further text make you think about the genre of the core text in a new way?

3 Exploring narrative openings

The beginning of a novel can be a vital way of setting up aspects of what is to follow, such as what the narrative is about, who the characters are, where the story is set and who is telling the story. It is the way that writers hook their readers and draw them into the world of their novel. The writer sets up a kind of 'contract' with the reader about what to expect – 'if you come on this reading journey with me you're going to have this kind or that kind of experience'. Narratives in a genre such as thriller, romance or detective fiction, often make the reader aware particularly clearly, right from the start, what type of story or genre they are reading.

Activity 5

1 Explore the five openings from novels on page 54. They are written in very different styles and told in a range of different ways. Fill in a copy of the chart below using a star-rating system to show your first responses (* = not really, ** = quite a lot, *** = very much).

	A	B	C	D	E
The opening focuses on the setting.					
We get a strong sense of what the characters are like.					
The **narrator** tells you a lot about him or herself.					
You're dropped right into the middle of the story.					
The opening makes us aware of the genre of the novel.					
The opening makes you want to read on.					

Text A: From *Restless* by William Boyd

When I was a child and was being fractious and contrary and generally behaving badly, my mother used
5 to rebuke me by saying: 'One day someone will come and kill me and then you'll be sorry'; or, 'They'll appear out of the blue and whisk me away – how would you like that?' or, 'You'll wake up one morning and I'll be gone.
10 Disappeared. You wait and see.'

Text B: From *The God of Small Things* by Arundhati Roy

May in Ayemenem is a hot, brooding month. The days are long and humid. The river shrinks and black crows gorge on bright mangoes in still, dustgreen trees. Red bananas ripen. Jackfruits burst. Dissolute bluebottles hum vacuously in the fruity air. Then they stun themselves
5 against clear windowpanes and die, fatly baffled in the sun.
   The nights are clear but suffused with sloth and sullen expectation.
   But by early June the south-west monsoon breaks and there are three months of wind and water with short spells of sharp, glittering sunshine that thrilled children snatch to play with. The countryside
10 turns an immodest green. Boundaries blur as tapioca fences take root and bloom.

Text C: From *The Road* by Cormac McCarthy

When he woke in the woods in the dark and the cold of the night he'd reach out to touch the child
5 sleeping beside him. Nights dark beyond darkness and the days more grey each one than what had gone before. Like the onset of some cold glaucoma dimming away the world. His hand rose and fell
10 softly with each precious breath. He pushed away the plastic tarpaulin and raised himself in the stinking robes and blankets and looked toward the east for any light but there was none.

Text D: From *Housekeeping* by Marilynne Robinson

My name is Ruth. I grew up with my younger sister, Lucille, under the care of my grandmother, Mrs. Sylvia Foster, and when she died, of her sisters-in-law, Misses Lily and Nona Foster, and when they fled, of her daughter, Mrs. Sylvia Fisher. Through all
5 these generations of elders we lived in one house, my grandmother's house, built for her by her husband, Edmund Foster, an employee of the railroad, who escaped this world years before I entered it. It was he
10 who put us down in this unlikely place.

Text E: From *The Spy Who Came in from the Cold* by John Le Carré

The American handed Leamas another cup of coffee and said, 'Why don't you go back to sleep? We can ring you if he shows up.'
   Leamas said nothing, just stared through the window of the checkpoint, along the empty street.
   'You can't wait for ever, sir. Maybe he'll come some other time. We can have the polizei contact the Agency: you can be back here in twenty minutes.'
5 'No,' said Leamas, 'it's nearly dark now.'
   'But you can't wait for ever; he's nine hours over schedule.'
   'If you want to go, go. You've been very good,' Leamas added. 'I'll tell Kramer you've been damn' good.'
   'But how long will you wait?'
   'Until he comes.'

Preparing for the exam (Section C)

Explore the openings of your texts, using what you have learned to analyse the writers' intentions, the techniques used and the impact on the reader. You could do this before reading your core text, so that right from the start you're thinking about it in relation to your second text.

Developing your analysis further

Activity 6

The writer Blake Morrison has tried to analyse novel openings by categorising them in different ways. Here is a summary of his categories:

- the plunge – launching you right into the middle
- the shocker – a big surprise or outrageous idea
- the intriguing narrator – you want to know more about the person (or animal) telling the story
- the epigram – a neat little phrase summing up an idea that will be important in the book
- the promise – telling the reader what they will be getting
- the omen – a warning of bad things to come
- the particulars – pinning down all the details, as if for a news report
- the self-referral – the narrator introduces him/herself.

Key terms

narrator
prologue
framing device
narrative voice

1   Look at the five novel openings on page 54 again and decide which of Morrison's categories (if any) best fits each opening. You can choose more than one category, if that seems appropriate, or add a category of your own, if you prefer.

2   Choose the opening you like best. Write a short statement about the opening in which you explain:

- how it grabs you as a reader
- what it focuses on (characters, setting, introducing the narrator or anything else)
- what sort of 'contract' you think it is setting up with the reader (eg 'it is saying if you read on you will find a novel that is …').

3   Using what you have learned, write one or two openings of your own, experimenting with different ways into a narrative. You could use a myth or legend or a film you have seen recently to provide you with the storyline itself, to allow you to concentrate on the *way* you tell it.

4   Read one of your openings to other people in the class, explaining what you were trying to do.

Take it further

- Find one other example of a novel opening that you think is particularly effective and quite different to the ones you have looked at so far. Share it with the rest of the class and explain how and why you think it works particularly well.
- Think about the effects of other strategies for starting a novel, such as epigrams (short quotations at the start), **prologues** (introductory passages) or **framing devices** (putting the main narrative inside another 'framing' one). Frames often introduce a character who will narrate the main story, giving the circumstances of how they first heard the story).
- Compare endings as well. You could create your own categories for types of endings, along the same lines as Blake Morrison's list. Perhaps your starting point could be to brainstorm the endings of books or films that you have particularly liked, which you then try to categorise.

4   Modes of telling: narrative voice and point of view

At GCSE you may well have come across the terms 'first', 'second' and 'third person **narrative voice**', to describe the way a novel or short story is told. At AS level, you need to look at this in a more detailed way, exploring the subtleties of how writers use narrative voice.

Finding out more

Some descriptions of different kinds of narrative voice are given on page 56. Don't worry about absorbing all the information at this stage. The activity that follows will allow you to make use of, and become familiar with, these ideas.

Key terms

first person narrative
unreliable narrator
stream of consciousness
third person narrative
ominiscient third person
  narrator
point of view
over-the-shoulder
  narration
free indirect style
tag
second person narrative

First person narrative

Narratives told in the first person are written in the voice of a character in the narrative, as if they are saying, 'This happened to me. I am telling you this story.'

First person narrators can be very different, from the narrator who introduces themselves at the beginning as the person telling a story in which they are not involved and then almost disappears from view, to the narrator whose life is at the heart of the story.

Some first person narrators are described as **unreliable narrators**, because the writer deliberately introduces an element of doubt as to the trustworthiness of their account of things. This makes the act of reading the story more complex, as the reader is not only following the twists and turns of the plot and getting to grips with themes and characters, but is also having to question the narrator and their judgement on everything that is presented.

Stream of consciousness is a form of first person narration, where the writer, through the narrator, tries to suggest the spontaneous outpouring of thoughts and feelings. It is as if the reader has direct access to the inner workings of the narrator's mind. Occasionally a 'stream of consciousness' style can also be used in a third person narrative voice.

Third person narrative

Third person narrators are not characters in the story. A **third person narrative** says, 'He did this' or 'She went there'. Conventionally, third person narration is thought to be more distanced and neutral than first person narration, but in fact there are different kinds of third person voice, as summarised below.

The **omniscient third person narrator** is a god-like, all-knowing narrator, who does not draw attention to him or herself and is able to tell you the thoughts and feelings of all of the characters, although often the story focuses on the **point of view** of just one or two characters. This is sometimes described as **over-the-shoulder narration** (see the comments on point of view, page 58). Omniscient third person narration is often regarded by readers as the author's voice, although as a student of literature you should try to keep the two separate in your discussion of the text. In some such narratives, the author's voice seems to be more explicit and obvious than in others.

In **free indirect style** the third person narrative voice shifts into something more like the thoughts and feelings of a character, expressed directly. It can be identified partly by a difference in the use of **tags** (how writers introduce or follow up direct speech, indicating who said it), for example: '"Why didn't she accept the flowers?" thought James, feeling rebuffed by her rejection', in free indirect style might simply say: 'Why didn't she accept the flowers? This was clearly a rebuff.' The difference in the second example is that James's feelings are presented without the distancing of the narrator telling us that these are James's thoughts rather than the narrator's account of it.

Free indirect style is especially clear where the reader knows that what is being said definitely is *not* what the third person narrator believes. In the example above, the narrator may have already made it clear to the reader that the girl suffers from a severe allergy to pollen, in which case the reader knows that James's feelings of rejection are not shared by the narrator. Many third person narratives slip in and out of the more detached style and free indirect style.

Second person narrative

Second person narrative is a form of narration where the reader is addressed as 'you'. It is quite rare for narratives to use it at all, but extremely rare to find it is used for a whole book, as it is really hard to maintain and equally hard to read.

Activity 7

1 Below is a well-known 'story'. Read the five re-tellings of it that follow. Read each one aloud to get a sense of the voice in which the story is told.

2 Using the information on narrative voice, discuss which kind of narrative voice would best describe each re-telling. (You may find that it is not always clear-cut and you should debate the reasons for choosing one or other description.)

3 Think of another nursery rhyme, fairytale or traditional story (eg Jack and Jill, Cinderella, Anansi). Write a short section of the story, just a paragraph or so, choosing what kind of narrative voice you're going to use.

4 As a class, read aloud your writing to see if other people can identify the story and the kind of narrative voice you chose to use.

Hey diddle diddle,
The cat and the fiddle,
The cow jumped over the moon.
The little dog laughed to see such fun
And the dish ran away with the spoon.

Re-telling A

It's been crazy around here all week - everything topsy-turvy. And just when I thought things were settling down, Mogsy takes it into her head that she wants to be a musician, the silly old cow from the upper field decides she's had enough of grass and fields and wants to be a high jump champion and Fido forgets his bark and gets a fit of the giggles. So me and the dish decide that enough's enough. We team up together, pack our bags and off we go to make a new life for ourselves somewhere a bit more chilled out, where we can raise a whole family of crockery and cutlery in peace and quiet!

Re-telling B

The Cat padded quietly towards the drawing room and slunk in. There sitting on a chair was the precious wooden instrument belonging to her mistress. With one spring she was up on the upholstered seat. She snuggled up into its soft curves. Light was fading fast. Blinking, she let her green eyes focus on the window and on the outline of the crescent moon. The cow was out again tonight, leaping skywards, while the farmer absent-mindedly cleaned out the shed. In the distance she heard the sound of laughter, the hoarse barking cackle of the farmer's dog. And from the kitchen came the clatter of cutlery, as her mistress washed up after dinner, searching for that last spoon and the little dish that always seemed to go astray.

Re-telling C

The cow was bored. Why was it always the same? Munch grass all day, swish off the flies with your tail, squelch about in a muddy field, plod home to the dairy. Life wasn't much fun, not if you were Daisy of Dunberry Farm. Not even a nice bit of romance to spice things up. Just a lonely return to the barn and the endless dark night on her own. She had had enough. And seeing those lucky birds flying up and free in the trees she decided to make her break for freedom. Why not give it a try? And that moon looked so very inviting.

Re-telling D

Dark sky and a cold chill in the air, my fur damp through and no dinner. NO dinner! They forgot my dinner! With all that fuss over a stupid cow and a silly old spoon they didn't put out my dinner. I went to the kitchen at the usual time but the dish wasn't there. And now I'm hungry. How dare they forget me like that? I think I'll go and sharpen my claws on their stupid old fiddle. A few good scratches and bit of a kick. That'll teach them a lesson! They won't forget my dinner again in a hurry.

Re-telling E

You may not believe me. That's up to you. But I definitely saw a pure white cow jumping over the moon, that's one hundred percent certain. I hadn't been drinking that night, I can assure you. The cat can vouch for me, and the dog as well. I'll kick him good and hard if he doesn't! Ok, perhaps I had a little drink but there certainly were strange goings on. It wasn't me imagining it. That stupid mutt really was playing the fiddle, the cow was up there frolicking in the sky and the silly cat was sat there laughing her head off. That much I can promise was true.

Point of view

Point of view is closely linked to, but *not the same as*, narrative voice. It is about 'whose eyes events are seen through'. For example, you could have a third person narrative voice where the events of the novel are mainly seen through the eyes of one particular character. The person whose point of view dominates is sometimes called the **focaliser**. The events of the narrative are focalised through that character.

Even in a first person narrative, writers can introduce other points of view through devices like:

* letters
* chapters written in another voice
* whole sections written in different voices
* a narrative introduced by someone who first tells their own story (a frame)
* documents before or after the main narrative, such as prologues, appendices or **epilogues**.

These devices can help to overcome the limitations of first person narratives, in only offering a single perspective.

Preparing for the exam (Sections A and C)

The examiners will be looking for a more precise comment than just first, second or third person. They will also want you to talk about the *effect* of the choices made by the writer.

Activity 8

Look back at the re-tellings of 'Hey diddle diddle' on page 57, as well as your own telling of a nursery rhyme. Decide from whose point of view each one is told. Is the point of view always the same as that of the narrator?

Activity 9

1   Read the four extracts from novels below.

Text A: From *Captain Corelli's Mandolin* by Louis de Bernières

That evening the captain noticed an exquisitely embroidered waistcoat hanging over the back of a chair in the kitchen. He picked it up and held it against the light; the velvet was richly scarlet, and the satin lining was sewn in with tiny conscientious threads that looked as though they could only have been done by the fingers of a diminutive sylph.
5   In gold and yellow thread he saw languid flowers, soaring eagles, and leaping fish. He ran his finger over the embroidery and felt the density of the designs. He closed his eyes and realised that each figure recapitulated in relief the curves of the creature it portrayed.
      Pelagia came in and caught him. She felt a rush of embarrassment, perhaps because she did not want him to know why she had made the article, perhaps because she
10   had been rendered ashamed of its imperfections. He opened his eyes and held out the waistcoat to her. 'This is so beautiful,' he said…

Text B: From *Mrs Dalloway* by Virginia Woolf

Mrs Dalloway said she would buy the flowers herself.
      For Lucy had her work cut out for her. The doors would be taken off their hinges; Rumpelmayer's men were coming. And then, thought Clarissa Dalloway, what a morning – fresh as if issued to children on a beach.
      What a lark! What a plunge! For so it has always seemed to her when, with a little squeak of the hinges,
5   which she could hear now, she had burst open the French windows and plunged at Bourton into the open air. How fresh, how calm, stiller than this of course, the air was in the early morning; like the flap of a wave; the kiss of a wave, chill and sharp and yet (for a girl of eighteen as she then was) solemn, feeling as she did, standing there at the open window, that something awful was about to happen; looking at the flowers, at the trees with the smoke winding off them and the rooks rising, falling; standing and looking until Peter Walsh
10   said, 'Musing among the vegetables?' – was that it? – 'I prefer men to cauliflowers' – was that it? He must have said it at breakfast one morning when she had gone out on to the terrace – Peter Walsh. He would be back from India one of these days, June or July, she forgot which, for his letters were awfully dull; it was his sayings one remembered; his eyes, his pocket-knife, his smile, his grumpiness and, when millions of things had utterly vanished – how strange it was! – a few sayings like this about cabbages.

Text C: From *The Curious Incident of the Dog in the Night Time* by Mark Haddon

I think I would make a very good astronaut.

To be a good astronaut you have to be intelligent and I'm intelligent. You also have to understand how machines work and I'm good at understanding how machines work. You also have to be someone who would like being on their own in a tiny spacecraft
5 thousands and thousands of miles away from the surface of the earth and not panic or get claustrophobia or homesick or insane. And I like really little spaces, so long as there is no one else in them with me. Sometimes when I want to be on my own I get into the airing cupboard in the bathroom and slide in beside the boiler and pull the door closed behind me and sit there and think for hours and it makes me feel calm.

10 So I would have to be an astronaut on my own, or have my own part of the spacecraft which no one else could come into.

And also there are no yellow things or brown things in a spacecraft so that would be OK, too.

And I would have to talk to other people from Mission Control, but we would do
15 that through a radio link-up and a TV monitor so they wouldn't be like real people who are strangers, but it would be like playing a computer game.

Also I wouldn't be homesick at all because I'd be surrounded by lots of things I like, which are machines and computers and outer space.

Text D: From *The Sea* by John Banville

Bun, I began to see, was far more sly and astute than I would at first have given her credit for. One is inclined to imagine that people who are fat must also be stupid. This fat person, however, had taken the measure of me, and, I was convinced, saw me clearly for what I was, in all my essentials. And what was it that she saw? In my life it never
5 troubled me to be kept by a rich, or richish, wife. I was born to be a dilettante, all that was lacking was the means, until I met Anna. Nor am I concerned particularly about the provenance of Anna's money, which was first Charlie Weiss's and is now mine, or how much or what kind of heavy machinery Charlie had to buy and sell in the making of it. What is money, after all? Almost nothing, when one has a sufficiency of it. So why was
10 I squirming like this under Bun's veiled but knowing, irresistible scrutiny?

But come now, Max, come now. I will not deny it. I was always ashamed of my origins, and even still it requires only an arch glance or a condescending word from the likes of Bun to set me quivering inwardly in indignation and hot resentment. From the start I was bent on bettering myself.

2 Use what you have learned to identify broadly what kind of narrative voice is used (first, second, third, omniscient, free indirect style and so on).

3 Explore each voice in more detail. For instance, is it the voice of a detached observer, is it intimate and close up, does it sound like the voice of the character speaking to the reader, perhaps using second person address, or does it sound like the thoughts of the character pouring out?

4 Use the list of prompts below to help you explore how the writer has created this voice:

- sentence length and structure
- what kinds of words are chosen (lexis)
- formality or informality
- how structured or unstructured it seems as a whole.

5 Now think about point of view. Is it clear whose point of view you are given? Is there a single point of view? Does there ever seem to be a gap between the narrator's point of view and that of the writer?

6 Finally, think about the effect on you as a reader, choosing some examples to show the effect.

Preparing for the exam (Section A)

You may be asked to write about narrative voice or point of view in Question a) or b). You will be expected to talk about one aspect, chosen for you by the examiner (eg the use of free indirect style in lines XX–XX.) Question c) is more general; you will have to choose which aspects to focus on. Study the commentary on Extract D in Activity 11, which is the kind of writing that you will be expected to do if Question c) is on narrative voice.

Key terms

focaliser

epilogue

Activity 10

This activity in creative writing will take your thinking further.

1   Individually, pick one of the extracts from Activity 9 and rewrite the first four or five sentences using a different kind of narrative voice, to see what difference this makes.

2   Read your changed versions aloud and talk about the impact of the changes. Talk about what this adds to your understanding of the voice and point of view in the original.

Activity 11

1   Read the commentary on Extract **D** below. Share what you notice about what has been included. Annotate a copy of the commentary to show:

- which features of narrative voice and point of view the writer of the commentary has identified
- whether and where the writer has explored the effect of these features or merely noticed them
- how well the writer has used evidence from the text
- anything extra that you think would be worth saying, or that you disagree with.

2   Write a commentary of your own on the use of narrative voice in one of the other extracts on pages 58–59.

3   Swap commentaries with other people in the class who have chosen the same extract to see how they have approached it.

Preparing for the exam (Section C)

Open your core text at a random page. See what you can say about the use of narrative voice on that page, using everything you have learned in this section. Present your findings to the rest of the group, either as an oral presentation or as a written presentation for display on the wall.

Extract D commentary

This is a first person narrative, in which the narrator remembers events in his life and reflects on his own behaviour, explaining to himself (and the reader) his motivation and trying to justify his actions. Aspects of the language give the flavour of him talking to himself (for example occasional informal expressions such as 'rich, or richish') but it is organised thoughts rather than stream of consciousness. The repeated questions, addressed to himself suggest thoughts, for instance, 'And what was it that she saw?' 'But come now, Max, come now' is speech-like and suggests inner conflict as he tries to be honest with himself. Generally the lexis is formal and precise – the writer uses words such as 'astute', 'essentials', 'dilettante', 'provenance', 'indignation' and so on, which suggest to the reader a particular kind of man, well-educated and used to reflection. However, this is strongly contrasted with his crude description of Bun as 'This fat person'. There is a bluntness about this that perhaps makes us wonder about the narrator. It creates a gap between what the reader (and perhaps the author?) thinks and the narrator's own view of himself. Although the point of view is the narrator's, we don't always share it.

By the end of the extract the narrator seems to have come full circle. From feeling hostility towards Bun and resisting her view of him, he ends up admitting to himself that he was always 'bent on bettering myself.'

5 Dialogue and voices

Narrative voice is the voice chosen to tell the story. Within most narratives there is also a range of other voices, usually presented to the reader through **dialogue**. The narrative voice (or occasionally voices) and the voices of characters in dialogue are often given their own unique styles of speech. The way someone speaks is used to reveal their character to us.

Writers can use a range of techniques to convey individual voices:

- the rhythm of their speech
- the level or degree of **formality** or **informality**
- repeated expressions and favourite phrases
- individual or unusual ways of speaking
- the length of their **utterances**
- their use of **Standard English**, **dialect**, **Received Pronunciation** or another accent
- signals of politeness or impoliteness (eg commands, abruptness and so on)
- indications of tone (eg using italics to show emphasis, dashes or exclamation marks)
- the use of tags (the way their speech is described by the writer in introducing their speech directly, eg 'she said, langorously' or 'he barked in his usual stentorian tone of voice')
- the way the speech is laid out on the page.

Key terms

dialogue
formality/informality
utterance
Standard English
dialect
Received Pronunciation

Activity 12

In this activity you will be writing a very short dialogue for three characters, to explore how writers can use dialogue to develop their characters. Below are eight thumbnail sketches for characters, which are deliberately exaggerated to allow you to quickly give an impression of what they are like through their speech.

1   Choose three characters from the thumbnails and write one or two lines of dialogue for each one, deciding how you are going to introduce their words as well as what they say. Try to give a flavour of each character in their speech. Don't use their names to give away who they are!

Here is one example to get you started. Which character do you think it is?

His voice trembled slightly. 'Er…I'm so…so very sorry but would you mind telling me where I'm supposed to be?'

2   Read your bits of dialogue out to a partner and see if they can guess who they are from the dialogue and/or the way you have introduced them.

Ivan Markovic

A rich Russian businessman living in London, who has decided to bid to take over a Premiership football team.

Salima Ahmed

A young wannabe actress, with attitude, who is determined to make it whatever it takes.

Colonel Blinkhorn

An English army man in his 80s, who now lives alone in a large house with his housekeeper.

Lorna Lewis

A dinner lady, who runs the canteen at a primary school and likes to rule the roost.

Timmy Dodds

A cheeky 15-year-old boy, who is frequently in trouble with his teachers.

Emma Macdonald

A housewife, living in Glasgow, who works hard at bringing up her three lively daughters.

Michael Maloney

A timid young man, who has just started his first job working in an office, alongside a boisterous group of other workers.

Davina Lloyd-Smith

A young woman in her 20s, brought up in a stately home in Kent, who enjoys partying with the sons and daughters of lords and dukes.

Analysing dialogue in a novel extract

Activity 13

1 Read the extract below from *Small Island* by Andrea Levy, which has been partially annotated to show how the author has conveyed the voices.

2 Add to the annotations, using the bullet points on page 61 to help you explore the techniques and their effects.

The writer signals Celia's shock with her use of an adjective, 'confused' and a precise verb 'squeaked'.

Sentence grammar indicates an Afro-Caribbean speaker.

The length of this utterance suggests that the speaker is controlling the conversation and enjoying that control.

'Well, hello again,' this man said – not to Celia but to me.

Celia, confused, almost squeaked, 'You have met before?'

I heard a plain voice – no lilting baritone – when the man said, 'This is the woman who likes to put pawpaw on her foot.'

5 I protested, 'I do not. I accidentally step in the fruit,' while Celia's eyes were fixed on me for an explanation.

But this man just kept on jabbering. 'You step in it? Let me tell you, Celia, about this woman. But wait, this woman is not the friend you tell me of?'

Celia, nodding, tried to say, 'We teach at the same – ' before this man was off again.

10 'Celia has told me of her good friend and it is you. Cha, man!' He sucked his teeth, shaking his head. 'You. So you remember me?'

I made no reply, which did not discourage him.

'Celia, let me tell you how I meet this woman. It was the day Busta speaking – by the corporation office. You know Busta? Bustemate? Everybody know Busta. So Busta

15 speaking. Suddenly one quarrel break out. Everything that could be pick up is flying through the air. Boy, the confusion, everyone running this way and that. And there in the middle of the mighty battle is this young woman looking like she strolling to church in her best hat. So I rescue her.'

'He rescued you?' Celia asked.

20 'You did what to me?' I shouted to this man. 'I did not need rescuing.'

'Oh. As I recall the situation something was about to bounce off your pretty head and knock you flat.'

'He rescued you?' Celia said once more.

'Yes, I rescue her. But the look on her face made me worry she gone turn round and

25 bite me.'

'And what about the pawpaw?' Celia wanted to know.

'Celia, I am glad you ask about the pawpaw – because I am sure your friend here does not tell you she likes to wear it on her foot.'

We waited quietly for this man to stop laughing at his joke.

Activity 14

1   Read the following short extract from *Trainspotting* by Irvine Welsh, in which the use of dialogue is particularly interesting.

2   Remind yourself of the bullet points on techniques, on page 61, and then read the extract again, annotating a copy of it with your thoughts about the voice and how it has been evoked.

3   Write one or two paragraphs exploring how the writer uses dialogue in this extract and its impact on you as a reader.

> Shite. Geoff was coming over to talk to her. She had once pointed him out to Shona, who said that he looked like Marti from Wet Wet Wet. Nina hated both Marti and the Wets, and, anyway, thought that Geoff was nothing like him.
>
> – Awright, Nina?
>
> 5   – Aye. It's a shame aboot Uncle Andy.
>
> – Aye, Whit kin ye say? Geoff shrugged his shoulders. He was twenty-one and Nina thought that was ancient.
>
> – Soo when dae ye finish the school? he asked her.
>
> – Next year. Ah wanted tae go now but ma Ma hassled us tae stey.
>
> 10   – Takin O Grades?
>
> – Aye.
>
> – Which yins?
>
> – English, Maths, Arithmetic, Art, Accounts, Physics, Modern Studies.
>
> – Gaunnae pass them?
>
> 15   – Aye. It's no that hard. Cept Maths.
>
> – Then whit?
>
> – Git a job. Or git oan a scheme.
>
> – No gaunnae stey oan n take Highers?
>
> – Naw.
>
> 20   – Ye should. You could go tae University.
>
> – Whit fir?
>
> Geoff had to think for a while. He had recently graduated with a degree in English Literature and was on the dole. So were most of his fellow graduates. – It's a good social life, he said.

Take it further

Wider reading will develop your understanding of the way writers create distinctive narrative voices and voices in dialogue. Texts with specially interesting narrative voices include: *The Hours*, Michael Cunningham; *English Passengers*, Matthew Kneale; *Vernon God Little*, D.B.C. Pierre; *Cloud Atlas*, David Mitchell. These narratives use dialogue particularly interestingly: *Cold Comfort Farm*, Stella Gibbons; *Paddy Clarke Ha Ha Ha*, Roddy Doyle; *Trainspotting*, Irvine Welsh.

Preparing for the exam (Sections A and C)

Compare the way the writers of your core text and your second text handle dialogue by choosing two short extracts, one from each text, and applying what you have learned. Share your findings and see whether you can make any general statements about the way each writer handles dialogue and the use made of it in the novels as a whole.

If you are asked to comment on dialogue in Section A of the exam, draw on the list of features on page 61 in your answers, selecting those that you find most relevant or adding other features that you notice. Note that dialogue might be one aspect of a broader question, such as how the writer creates a character.

6 Narrative structure

Narrative and chronological time

If you unravel the plot of a novel, you can work out the sequence of what happens in **chronological time** – in other words, first this happens, then this, then this. The order in which the story unfolds for the reader (**narrative time**) can differ from chronological time.

Activity 15

1   Look at this short example of the chronology of a story.

> **Chronological time**
>
> - Jack had been selected for his local football team, for the first time.
> - The game started. At first he felt nervous and did not play his best.
> - Just before half time he scored a goal.
> - During the break an opposing player muttered a threat in his ear.
> - In the second half he scored again.
> - A few minutes later, the opposing player fouled him viciously.
> - In falling, Jack tore a ligament in his knee.
> - He was taken off to hospital.

In telling the story of the football game, a writer may well choose not to follow chronological time exactly. For instance:

> **Narrative time**
>
> - The story starts with Jack in hospital, looking back bitterly on events that afternoon.
> - It moves to the opening of the game, his nerves and failure to score.
> - It flashes back to his selection for the team and his feelings that he must do himself justice.
> - It returns to the game itself and his first goal.
> - It follows chronological sequence with the whispered threat during the half-time break and the second half goal.
> - It returns to the present with him in the hospital.
> - It ends with the scene where the boy fouls him.

2   Write your own five to eight sentence 'bare bones' sequence of events for a story, in chronological order.

3   Then decide on a different narrative sequence, using **flashbacks** or other ways of using time.

4   Talk about why you think a writer might choose to use narrative time in each of the following ways:

   a   starting with the ending, rather than the beginning of the story

   b   using repeated jumps in time, such as flashbacks or **flash forwards**

   c   setting different parts of the story in different time periods

   d   telling the entire story in reverse, from end to beginning.

Key terms

chronological time
narrative time
flashback
flash forward

Exploring shifts in narrative time in a text

Activity 16

1 Read the extract below from *Wise Children* by Angela Carter.

2 What are your first reactions to it? What effects do you think the writer is trying to achieve?

> She fixed Tristram with a suspicious eye, for he was no kin of hers, while the picture settled down on a flight of neon steps in a burst of canned applause as he came bounding down with his red hair slicked back, his top-of-the-milk-coloured rumpled linen Georgio Armani whistle and flute, Tristram Hazard, weak
> 5 but charming, game-show presenter and television personality, last gasp of the imperial Hazard dynasty that bestrode the British theatre like a colossus for a century and a half. Tristram, youngest son of the great Melchior Hazard, 'prince of players'; grandson of those tragic giants of the Victorian stage, Ranulph and Estella 'A star danced' Hazard. Lo, how the mighty have fallen.
> 10 'Hi, there! I'm Tristram!'
> The camera closes in as he sings out, 'Hi, there, lolly lovers! I'm Tristram Hazard and I've come to bring you …' Now he throws back his head, showing off his throat, he's got a real old-fashioned, full-bodied, Ivory Novello-type throat, he throws his head back and cries out in the voice of an ecstatic: 'LASHINGS OF
> 15 LOLLY! LASHINGS OF LOLLY!'
> The show begins.
>
> Freeze frame.
> Let us pause awhile in the unfolding story of Tristram and Tiffany so that I can fill you in on the background. High time! you must be saying. Just who
> 20 is this Melchior Hazard and his clan, his wives, his children, his hangers-on? It is in order to provide some of the answers to those questions that I, Dora Chance, in the course of assembling notes towards my own autobiography, have inadvertently become the chronicler of all the Hazards …

3 Think of six adjectives to describe the writing, then compare your ideas with those of others.

4 Look more closely at the way the writer is using narrative time. How does she make us aware of the transitions? Why do you think she makes the shift and why do you think she chooses to draw attention to it in the way that she does?

5 Choose two of the following statements about the extract that you feel most in agreement with or find most interesting. Find a piece of evidence from the extract to support each of your chosen statements.

  a The writer is playing with the reader, giving titbits of information and then backtracking so that she fills us in with the 'history' once the reader has become interested to know more.

  b The jump back to a previous time is confusing and part of the writer's deliberate creation of a sense of chaos.

  c The jumps in time echo the narrator's jumbled process of putting together her own autobiography.

  d The writer uses film techniques to play with time in the narrative.

  e The use of time is closely connected to the character of the narrator and the narrative voice.

  f The use of time makes the text uncomfortable and difficult for a reader.

6 Use the statements and evidence to write a paragraph on how Angela Carter makes use of shifts in time in the extract.

Preparing for the exam (Section C)

You might want to track key chronological events and plot them against narrative time (in other words the order in which they are told). You could do this as a chart, where the first column is chronological and the second is narrative time, with arrows from one to the other.

Preparing for the exam (Section C)

While you are reading your core text and your second text, think about which narrative structures each writer is using and what effect this has. You could start doing this by comparing the opening chapters of your texts, to see what you can discover about the unfolding structure.

Big structures: the whole text

The use of narrative time is just one element of the way novels are structured. The writer has a number of options available when choosing the overall structure of a narrative. Here are some of the kinds of structural devices that novelists have used:

- a **frame story**, where a narrative is embedded in another narrative. The frame story is often the story of how the main narrative came to be told. Other framing devices are prologues, epilogues, additional documents, appendices or other additions to the main narrative

- an **episodic structure**, where the narrative moves from one episode to the next, without always having a direct connection between the two. Fictional autobiographies, rites of passage novels or journeys are well suited to this structure

- **parallel** or **connected narratives**, where several different characters or groups of characters are followed alternately. In linked narratives, they come together at key moments

- a structure of one story told through **linked parts**, for instance, three tellings of the same story in different voices

- a deliberate **anti-structure**, approach, in which the story emerges from the seemingly incoherent thoughts of a narrator, apparently without an overall plan or coherent shape

- a **generic structure**, such as that of the thriller or detective story, where the genre itself determines the conventional pattern of how events unfold. In the detective genre, for example, the structure is often based on a death followed by an unravelling of clues to how and why it happened. Other generic structures might be the fairytale, romance or horror story.

Exploring the structure of a whole short narrative

Activity 17

1 Read the short whole narrative below, 'Interchapter VII, *In Our Time*' by Ernest Hemingway, and work on a copy of it in the following ways.

    a Underline or highlight any contrasts or oppositions.

    b Remove the last two sentences. What difference would it make to end the story here?

    c What difference does the very last sentence make to the story?

    d Write one extra sentence of your own, drawing out the moral of the story more explicitly. What difference do you think it makes to add this more explicit ending?

2 Use the ideas raised by these tasks to help you write a short paragraph on the way Hemingway has structured this short story.

> While the bombardment was knocking the trench to pieces at Fossalta, he lay very flat and sweated and prayed oh jesus christ get me out of here. Dear jesus please get me out. Christ please please please christ. If you'll only keep me from getting killed I'll do anything you say. I believe in you and I'll tell every one in the world that you are the only one that matters. Please please dear jesus. The shelling moved further up the line. We went to work on the trench and in the morning the sun came up and the day was hot and muggy and cheerful and quiet. The next night back in Mestre he did not tell the girl he went upstairs with at the Villa Rossa about Jesus. And he never told anybody.

Preparing for the exam (Section A)

When considering the structure within an extract, think about these kinds of issues:

- use of recurring patterns of language (such as repetitions, or contrasts and **oppositions**)
- the use of symbols or motifs (see page 69)

- the way the extract develops (shifts, connections, coherence)
- shifts in narrative voice or point of view
- how it works as part of the overall structure of the text (eg if it is the beginning, the end or the start of a new section).

If you are given a very brief short story in its entirety, you might be expected to comment on any of the above, as well as:

- how it begins and ends, and how the two tie up
- whether it follows a generic structure, such as a fairytale or fable.

Tenses

Here is an outline for a story.

> A small child in a crowded shopping centre gets separated from her parents.

To turn this into a novel or short story you are faced with a number of choices, one of which is the choice of **tense**.

The tense used by the writer is what places the story in time, letting the reader know when it took place. The two main choices a writer has are to tell the story in the **past tense** as though the events are now over, or in the **present tense** as though they are still happening. Occasionally writers may slip into the **future tense** for short bursts.

<aside>

Key terms

frame story
episodic structure
parallel/connected
 narratives
linked parts
anti-structure
generic structure
opposition
tense
past tense
present tense
future tense

</aside>

Activity 18

1 On your own, write the first three or four sentences of the story of the child in the shopping centre, first in the present tense and then in the past tense. (Half the class should write their versions in the first person and the other half in the third person.)

2 In small groups (each containing at least one first and third person writer), take it in turns to read out your two versions and talk about the effects of the choice of tense. Did the use of first or third person make any difference to the effects of the tenses?

3 The boxes below give some reasons why writers might use different tenses. Read the information in each box and see how far it matches what you have discovered for yourselves and what else it adds.

Present tense	Past tense	Future tense
The story is told as though the events are still happening. This might make things seem uncertain as though even the narrator does not yet know how things will end.	It creates the impression that the action is over and that the events or experience are being reflected on.	It tells what will happen in the future.
It can seem slightly odd (the events and the telling of them are supposedly happening at the same time).	The narrator is imposing a pattern on events, leading the reader towards a conclusion.	A novel told wholly in the future tense would be very unusual and experimental, a series of predictions or speculative imaginings, or perhaps a set of instructions.
It can create a sense of immediacy.	While everything may seem uncertain to the reader, there is a sense that things will be resolved, although not necessarily happily.	Novelists may exploit this tense in small doses for particular effects.
It is more common in first than in third person narratives.		
It can also be used to create a sense of timelessness, as though everything has always been this way.		

A writer is not restricted to using one tense. Writers often choose to shift between past, present and future to create particular effects, as John Mullan explains here:

> This making of the past present, as if re-enacting it, is a device discovered by some 19th-century novelists. Charlotte Brontë's *Jane Eyre* uses it to memorable effect. When Brontë's narrator recalls episodes of special significance she suddenly shifts into the present tense, tasting delight or pain afresh.

Some writers even include short passages without a main verb, making it unclear whether what is happening is in the past or the present. This can create a timeless feel.

Activity 19

The following extracts are taken from Hilary Mantel's autobiography, *Giving Up the Ghost*. In both she describes a childhood memory.

1   Read the extracts and, in pairs, identify the tenses Mantel uses.

2   Talk about why you think Mantel uses different tenses in each extract and, in each case, what the effect is on you as a reader.

Hilary Mantel

Preparing for the exam (Section C)

Choose three short extracts, ranging across your core text, showing the writer's choice of tenses and how that affects meaning. You could go on to do the same with your second text to see whether there are any interesting points of comparison.

Extract 1

This is the first thing I remember. I am sitting up in my pram. We are outside, in the park called Bankswood. My mother walks backwards. I hold out my arms because I don't want her to go. She says she's only going to take my picture. I
5 don't understand why she goes backwards, back and aslant, tracking to one side. The trees overhead make a noise of urgent conversation, too quick to catch; the leaves part, the sky moves, the sun peers down at me. Away and away she goes, till she comes to a halt. She raises her arm and partly
10 hides her face. The sky and trees rush over my head. I feel dizzied. The entire world is sound, movement. She moves towards me, speaking. The memory ends.

Extract 2

When I was a child we used to play with toys called Magic Slates. There was a coloured cardboard frame, like a picture frame, which held a rectangle of carbon paper covered by a sheet of clear plastic. You had a writing implement like a
5 short knitting needle, with which you inscribed the plastic sheet. Behind the clear panel, your secret writing appeared; then you pulled up a cardboard tab, swished up the 'slate', and the marks vanished.

   The magic slate was a favourite toy of mine. I could
10 write anything I liked, but if someone loomed into view I could disappear it in an instant. I wrote many thoughts and observations, and letters from an imaginary me to an imaginary someone. I believed I was doing it in perfect safety.

7 Symbols and motifs

Symbols and **motifs** function in a range of ways in a narrative. They are closely related to the **themes** of the text, helping to signpost key ideas. As you read, the symbol or motif keeps gaining added meaning. They often also help to structure a narrative, providing continuity and coherence.

A symbol is something that represents another thing. For instance, white often symbolises purity, a dove is often used as a symbol for peace and a crown is the symbol of kingship. Unlike a motif, a symbol can be used on a single occasion and never mentioned again.

A motif is a recurring idea, running through a text. It might be an image or symbol that keeps cropping up, or it could be just a word, phrase or idea that keeps returning, for example, the repetition of the word 'darkness' in Joseph Conrad's novel, *Heart of Darkness*.

Activity 20

1   Think about the colour red. Draw a spider diagram to show phrases you have brainstormed in which red often appears. Now, in a different colour, add the **connotations** of red, in other words what red has come to represent. Use the examples below to start you off.

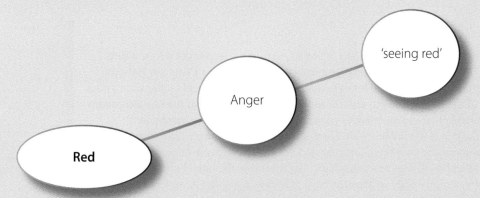

2   Create a quick thumbnail sketch of a character for whom red might be a good symbolic colour. Share your sketches with other students.

3   Think about one of these characters from narratives (or choose an example of your own). How has the colour red been used in relation to that character?

- Little Red Riding Hood
- Scarlet O'Hara in *Gone with the Wind*
- Dorothy in *The Wizard of Oz*
- The women in *The Handmaid's Tale*
- Snow White
- Amy Denver in Toni Morrison's *Beloved*
- the little girl in the film *Schindler's List*.

4   All the characters listed above are female. Can you think of any male characters with whom red has been associated? Explore your ideas about your findings.

Preparing for the exam (Section C)

While you are reading your core text and your second text, look out for any symbols and motifs, and keep track of them. After reading the novels, look back to see if you can trace the way the symbols and/or motifs develop across the novel and what use the writer makes of them to develop key themes, develop characters or structure the narrative.

Key terms

symbol

motif

theme

connotation

Exploring symbols and motifs in written narratives

Activity 21

Take it further

Use your knowledge of symbols and motifs in literary texts to explore their use in films or TV drama. For instance, you might notice the use of colour as a visual motif or the use of visual or sound symbolism in relation to different characters.

Michael Frayn's novel, *Spies* tells the story of two boys living in wartime England. There are several recurring symbols and motifs. One of these is a tunnel.

Here are some possible connotations for the tunnel:

- passing from one world to another (eg from child to adult; innocence to experience; innocence to corruption; safety to danger; urban to rural; suburban to slum)
- going from the known to the unknown
- moving from light into darkness or darkness into light (knowledge to ignorance, or vice versa)
- trial or quest
- fear
- adventure
- entrapment
- escape from the world.

Read the two short extracts from Spies below and talk about which connotations of the tunnel are being used and how Frayn seems to be using the tunnel symbolically. Are there any differences in its use in the two extracts?

Extract 1

Beyond the abandoned farm was a desolate no man's land half marked out as builder's lots, where colonisation approaching from the next settlement along had been halted for the Duration. Between the line of the railway and the wasteland of the lots, preserved for a few more years by the sifting tides of history, the last pocket of the rural world pursued its ancient, secret life. Each of the rare excursions

5   we made into it was a frightening adventure, a series of ordeals to test our coming manhood.

And the first of the ordeals was the tunnel itself. Once again I hear our uneasy cries drowned by the huge thunder of the train passing overhead. Once again I see the circle of unwelcoming daylight at the end doubled by its reflection in the great lake that collected inside the tunnel after rain. Once again I feel the awkward twist of my body as I turn to edge sideways along the narrow causeway left

10   at the edge of the lake, and simultaneously lean away from the glistening, dripping, wetness of the brickwork. Once again I feel the dank touch of the walls on my hair and shoulder, and brush at the foul exudations they've left. Once again I try to wipe the dark-green slime off my hands.

Extract 2

I put the cigarette into my mouth. The cork tip is moist from her lips, like the flap of her purse. Very carefully I suck in a little smoke. I feel the presence of it inside my mouth, as if it were something solid. She takes her hands away from her eyes and watches me, weeping and blinking. I hold the smoke in my mouth for a few moments, careful not to get it into my throat. It tastes of importance and of being grown

5   up. I lift my head, as I've seen Geoff do, and blow the smoke out again. I sigh with satisfaction.

She takes the cigarette back. 'How do you do it?' she asks humbly.

'You just have to get used to it.'

She screws up her eyes and takes another little puff.

'Now blow it out,' I instruct her. She blows the smoke out, and jerks her head back to keep her eyes

10   away from it.

She hands me the cigarette, and watches as I take another little mouthful.

'Do you feel all right?' she asks. 'It's supposed to make you feel sick.'

Do I feel all right? I feel … *something* disturbing. I don't think it's sick. I think it's … a kind of soaring sensation. I have a sense of freedom, as if I'm no longer bound by the rules and restrictions of childhood.

15   I can open locked boxes and break meaningless oaths with impunity. I'm on the verge of understanding mysteries that have been closed to me. I'm emerging from the old dark world of tunnels and terrors, and coming to a broad upland where the air's bright, and remote blue horizons open all around.

8 Prose style

The style of a narrative comes partly from issues already explored but also from something more basic about the way the writer uses language. The prose style might include features such as:

- Balance of narration and dialogue
- Balance of description, exploration of thoughts and feelings and action
- Construction of sentences (eg long or short; simple, compound or complex; questions, statements, exclamations or commands)
- Use of **vocabulary** (eg poetic, colloquial, scholarly, plain, monosyllabic or polysyllabic)
- Amount of and kind of **figurative language** (eg metaphors, similes, symbols)
- Use of punctuation (eg dashes or colons, full speech **punctuation** or just dashes, use of commas)
- Length of paragraphs
- Other features unique to the voice of a writer (eg use of repetition, particular **idioms** or a rhythm that mimics the speaking voice)

Key terms

vocabulary

figurative language

punctuation

idiom

Activity 22

1   On your own, read the extract below from Cormac McCarthy's *The Road* and jot down a few first thoughts about your impressions of the style. This could be a list of five or six adjectives or short phrases.

> He studied the sky. There were days when the ashen overcast thinned and now the standing trees along the road made the faintest of shadows over the snow. They went on. The boy wasn't doing well. He stopped and checked his feet and retied the plastic. When the snow started to melt it was going to be hard to keep their feet dry. They
> 5   stopped often to rest. He'd no strength to carry the child. They sat on the pack and ate handfuls of the dirty snow. By afternoon it was beginning to melt. They passed a burned house, just the brick chimney standing in the yard. They were on the road all day, such day as there was. Such few hours. They might have covered three miles.
>   He thought the road would be so bad that no one would be on it but he was wrong.
> 10   They camped almost in the road itself and built a great fire, dragging dead limbs out of the snow and piling them on the flames to hiss and steam. There was no help for it. The few blankets they had would not keep them warm.

2   Now listen to the extract being read aloud. On your own, make an instant judgement about which features of prose style you think contribute most to your first impressions, using the list in the box above.

3   Share your first impressions and your instant judgements to see how much agreement there is across the class.

4   Now look back at the list of features in the box above and work through them more systematically. Share out the features among individuals or pairs in the class, so that every individual or pair focuses on a different feature and reports back on what they notice.

5   As a whole class, rank order the features to identify which you think is most significant in terms of creating the style of the extract.

Creative experiments with prose style

Activity 23

One way of getting a really good feel for prose style and for the choices writers make is to rewrite a piece of prose in an entirely different style. To do it well, you need to look closely at the features in order to make changes to the style. **Parody** (copying and exaggerating a writer's style for comic effect) is one example of this. You can either imitate the style of a text you are reading or turn another piece of writing into the style of the text you are reading.

Here is an example to show you the kind of thing you might do, rewriting the opening of *Pride and Prejudice* in the style of Cormac McCarthy's *The Road*.

> A man had come to the neighbourhood. Alone. He wanted a wife, or at least that's what the local people thought. The big house had been let and the woman found that interesting. She had heard all about it from her neighbour. She tried to interest her husband in the subject but he
> 5 didn't seem to want to know. She kept coming back to it: the house, the man and the man's desire, his yearning for a wife. Again and again she told him. The husband grew tired of her words. She wanted him to visit the man but stubbornly he refused. He was weary and unwilling to go, out to the far side of the village, in the greyness, with the rain falling.

Key term

parody

1   Talk about how well this writer has parodied McCarthy's style, using all that you have discovered from the previous activity. (If you see flaws, you might like to make a few changes of your own to improve it.)

2   Choose a short extract from another text, perhaps one of your set texts or a text you studied for GCSE. Try rewriting it in McCarthy's style or try rewriting the extract from *The Road* in the style of your core text or your second text.

Writing about prose style

Activity 24

1   Use a chart like the one below to help you analyse the extracts on page 73. You could look at each one or share them out among the class, and then take turns to report back on your extract.

Features	Extract 1	Evidence or quote	Extract 2	Evidence or quote	Extract 3	Evidence or quote
Narrative versus dialogue						
Description, thoughts, feelings or action						
Construction and kinds of sentences						
Vocabulary						
Figurative language						
Punctuation						
Paragraphing						
Anything else						

Extract 1: From *The Shipping News* by E. Annie Proulx

A year came when this life was brought up sharply. Voices over the wire, the
crump of folding steel, flame.

It began with his parents. First the father, diagnosed with liver cancer, a
blush of wild cells diffusing. A month later a tumour fastened in the mother's
5 brain like a burr, crowding her thoughts to one side. The father blamed the
power station. Two hundred yards from their house sizzling wires, thick as
eels, came down from northern towers.

They wheedled barbiturate prescriptions from winking doctors, stockpiled
the capsules. When there were enough, the father dictated, the mother typed
10 a suicide farewell, proclamation of individual choice and self-deliverance
– sentences copied from the newsletters of The Dignified Exit Society. Named
incineration and strewing as choice of disposal.

It was spring. Sodden ground, smell of earth. The wind beat through twigs,
gave off a greenish odor like struck flints. Coltsfoot in the ditches; furious
15 dabs of tulips stuttering in gardens. Slanting rain. Clock hands leapt to pellucid
evenings. The sky riffled like cards in a chalk-white hand.

Extract 2: From *On Beauty* by Zadie Smith

*Jack is a Head of Department at an American university, discussing a difficult
student with his colleague, Claire.*

'Jack, darling,' said Claire, shaking her head, 'you send these websites your
shopping lists and they put them up. They'll take *anything.*'

Jack retrieved the printouts from Claire and slipped them back in his
drawer. He had tried reason and plea and rhetoric, and now he must introduce
5 reality into the conversation. It was time, once again, to walk round the desk,
perch on the end and cross one leg over the other.

'Claire …'

'My God, what a piece of work that girl is!'

'Claire, I really can't have you making those kind of …'

10 'Well, she *is*.'

'That's as may be, but …'

'Jack, are you telling me I have to have her in my class?'

'Claire, Zora Belsey is a very good student. She's an *exceptional* student, in
fact. Now, she may not be Emily Dickinson …'

15 Claire laughed. 'Jack, Zora Belsey couldn't write a poem if Emily
Dickinson herself rolled out of her grave, put a gun to the girl's head and
demanded one. She's simply untalented in this area. She refuses to *read poetry*
– and all I get from her are pages from her journal aligned down the left-hand
margin. I've got *a hundred and twenty* talented students applying for *eighteen*
places.'

Extract 3: From *May Day* by F. Scott Fitzgerald

There had been a war fought and won and the great city of the conquering
people was crossed with triumphal arches and vivid with thrown flowers of
white, red, and rose. All through the long spring days the returning soldiers
marched up the chief highway behind the strump of drums and the joyous,
resonant wind of the brasses, while merchants and clerks left their bickerings
and figurings and, crowding to the windows, turned their white-bunched faces
gravely upon the passing battalions.

5

    Never had there been such splendour in the great city, for the victorious
war had brought plenty in its train, and the merchants had flocked thither from
the South and West with their households to taste of all the luscious feasts and
witness the lavish entertainments prepared – and to buy for their women furs
against the next winter and bags of golden mesh and varicoloured slippers of
silk and silver and rose satin and cloth of gold.

10

2   Using the notes on your chart and points raised in discussion, write three or four statements
about the prose style of one of the extracts, selecting what you think is worth focusing on.

3   Develop your statements into a paragraph by adding one piece of evidence from the text to
justify each one, followed by one further bit of analysis or exploration. For example:

> In Extract X, the writer uses short sentences to create an
> emotionless, detached style. This is particularly noticeable in the
> phrase, '___'. Here his use of the word '___' and his technique of '___'
> contribute to a sense of '___', which has '___' effect on the reader.

Take it further

Find two or three short examples of your own, where the
writer's prose style is very distinctive. Share your examples
as a whole group.

Preparing for the exam (Sections A and C)

- Preparing for Section A, You should read a range of
  different styles of narrative, so you become expert at
  analysing their prose style.

- Preparing for Section C, choose a random page
  from your core text or second text and analyse it,
  using the chart on page 72 to help you. Share your
  findings across the group. Drawing on what you have
  discovered, write a paragraph about each feature in
  the chart, summarising the key features of the prose
  style of your core text or your second text.

9 Methods of characterisation

There is no one kind of **character** or method of creating a character. Writers use a huge variety of techniques, many of which you have already learned about, such as the use of narrative voice, dialogue, symbols and so on. This section pulls together what you already know, but also adds a few more techniques and issues for you to think about.

In thinking about characters, readers and critics are most interested in:

- what kind of character it is and what makes them interesting within the narrative
- what **role** the character plays in the narrative
- how the writer has constructed the character.

Focusing on these issues allows you to comment on a writer's **characterisation** and prevents you from writing about characters as if they are real people.

Key terms

character
role
characterisation
realistic
caricature
foil
representative
stereotype

Kinds of characters

Characters in novels fall into different types. Not every character is constructed in the same way or is of equal importance. Some are more fully developed than others. Some are highly **realistic**, so that the reader begins to think about them as if they are real people. Others, such as characters in fairy tales, depend on not being entirely realistic but fitting into types, such as villains or heroes.

The kind of character often goes with the kind, or genre, of narrative. For example:

- if you are reading a fictional autobiography, you might expect the hero or heroine to be fully developed, with changing characteristics and attitudes as the novel develops
- if you are reading a short story, the characters might be quickly sketched and more one-dimensional, focusing on one or two major personality traits
- if you're reading a comic novel, the characters may be **caricatures** – exaggerated characters who are presented satirically, for your amusement.

Activity 25

Look at the kinds of characters listed below. Think of one or two characters from a novel or story you have read or from films or TV programmes that seem to you to fit each description, and fill in a copy of the chart.

Characters	Examples
A main protagonist – the central character at the heart of the story	
A realistic character	
A caricature – an exaggerated figure of fun	
A minor character – an 'extra' who only appears briefly	
A **foil** – a character whose key role is to reveal something about the main character	
A character who works by contrast with others who all have something in common (eg fathers, heroes, suitors, friends)	
A character who develops and changes over the course of the book or film	
A **representative** – a character who represents an idea (eg capitalism, repression, youth)	
A **stereotype** – a character who fits into a conventional character type (eg romantic heroine, villain, orphan)	

Listed below are some of the main techniques used by writers to construct characters. Many are ones you should now be familiar with.

- Naming
- Use of the narrative voice and point of view
- What the character says in dialogue and how they say it
- What other characters say about them
- Description of their physical and emotional qualities
- Their actions
- Contrast and comparison with other characters
- Use of images, symbols or motifs
- Setting or physical environment

Take it further

Choose a character from a novel you have enjoyed. Pick one short extract in which the character is strongly evoked. Identify three or four techniques used in the characterisation. Present your character, your extract and your analysis to other students in your group.

Activity 26

1 Read the depiction of a character below from the short story, 'Shoemaker Arnold' by Earl Lovelace.

Shoemaker Arnold

Shoemaker Arnold stood at the doorway of his little shop, hands on his hips, his body stiffened in that proprietory and undefeated stubbornness, announcing, not without some satisfaction, that if in his life he had not been triumphant, neither had the world defeated him. It would be hard,
5   though, to imagine how he could be defeated, since he exuded such hard tough unrelenting cantankerousness, gave off such a sense of readiness for confrontation, that if trouble had to pick someone to clash with, Shoemaker Arnold would not be the one. To him, the world was his shoemaker's shop. There he was master, and, anyone entering would have to surrender not
10 only to his opinion on shoes and leather and shoemaker apprentices, but to his views on politics, women, religion, flying objects, or any of the myriad subjects he decided to discourse upon, so that over the years he had arrived at a position where none of the villagers bothered to dispute him, and to any who dared maintain a view contrary to the one he was affirming, he was
15 quick to point out, 'This place is mine. Here, do as I please, I say what I want. Who don't like it, the door is open.'

Preparing for the exam (Sections A and C)

Avoid writing about the characters as if they are real people. Focus on characterisation, in other words all the techniques a writer uses to create and develop characters. Step back and think about the role a character is playing in the text – what kind of character they are and what their significance is.

When exploring characters in your set texts for Section C, think about the kind of character they are, their role in the novel and the ways in which they have been constructed, using the ideas in this book to help you.

2 Decide which of the statements below is true.

   a The character is revealed through dialogue.

   b The narrative voice guides the reader's view of the character.

   c The ironic voice of the narrator raises doubts about the character.

   d The point of view is that of the character.

   e The point of view is external to the character.

   f Description of the character's physical attributes plays an important part.

   g The character's behaviour contributes strongly to our view of him.

   h The setting is important in constructing the character.

   i The naming of the character is significant.

3 Put the statements you have chosen in rank order, to show which you think is most significant. Share your ideas, justifying why and how you came to your decisions.

10 Presentation of themes

What is the difference between the story and the themes?

What happens in a novel (the events and the characters involved in these events) is the story. The ideas and issues explored through the telling of these events – what we interpret the story as being *about* – point us to its themes.

The writer Ian McEwan suggests that while a novelist might start off with some ideas he wants to raise through the telling of the story, it is the reader's role to recognise the underlying themes in a novel.

> Themes are what readers have to address, rather than writers. You're dealing, as a writer, with generating a reality out of these scraps, and they come together in a haphazard way. And slowly over months, or a year, or two or three years, you impose a kind of order, so that you have an intact world. And then you discover that you've addressed certain matters, and that they repeat themselves throughout.
>
> Ian McEwan, English and Media Centre interview

This is one of the ways in which different readers create different readings of a text.

Activity 27

1   As a class, choose three well-known drama series (for example, *The West Wing*, *The Sopranos*, *Heroes*, *Skins*, etc). For each one, write down two or three words summing up what you think it is about – that is, the themes it explores – and share these as a class.

2   Do some of your dramas include the same themes? If so, do they lead the viewer to different conclusions? (For example, one drama might suggest that revenge is *never* justified, while another might suggest that sometimes it might be.)

How themes are explored in narratives

Narratives often share themes. For instance, many novels could be summed up as being about family life or relationships between men and women, or inequality or growing up. What is interesting for critics and readers is the particular way the novelist explores the theme and the way in which the reader's response is shaped: *what* does the writer seem to be saying and *how*?

Themes are created and revealed through:

- what happens
- what the characters do and say
- the way in which the story is told, including repetitions, contrasts, symbols and motifs.

To identify themes and analyse the role they play in a novel, you will need to bring to bear all you have learned in the unit about narrative and the ways writers use language.

Preparing for the exam (Section A)

If you are asked to explore the ways in which a particular theme is developed in an unseen extract, remember that it is the way the writer presents the theme (not just *what* but also *how*) that will gain you good marks in the exam.

Activity 28

Key term

setting

1 Read the extract below, taken from *A Room With a View* by E.M. Forster.

2 In pairs, tell each other the story of what happens. (This may be very brief.)

3 Then share your response to the passage and your interpretation of what it is about, in other words, its *themes*. Feedback your ideas as a class.

4 Some of the themes a reader might recognise in this passage include: freedom, love, hope, repression, life and conventionality. Re-read the extract, choosing a short section to illustrate one or two themes that you think are particularly important.

5 Annotate a copy of the extract to show the techniques Forster is using to explore the themes and direct the response of the reader, using the list below. Two annotations have been given to get you started.

- narrative voice
- the use of **setting**
- presentation of the character
- language
- use of oppositions (eg male versus female)
- imagery.

A group of English tourists staying at a small hotel in Florence have gone on a day trip into the countryside. Lucy is travelling with her older cousin and chaperone, Miss Bartlett. Lucy has wandered off away from the main group. The man described in the extract as 'her companion' is one of the young Italian drivers whom she has asked to take her to the 'buoni uomini', the 'good men'. George is one of the other English tourists.

The contrasting of characters' responses brings out the opposition between conventionality and unconventionality, freedom and repression.

The themes of freedom and hope are explored here through the choice of lexis with 'brink' and the simile of 'like a swimmer' – suggesting launching out into the open.

At the same moment the ground gave way, and with a cry she fell out of the wood. Light and beauty enveloped her. She had fallen out onto a little open terrace, which was covered with violets from end to end.

'Courage!' cried her companion, now standing some six feet above. 'Courage and love.'

She did not answer. From her feet the ground sloped sharply into the view and violets ran down in rivulets and streams and cataracts, irrigating the hillside with blue, eddying round the tree streams, collecting into pools in the hollows, covering the grass with spots of azure foam. But never again were they in such profusion; this terrace was the well-head, the primal source whence beauty gushed out to water the earth.

Standing at its brink, like a swimmer who prepares, was the good man. But he was not the good man that she had expected, and he was alone.

George had turned at the sound of her arrival. For a moment he contemplated her, as one who had fallen out of heaven. [1]He saw radiant joy in her face, he saw the flowers beat against her dress in blue waves. The bushes above them closed. He stepped quickly forward and kissed her.

Before she could speak, almost before she could feel, a voice called, 'Lucy! Lucy! Lucy!' The silence of life had been broken by Miss Bartlett, who stood brown against the view.

5

10

15

Preparing for the exam (Section C)

Keep a record of themes you think are important while you are reading your core text and second text. Remember to think about what is special about the *way* the writer has explored those themes, as well as the ideas themselves.

In conclusion

Throughout the 'Exploring prose' section you have explored the different choices writers make and the effects these choices can have both on the texts they create and on the readers who engage with them.

Reflect on the development of your understanding of the techniques and key genre features of prose, with a partner or your teacher. Which aspects do you feel more confident about now? Which do you feel are your current areas of strength? Which areas do you think you need further work?

Part 3   Preparing for the exam

Content

This part of the book provides step-by-step guidance for tackling each Section of the exam.

In **Section A** of the exam you have to answer three questions on EITHER a poetry extract OR a prose extract, neither of which you will have seen before.

In this part, you will learn:

- how to tackle an 'unseen' poem or prose passage
- how to write about style and technique rather than content
- how to meet the Assessment objectives for Section A (AO1 and AO2)
- how to write in a style examiners will reward.

In **Section B** of the exam you have to write an essay that compares and contrasts at least two poems on a common topic. These are taken from a poetry selection you have studied.

In this part, you will learn:

- how to analyse the key features of your poems
- how to find links between one poem and another
- how to bring out the similarities and differences between them
- how to meet the Assessment objectives for Section B (AO1, AO2 and AO3)
- how to write in a style examiners will reward.

In **Section C** of the exam you have to write an essay discussing two novels – your core novel and a second novel. Your novels will be related in theme, style or structure.

In this part you will learn:

- how to analyse the key features of your novels
- how to find links between them in theme, style and structure
- how to build up a discussion relating your novels together
- how to meet the Assessment objectives for Section C (AO1 and AO2)
- how to write in a style examiners will reward.

Additional support

The **Teaching and Assessment CD-ROM** provides detailed material for studying all the prescribed poetry groupings and all the prescribed novel groups in Sections B and C. It is designed to be used alongside this book.

Section A: Unseen Poetry

In Section A of the exam, you will choose to answer questions on EITHER a poetry extract OR a prose extract, neither of which you will have seen before. Short questions will ask you to comment on key features of either poetry or prose.

An example of the kind of question you can expect is given in Activity 5 on page 84. Section A is worth 20 marks (20% of the total marks for Unit 1).

The following pages will develop your analytical skills, which are essential when approaching any unseen poem. Most of them will be familiar from GCSE.

Assessment objectives

To assess your answers on unseen poetry, the examiners use a mark scheme based on two Assessment objectives.

- In Question a), AO1 is assessed: Articulate creative, informed and relevant responses to literary texts, using appropriate terminology and concepts, and coherent, accurate written expression. (5 marks)
- In Question b), AO2 is assessed: Demonstrate detailed critical understanding in analysing the ways in which structure, form and language shape meanings in literary texts. (5 marks)
- In Question c), AO1 and AO2 are both assessed. (10 marks)

Analysing an unseen poem

Activity 1

The following activities show you ways of exploring and analysing a poem when you read it for the first time. You will develop important skills and understand what the examiner is looking for when assessing your answer in the exam.

Read the poem by Philip Larkin. Then answer the questions, which ask you to discuss and make notes on two of its key features: use of setting and use of imagery.

Afternoons

Summer is fading:
The leaves fall in ones and twos
From trees bordering
The new recreation ground.
In the hollows of afternoons   5
Young mothers assemble
At swing and sandpit
Setting free their children.

Behind them, at intervals,
Stand husbands in skilled trades,   10
An estateful of washing,
And the albums, lettered
Our Wedding, lying
Near the television:
Before them, the wind   15
Is ruining their courting-places

That are still courting-places
(But the lovers are all in school),
And their children, so intent on
Finding more unripe acorns,   20
Expect to be taken home.
Their beauty has thickened.
Something is pushing them
To the side of their own lives.

Philip Larkin

1. As a class, discuss and make notes on the use of the setting in this poem, on a chart like the one below.

Use of setting

Point or statement	Evidence or quotation	Explanation or comment
Autumnal setting	'The leaves fall in ones and twos'	This shows that the seasons of new life and growth are coming to an end.

You may want to make reference to the following points.

- The autumnal setting reflects the course of the women's lives: although 'Young', they are already 'fading'.
- The autumn wind blows away memories of their youth: '… the wind/Is ruining their courting-places' (lines 15–16).
- Now married, the women live uniform lives in uniform houses: 'estateful of washing' (line 11).
- A highlight of the women's lives is now set aside; the excitement of the wedding day gives way to ordinariness: 'Our Wedding, lying/Near the television' (lines 13–14).

2. Now discuss the poet's use of imagery and make notes on it in a similar way.

Use of imagery

Point or statement	Evidence or quotation	Explanation or comment
Nature is linked with the young mothers' lives.	'Summer is fading'	The young mothers' lives are 'fading' into dull routine.

Consider the following questions as you draw up your notes.

- Autumn is used as an extended metaphor. What does this suggest about the women's lives?
- What does the metaphor 'In the hollows of afternoons' (line 5) suggest about the women's lives?
- What does 'unripe acorns' (line 20) suggest about the children?
- What does the metaphor, 'Something is pushing them/To the side of their own lives' (lines 23–24), suggest about the control that the women have over their lives?

3. Use all your notes to write one paragraph on the use of the setting in the poem and one paragraph on the use of imagery. You will have assembled a lot of detail. Select from it what you consider to be the most important points for your two paragraphs.

4. Poets construct poems in ways that are suited to their subject matter. Write two paragraphs commenting on the stanza form of 'Afternoons' and saying how it matches the subject matter.

Here are some sample notes, which could form the basis of your analysis.

- Three stanzas reflect the stages in the young mothers' lives: Stanza 1 = present, Stanza 2 = past and present, Stanza 3 = present and future. Time brings about change and a sense of loss.
- Stanza 1, the present: the women 'assemble', the collective term 'young mothers' showing how they have given up their individuality – now just mothers
- Stanza 2, the past and present: the women's lives now regulated by marriage ('Our Wedding') and domestic chores ('An estateful of washing')
- Stanza 3, the present and the future: the women's lives are dominated by parenthood, now and in future
- Overall structure: describes process of change in the women's lives; whatever they gain by marriage and motherhood, there is also a loss.

Writing in the exam

As for GCSE, use the PEE (point, evidence, explanation) method as a starting point when building up your analysis of a poem. For example:

Larkin's metaphor 'the hollows of afternoons' conveys the impression that there is an emptiness in the women's lives. They have succumbed to a dull, domestic routine, symbolised by 'An estateful of washing' and 'the television'.

Identifying key features of poetry

Setting, imagery and structure are, of course, not the only features that you should be prepared to comment on when you are given an unseen poem. A full list includes the following, covered in 'Exploring Poetry' in part 1 of the book:

- the choice of a particular poetic form and structure (such as a lyric, a sonnet, free verse or rhymed couplets) to convey meaning (pages 12–24)
- how rhyme and rhythm are used to create particular effects (pages 24–30)
- how the sound of words is used to reinforce meaning (pages 31–34)
- how language and imagery is used in striking and original ways to convey particular effects (pages 31–37)
- the use of a distinctive voice, either the poet's own or that of a persona (adopted personality), to convey their attitude to the reader (pages 38–41)
- how the poet creates mood and atmosphere (pages 42–48)
- whether strong feelings are aroused in the reader and why that is (pages 42–48).

Activity 2

1 In a small group, use the list of key features above to draw up a chart like the one below.

Feature of the poem	What this means	Things to look for in the poem
Use of imagery	Comparisons in the form of simile, metaphor or personification: how do they help convey meaning?	• the words 'like' or 'as' used to compare • a direct comparison: eg 'the bladed wind' • what is being compared with what? • what impression do the comparisons give?
Use of voice	The poet's own voice or the voice of a persona: what attitudes and feelings does the voice express?	• choice of speaker's language (**idiolect**) • tone of voice (**register**) • What 'character' does the voice suggest? • What are the speaker's emotions?

2 As a class, compare your charts. Add other points to your own copy, especially in column 3. Use your completed chart as a checklist for particular features of poetry each time you do a practice unseen.

Key terms
idiolect
register

Activity 3

Read the following poem by Vernon Scannell.

Gunpowder Plot

For days these curious cardboard buds have lain
In brightly coloured boxes. Soon the night
Will come. We pray there'll be no sullen rain
To make these magic orchids flame less bright.

Now in the garden's darkness they begin
To flower: the frenzied whizz of Catherine-wheel
Puts forth its fiery petals and the thin
Rocket soars to burst upon the steel

Bulwark of a cloud. And then the guy,
Absurdly human phoenix, is again
Gulped by greedy flames: the harvest sky
Is flecked with threshed and glittering golden rain.

'Uncle! A cannon! Watch me as I light it!'
The women helter-skelter, squealing high,
Retreat; the paper fuse is quickly lit,
A cat-like hiss and spit of fire, a sly

Falter, then the air is shocked with blast.
The cannon bangs and in my nostrils drifts
A bitter scent that brings the lurking past
Lurching to my side. The present shifts,

Allows a ten-year memory to walk
Unhindered now; and so I'm forced to hear
The banshee howl of mortar and the talk
Of men who died; am forced to taste my fear.

I listen for a moment to the guns,
The torn earth's grunts, recalling how I prayed.
The past retreats. I hear a corpse's sons –

'Who's scared of bangers!' 'Uncle, John's afraid!'

Vernon Scannell

(line numbers: 5, 10, 15, 20, 25)

1 Form groups of three. Each group should choose one of the following features of the poem to analyse and comment on, and write one paragraph about it using the PEE method:

   - the poet's use of settings
   - how imagery helps to convey the themes and ideas of the poem
   - how the sound of the words helps to convey meaning.

2 Now peer review with your partners. Check what you have written against the chart you drew up in Activity 2. Add any points other people have made which you agree are important.

Activity 4

1 Individually, review all the work you have done so far on unseen poetry. Make a chart of your strengths and weaknesses, like the one below.

Unseen poetry: my strengths and weaknesses			
Aspect of unseen poetry (see list of key features, page 82)	What I can do confidently and well	What I can do fairly well but need to practise more	What I get stuck with

2 Use your chart to discuss with your teacher the specific ways in which you can improve your writing about unseen poetry. Prioritise three areas.

Tackling unseen poetry in Section A of the exam

In Section A of the exam, you can choose to answer questions on EITHER the unseen poetry OR the unseen prose. You have to write two short answers and one longer answer. Each of the short answer questions on poetry asks you to identify one feature of the given poem and comment on its use. The longer question requires you to explore a feature of the poem in more depth.

A suggested approach

- Allow yourself around 35 minutes. Use your time in a way that reflects the marks available. For Questions a) and b) 5 marks each are available and for Question c) 10 marks are available. There is space on the question paper for your answer.

- Make sure you correctly identify the *focus* of each question. Underline the key words on your question paper (eg 'choice of setting', 'use and effect of imagery', 'use and effect of rhyme').

- Remember, the instruction 'comment on' means 'show how this aspect of style is created and used by the writer'. It does *not* mean 'explain the meaning of the poem'.

Assessment objectives

In Question a), AO1 is assessed: Articulate creative, informed and relevant responses to literary texts, using appropriate terminology and concepts, and coherent, accurate written expression. (5 marks)

In Question b), AO2 is assessed: Demonstrate detailed critical understanding in analysing the ways in which structure, form and language shape meanings in literary texts. (5 marks)

In Question c), AO1 and AO2 are both assessed. (10 marks)

Activity 5

1   In a small group or as a class, do the following practice unseen. First read the poem *Hospital Visit* by John Walsh. Then answer these questions on it.

   a   Poets sometimes want to arouse strong feelings in the reader towards what they describe. Comment on the way this poem appeals to your feelings and how you react. Focus on two or three examples. (5 marks)

   b   Poets construct poems in ways that are suited to their subject matter. Comment on the stanza and line structures in this poem and how they match the subject matter. Focus on two or three examples. (5 marks)

   c   Poets use imagery to create particular effects. Comment on the poet's use of imagery and the effects it achieves. (10 marks)

Hospital Visit

The hospital smell
combs my nostrils
as they go bobbing along
green and yellow corridors.

5 What seems like a corpse
is trundled into a lift and vanishes
heavenwards.

I will not feel, I will not
feel, until
10 I have to.

Nurses walk lightly, swiftly,
here and up and down and there,
their slender waists miraculously
carrying their burden
15 of so much pain, so
many deaths, their eyes
still clear after
so many farewells.
Ward 7. She lies

20 in a white cave of forgetfulness.
A withered hand
Trembles on its stalk. Eyes move
behind eyelids too heavy
to raise. Into an arm wasted
25 of colour, a glass fang is fixed,
not guzzling but giving.
And between her and me
distance shrinks until there is none left
but the distance of pain that neither she nor I
30 can cross.

She smiles a little at this
black figure in her white cave
who clumsily rises
in the round swimming waves of a bell
35 and dizzily goes off, leaving behind only
books that will not be read
and fruitless fruits.

John Walsh

---

2 As a class, assess the following responses to Questions a) and b). Use AO1 to award up to a maximum of 5 marks for a) and AO2 to award up to a maximum of 5 marks for b). See page 84 for details of AO1 and AO2.

Response to Question a)

The poem arouses feelings of sympathy for both the visitor and the patient. The visitor feels upset but is determined not to show it: 'I will not feel, I will not/feel, until/I have to'. The lines are broken up to show how his feelings are bubbling to the surface but how he is keeping them in check by the emphasis on 'not'. The patient seems to be dying, which makes us feel sorry for her, since her hand is 'withered' like a flower on a 'stalk', ie her arm. She is drugged, which puts her into a 'white cave' of half-consciousness. In this state she can feel nothing for the pain, which is like a space 'that neither she nor I/can cross'. It is sad that the two of them are kept apart by this 'distance' of pain. The fruit that he brings is 'fruitless' – it will not be eaten and it symbolises the death of their relationship.

Response to Question b)

The stanzas in this poem reflect the visitor's journey to 'Ward 7' and his departure from it at the end. The first four stanzas show him getting progressively nearer to the patient, 'bobbing along/green and yellow corridors' and passing the nurses on his way to Ward 7. When he gets there, there is a break between stanzas 5 and 6 to underline 'the distance of pain that neither she nor I/can cross'. The lines are often short, perhaps to represent how the patient has only a short time left to live: 'heavenwards'/'so many farewells'. Line 29 is much longer to show the large gap between the two of them, followed by a short line to show how near they are physically but how far apart they are emotionally.

---

3 Assess a partner's answer to Question c). Use a combination of AO1 and AO2 to award a maximum of 10 marks. Then explain the reasons for your assessment.

Section A: Unseen Prose

In Section A of the exam, you will choose to answer questions on EITHER a poetry extract OR a prose extract, neither of which you will have seen before. Short questions will ask you to comment on key features of either poetry or prose.

An example of the kind of question you can expect is given in Activity 10 on page 89. Section A is worth 20 marks (20% of the total marks for Unit 1).

The following pages will develop your analytical skills, which are essential when approaching any unseen prose extract. Most of them will be familiar from GCSE.

Assessment objectives

To assess your answers on unseen prose, the examiners use a mark scheme based on two Assessment objectives.

In Question a), AO1 is assessed: Articulate creative, informed and relevant responses to literary texts, using appropriate terminology and concepts, and coherent, accurate written expression. (5 marks)

In Question b), AO2 is assessed: Demonstrate detailed critical understanding in analysing the ways in which structure, form and language shape meanings in literary texts. (5 marks)

In Question c), AO1 and AO2 are both assessed. (10 marks)

Analysing an unseen prose extract

The following activities show you ways of exploring and analysing a piece of prose when you read it for the first time. You will develop important skills and understand what the examiner is looking for when assessing your answer in the exam.

Activity 6

1 Read the extract below from the opening of Jeanette Winterson's novel *Oranges Are Not the Only Fruit*. Then answer the questions, which ask you to discuss and make notes on two of its key features: narrative point of view and structure.

Like most people I lived for a long time with my mother and father. My father liked to watch the wrestling and my mother liked to wrestle; it didn't matter what. She was in the white corner and that was that. She hung out 5 the largest sheets on the windiest days. She *wanted* the Mormons to knock on the door. At election time in a Labour mill town she put a picture of the Conservative candidate in the window.

She had never heard of mixed feelings. There were 10 friends and there were enemies.

Enemies were:	The Devil (in his many forms)
	Next Door
	Sex (in its many forms)
	Slugs
15 Friends were:	God
	Our dog
	Auntie Madge
	The Novels of Charlotte Bronte
	Slug pellets

20 and me, at first. I had been brought in to join her in a tag match against the Rest of the World. She had a mysterious attitude towards the begetting of children; it wasn't that she couldn't do it, more that she didn't want to do it. She was very bitter about the Virgin Mary getting there 25 first. So she did the next best thing and arranged for a foundling. That was me.

I cannot recall a time when I did not know that I was special. We had no Wise Men, but we had sheep. One of my earliest memories is me sitting on a sheep at Easter 30 while she told me the story of the Sacrificial Lamb. We had it on Sundays with potato.

2 As a class, make notes on the narrative point of view in the extract, using a chart like the one below.

Narrative point of view		
Point or statement	**Evidence or quotation**	**Explanation or comment**
Written in the first person	'I lived for a long time with my mother and father'	We see events from the narrator's perspective as an adult, looking back on her childhood.

You may want to make reference to the following points.

- The narrator establishes a personal point of view: 'I' and 'we'.
- The narrator looks back on childhood from an adult point of view: 'I cannot recall a time when I did not …'.
- An adult point of view allows the narrator to provide insights into mother's character.
- An adult point of view allows the narrator to *comment* on events, not just describe them.

3 Now discuss the writer's use of paragraphing and sentence structure, and make notes in a similar way.

Paragraphing and sentence structure in lines 1–20		
Point or statement	**Evidence or quotation**	**Explanation or comment**
Mother is the subject of most sentences in the text.	'She was …', 'She *wanted* …', 'She hung out …'	Shows mother was the dominant figure in the narrator's life

Consider the following questions as you draw up your notes.

- What effect do the short, grammatically simple sentences have?
- How does the listing technique in lines 11–19 'Enemies were …, Friends were …' reflect the mother's view of the world?
- What question does the phrase 'and me, at first' (line 20) raise in our minds?
- How do the writer's sentences combine references to everyday affairs with religion?

4 Use all your notes to write one paragraph on the narrative point of view and one paragraph on the structure of the extract. You will have assembled a lot of detail. Select from it what you consider to be the most important points for your two paragraphs.

5 Write two paragraphs on the way Jeanette Winterson begins her novel and how effective you find it as an opening.

Here are some sample notes, which could form the basis of your analysis.

- The narrator parodies the typical opening to an autobiography: 'Like most people, I lived for a long time with my father and mother' – a humorous, ironic tone – this is not going to be like most people's life story.
- Reader's curiosity aroused by some intriguing yet-to-be-answered questions: eg 'she… arranged for a foundling' (why? how?), 'Enemies were… Sex (in its many forms), Slugs' (does mother see a link?).
- An unusual story lies ahead: father almost anonymous ('liked to watch the wrestling'), mother a fierce Christian who sees the narrator in a religious framework ('she told me the story of the Sacrificial Lamb').
- A very brisk opening: reader is plunged straight into the narrator's strange family life – sentences fast-paced ('She had never heard of mixed feelings').
- The narrator uses a wry, humorous tone, eg extended metaphor for mother's view of life as a 'tag match against the Rest of the World' – this is appealing.

> **Writing in the exam**
>
> As for GCSE, use the PEE (point, evidence, explanation) method as a starting point when building up your analysis of a prose extract. For example:
>
> The use of capital letters ('The Devil', 'Next Door') suggests that these few preoccupations are of huge importance to mother, reinforcing the impression that she is an obsessive personality.

Identifying key features of prose

Narrative point of view, structure and openings are, of course, not the only key features of prose that you should be prepared to comment on when you are given an unseen extract. A full list includes the following covered in 'Exploring Prose in part 2 of this book):

- how the style relates to genre (pages 51–53)
- how the narrative starts (pages 53–55)
- narrative voice and point of view (pages 55–60)
- use and effect of dialogue and voice (pages 61–63)
- how the narrative is structured (pages 64–68)
- use of symbols and motifs (pages 69–70)
- use of particular features of prose style (pages 71–74)
- use of different techniques to convey character (pages 75–76)
- presentation of themes (pages 77–78).

Activity 7

1   In a small group, use the list of key features above to draw up a chart like the one below.

Feature of the extract	What this means	Things to look for in the extract
Use of dialogue	Direct speech between the characters – conversation: what impression does this make on us?	• characters' use of language • characters' tone of voice (register) • balance between dialogue and description
Techniques for creating character: characterisation	How is the character conveyed to us (not what their personality is like)?	• description of physical appearance • distinctive way of speaking (idiolect) • relationship with other characters

2   As a class, compare your charts. Add other points to your own copy, especially in column 3. Use this chart as a checklist for particular features of prose each time you do a practice unseen.

Activity 8

1   Read the opening of Nick Hornby's novel *About a Boy*.

'Have you split up now?'

'Are you being funny?'

People quite often thought Marcus was being funny when he wasn't. He couldn't understand it. Asking his mum
5   whether she'd split up with Roger was a perfectly sensible question, he thought; they'd had a big row, then they'd gone off into the kitchen to talk quietly, and after a little while they'd come out looking serious, and Roger had come over to him, shaken his hand and wished him luck at his new
10   school, and then he'd gone.

'Why would I want to be funny?'

'Well, what does it look like to you?'

'It looks to me like you've split up. But I just wanted to make sure.'

15   'We've split up.'

'So he's gone?'

'Yes, Marcus, he's gone.'

He didn't think he'd ever get used to this business. He had quite liked Roger. And the three of them had been out a few
20   times; now, apparently, he'd never see him again. He didn't mind, but it was weird if you thought about it. He'd once shared a toilet with Roger, when they were both busting for a pee after a car journey. You'd think that if you'd peed with someone you ought to keep in touch with them somehow.

25   'What about his pizza?' They'd just ordered three pizzas when the argument started, and they hadn't arrived yet.

'We'll share it. If we're hungry.'

'Or we could pick the pepperoni off. I don't think they give you much of it anyway. It's mostly cheese and tomato.'

30   'Marcus, I'm not really thinking about pizzas right now.'

'OK. Sorry. Why did you split up?'

'Oh … this and that. I don't really know how to explain it.'

2 Form groups of three. Each group should choose one of the following features to analyse and comment on, and write one paragraph about it using the PEE method:

- the writer's use of dialogue
- how the writer guides your response to the characters
- the writer's point of view.

3 Now peer review with your partners. Check what you have written against the chart you drew up in Activity 7. Add any points other people have made which you agree are important.

Activity 9

1 Individually, review all the work you have done so far on unseen prose. Make a chart of your strengths and weaknesses, like the one below.

Unseen prose: my strengths and weaknesses			
Aspect of unseen poetry (see list of common features, page 88)	What I can do confidently and well	What I can do fairly well but need to practise more	What I get stuck with

2 Use your chart to discuss with your teacher the specific ways in which you can improve your writing about unseen prose. Prioritise three areas.

Tackling unseen prose in Section A of the exam

In Section A of the exam, you can choose to answer questions on EITHER the unseen prose OR the unseen poetry. You have to write two short answers and one longer answer. Each of the short answer questions on prose asks you to identify one feature of the given prose extract and comment on its use. The longer question requires you to explore a feature of the extract in more depth.

A suggested approach

- Allow yourself around 35 minutes. Use your time in a way that reflects the Marks available. For Questions a) and b) 5 marks each are available and for Question c) 10 marks are available. There is space on the question paper for your answer.
- Make sure you correctly identify the *focus* of each question. Underline the key words on your question paper (eg 'use of dialogue', 'choice of sentence structure', 'use and effect of imagery').
- Remember, the instruction 'comment on' means 'show how this aspect of style is created and used by the writer'. It does *not* mean 'explain the meaning of the text'.

Activity 10

1 In a small group or as a class, do the following practice unseen. First read the extract from *A Short History of Tractors in Ukranian*. Then answer these questions on it.

> **a** Writers choose different tenses (past, present or future) in which to write. Identify and comment on the effect of tense choices in one or two places in this extract. (5 marks)
>
> **b** Writers use imagery to create particular effects and impressions. Identify and comment on one or two examples of imagery in this extract. (5 marks)
>
> **c** Comment on the effectiveness of this extract as the opening of a novel. (10marks)

Assessment objectives

In Question a), AO1 is assessed: Articulate creative, informed and relevant responses to literary texts, using appropriate terminology and concepts, and coherent, accurate written expression. (5 marks)

In Question b), AO2 is assessed: Demonstrate detailed critical understanding in analysing the ways in which structure, form and language shape meanings in literary texts. (5 marks)

In Question c), AO1 and AO2 are both assessed. (10 marks)

Two years after my mother died, my father fell in love with a glamorous blonde Ukranian divorcee. He was eighty-four and she was thirty-six. She exploded into our lives like a fluffy pink grenade, churning up the murky water, bringing to the surface a sludge of sloughed-off memories, giving the family ghosts a kick up the backside.

It all started with a phonecall.

My father's voice, quavery with excitement, crackles down the line. 'Good news, Nadezhda. I'm getting married!'

I remember the rush of blood to my head. Please let it be a joke! Oh, he's gone bonkers! Oh, you foolish old man! But I don't say any of those things. 'Oh, that's nice, Pappa,' I say.

'Yes, yes. She is coming with her son from Ukraine. Ternopil in Ukraina.'

Ukraina: he sighs, breathing in the remembered scent of mown hay and cherry blossom. But I catch the distinct synthetic whiff of New Russia.

Her name is Valentina, he tells me. But she is more like Venus. 'Botticelli's Venus rising from waves. Golden hair. Charming eyes. Superior breasts. When you see her you will understand.'

The grown-up me is indulgent. How sweet – this last late flowering of love. The daughter me is outraged. The traitor! The randy old beast! And our mother barely two years dead. I am angry and curious. I can't wait to see her – this woman who is usurping my mother.

'She sounds *gorgeous*. When can I meet her?'

'After marriage you can meet.'

Marina Lewycka

2   As a class, assess the following responses to Questions a) and b). Use AO1 to award up to a maximum of 5 marks for a) and AO2 to award up to a maximum of 5 marks for b) See page 86 for details of AO1 and AO2.

Response to Question a)

There is an interesting shift in tenses, from past to present after the sentence, 'It all started with a phone call', where the writer tells us what happens in the phone call with her father. The use of the past tense at the very beginning sets up the background to the story, in a fairly conventional way. The shift in tense plunges us into the event that sets the story in motion and gives it a directness and sense of immediacy, as if it is happening there and then. The 'excitement' of the father's voice is conveyed by the present tense verb 'crackles'.

Response to Question b)

In the first paragraph of the story, the comparison starts as a surprising simile – 'she exploded into our lives like a fluffy pink grenade'. 'Pink' and 'grenade' are odd juxtapositions and by putting them together, the writer suggests, humorously, how potentially dangerous this seemingly soft and harmless woman is going to be. The writer does not stop there. The imagery is taken several stages further, by adding the idea of the grenade churning up waters and then introducing a quite different piece of imagery about the family ghosts being 'kicked up the backside'. By piling the images one on top of the other...

3   Assess a partner's answer to Question c). Use a combination of AO1 and AO2 to award up to a maximum of 10 marks. Then explain the reasons for your assessment.

Section B: Poetry

In Section B of the exam, you have to compare two or more poems on a common topic. This section uses a range of examples from the prescribed poems to help you develop the following skills:

- making links between one poem and another
- bringing out the similarities and differences between poems
- analysing their key features
- writing your examination response.

Examples of the kind of question you can expect are given in Activity 16 on page 95. Section B is worth 40 marks (40% of the total marks for Unit 1).

Finding links between your poems

For Section B of the exam, you have to read a selection of poems within one of these three topics: Home, Land or Work. There are about 16 poems in each grouping. You will need to make connections and comparisons between poems that illustrate your chosen topic in different ways and poems that demonstrate a range of forms and styles.

Assessment objectives

To assess your answer on your chosen poems, the examiners use a mark scheme based on three Assessment objectives:

AO1: Articulate creative, informed and relevant responses to literary texts, using appropriate terminology and concepts, and coherent, accurate written expression. (15 marks)

AO2: Demonstrate detailed critical understanding in analysing the ways in which structure, form and language shape meanings in literary texts. (5 marks)

AO3: Explore connections and comparisons between different literary texts, informed by interpretations of other readers. (20 marks)

Activity 11

1   As a class, look over your selection of poems. Choose *three* poems to focus on to begin with. They should be poems that:

- deal with different aspects of the set topic
- differ in form
- differ in style.

2   Now work together to make a detailed analysis of two of them. Concentrate on how each poet presents the theme by looking closely at:

- the choice of language, including imagery: how does this direct us to the poem's theme?
- the voice created in the poem: how does it convey the poet's attitude to the topic?
- the use of language devices (eg alliteration, onomatopoeia, assonance, sibilance): how do these help to highlight the poet's attitude?
- the choice of form (eg quatrains, other kinds of stanzas, sonnet, ballad, free verse): how does form help to reinforce meaning?
- structural elements (eg rhyme, line-lengths, punctuation, rhythm): how do these help to reinforce meaning?

3   In a small group, look back over your two analyses. Use them to fill in a copy of the comparison chart below.

Chosen topic (Home/ Land/Work)	Key aspects of chosen topic highlighted	Key features of style and language	Key features of form and structure
Poem A title			
Poem B title			

4   Individually, write an analysis of the third poem of your choice (Poem C), using the above method. Then add details about Poem C to your comparison chart.

Grouping your poems by theme

Activity 12

1 Read through the rest of your chosen poems.

2 In a small group, start arranging them by theme (that is, the aspect(s) of the chosen topic they deal with). For example, the poems on the topic of Land could be grouped as follows:

Aspect of the topic	Individual poems
Poems that celebrate where the poet lives	
Poems that express a negative attitude to where the poet lives	
Poems that link the land with memories	
Poems that show the land to be neglected	
Poems that show the land to be something special	

Some poems will cover one aspect; some will cover two or more. Some poems may need to be put under further headings.

3 As a class, share your findings.

4 Then look ahead to the typical exam questions listed in Activity 16 (page 95). Use your chart above to devise possible exam questions on your selection of poems.

Grouping your poems by form and style

To help you compare and contrast, you need to select poems that are sufficiently different in form and style for you to make a *range* of comments on them and avoid repeating yourself.

Activity 13

1 In a small group, look over your selection of poems. Then copy and complete the chart below. Include notes on three of your poems.

Poems grouped by form and style		
Poem titles	**Key elements of form and structure**	**Key elements of style and language**
Poem X		
Poem Y		
Poem Z		

For example, this is how the chart might be completed for three poems in the topic area of Home.

Poems grouped by form and style		
Poem titles	**Key elements of form and structure**	**Key elements of style and language**
'The Ballad of Rudolph Reed'	• Ballad form with a simple moral • Narrative structure: third person voice • Regular rhyming stanzas (disrupted for effect in the last stanza)	• Mixture of third and first person voices • Deliberately archaic language at times, typical of ballads • Archaic language set against modern context for effect
'Death in Leamington'	• Narrative structure: takes the form of an elegy • Regular strongly – rhymed quatrains • Poet's narrative voice provides comment on the woman's death	• Mixture of poetic diction and everyday language for effect • Simple narrative style is used ironically: this is a tragic event • Language of 'things' offset against the language of feeling
'Baby Song'	• Persona poem: first person voice • Rhymed couplets • Alternate lines of each couplet used to create a contrast	• Lyrical language of 'Song' used ironically: birth not a happy event • Language contrasts: baby in the womb, baby in the world • Mixture of colloquial and figurative language

2 As a class, compare the points you have made on your charts. Add to or revise them in the light of discussion.

Comparing your chosen poems: planning

The following section gives you guidance and practice in:

- choosing poems that compare and contrast well
- drawing out the similarities between poems
- drawing out the differences between poems
- creating a balanced answer that incorporates two or more poems.

Planning your comparison

As shown on the comparison chart of poems you completed for Activity 12, there are *three* considerations to make when choosing poems to compare:

- the poets' attitudes towards the topics of Land, Home or Work
- key features of the poems' style and language
- key features of the poems' form and structure.

Any comparison will work well if the poems you choose show both similarities and differences in at least two of these areas.

Activity 14

Individually, make a paragraph plan for an answer based on two poems you have decided will compare well. Devise your own title.

There follows an example of a paragraph plan for a comparison of two poems on the topic of Land. Use it to help you with your own. Note that the plan goes into considerable detail to illustrate the range of points that could be made; an exam-length answer would need to *select* from these.

Poem A: Stopping by Woods on a Snowy Evening

Whose woods these are I think I know,
His house is in the village though;
He will not see me stopping here
To watch his woods fill up with snow.

5 My little horse must think it queer
To stop without a farmhouse near
Between the woods and frozen lake
The darkest evening of the year,

He gives his harness bells a shake
10 To ask if there is some mistake.
The only other sound's the sweep
Of easy wind and downy flake.

The woods are lovely, dark and deep,
But I have promises to keep,
15 And miles to go before I sleep,
And miles to go before I sleep.

Robert Frost

Poem B: The Way through the Woods

They shut the road through the woods
Seventy years ago,
Weather and rain have undone it again,
And now you would never know
5 There was once a path through the woods
Before they planted the trees,
It is underneath the coppice and heath,
And the thin anemones.
Only the keeper sees
10 That, where the ring-dove broods,
And the badgers roll at ease,
There was once a road through the woods.

Yet, if you enter the woods
Of a summer evening late,
15 When the night-air cools on the trout-ring'd pools
Where the otter whistles his mate,
(They fear not men in the woods
Because they see so few)
You will hear the beat of a horse's feet
20 And the swish of a skirt in the dew,
Steadily cantering through
The misty solitudes,
As though they perfectly knew
The old lost road through the woods …
25 But there is no road through the woods.

Rudyard Kipling

Detailed paragraph plan for the poems on page 93	
POEM A	**POEM B**
Paragraphs 1 and 2: Similarities	
• Frost is struck by the unspoiled beauty of the woods: 'the woods are lovely', 'easy wind and downy flake'. • Frost is attracted by the 'dark and deep' mysteriousness of the woods – they tempt him to remain there, but practical concerns call him away: 'But I have promises to keep'.	• Kipling also emphasises the unspoiled beauty of the woods: 'When the night-air cools on the trout-ring'd pools/Where the otter whistles his mate' – the woods are Nature's domain. • Kipling also creates a sense of mysteriousness and timelessness around the woods: 'You will hear the beat of a horse's feet' – the past lives on in the woods.
Paragraphs 3 and 4: Differences of emphasis	
• Frost's focus is on the prospect of finding rest, and perhaps oblivion, for himself in the woods – he is tempted to forget his 'promises' and the 'miles [he has] to go' and surrender himself to 'The darkest evening of the year', possibly through death. • The woods are a private place in which Frost can simply 'watch [them] fill up with snow', not needing to act, and contemplate the prospect of a release from the cares of life.	• Kipling's focus is less personal – for him the woods are entrancing because they affirm the power of Nature to withstand man's attempts to impose 'the road', 'the trees', 'the coppice' upon them: 'Weather and rain have undone it again,/And now you would never know …'. • The woods, therefore, are to be celebrated because they represent the triumph of natural life over the man-made: 'where the ring-dove broods,/And the badgers roll at ease'.
Paragraphs 5 and 6: Style and language	
• Frost's language is metaphorical as well as literal: '<u>his</u> woods' become '<u>the</u> woods', developing symbolic overtones; 'darkest evening of the year' and 'frozen lake' suggest death and oblivion; 'miles to go before I sleep' connotes Frost's journey through life. • The language is simple, lyrical, almost childlike: 'My little horse', 'He gives his harness bells a shake' – this gives the impression of the poem as a fable with a timeless theme. • Soft alliteration and assonance ('sound's the sweep/ Of easy wind') evoke an impression of the deep tranquillity of the woods, an impression heightened by the smooth, undisturbed rhythms of the lines.	• Kipling's voice addresses the reader directly: 'And now you would never know', 'Yet, if you enter the woods … You will hear' – this is a more public voice than Frost's (who muses aloud to himself), announcing a theme for which the poet is spokesman: 'There was once a <u>path</u> through the woods … , But there is no <u>road</u> through the woods'. • The language establishes a clear contrast running throughout the poem between man ('They shut the road … They planted the trees') and Nature ('The badgers roll at ease', 'They fear not men in the woods') – man intrudes and inhibits, Nature inhabits and lives freely. • Soft alliteration and assonance ('And the swish of a skirt in the dew/Steadily cantering through/The misty solitudes') evokes an impression of timeless mystery, an impression heightened by the smooth, undisturbed rhythms of the lines in stanza 2.
Paragraphs 7 and 8: Form and structure	
• Frost's four stanzas show him being drawn progressively deeper into the woods in sympathy, so that by the start of stanza 4 he seems ready to yield himself to their 'lovely, dark and deep' attractions – the three consecutive adjectives here underline the strength of his desire to retreat from life into a more peaceful existence. • The pivotal word 'But' in line 14, emphasised by its placing at the start of the line, shows Frost pulling himself reluctantly away to face the 'promises' he has to 'keep'. • The repetition in lines 15 and 16 can be taken to show either Frost's determination 'to go' or his profound weariness with life, or both.	• Kipling's 2 stanzas provide a contrast and a development: stanza 1 describes the present, stanza 2 describes how the past lives on in the present. The purpose is to show that the sounds and sights of the past are not 'old' or 'lost' but remain preserved in the woods for all time. • The refrain 'road through the woods' echoes through the poem. Stanza 2 has an extra line at the end, emphasising the poem's contrast between 'road' and 'path' or (as in the title) 'way' – a 'road' is made by man, a 'path' or 'way' is created naturally, and Nature prevails.

Turning plans into exam answers

Activity 15

1 Individually, turn your paragraph plan into an exam answer of six to eight paragraphs. Follow the paragraph structure of the example in Activity 14 and pay a roughly equal amount of attention to:

- similarities/differences of emphasis
- style and language
- form and structure.

2 At the end of your work, add a list of bullet points identifying the parts of this task you found the most straightforward and those you found the most difficult. Be totally honest. If the second list is longer than the first one, you will be giving your teacher useful feedback about what to concentrate on next.

Activity 16

1 Here is a list of possible exam questions. Identify your chosen topic and the question on it.

Home: 'Home is where the heart is'. Compare and contrast at least two poems in the light of this statement.

Suggested poems:

The House by Matthew Sweeney

Frost at Midnight by Samuel Taylor Coleridge

The Hill Wife by Robert Frost

I Remember, I Remember by Thomas Hood

End of Another Home Holiday by D.H. Lawrence

To My Mother by George Barker

Autobiography by Louis MacNeice

My Father played the Melodeon by Patrick Kavanagh

Piano by D.H. Lawrence

Land: 'Poets associate particular places with strong personal memories'. Compare and contrast at least two poems in the light of this statement.

Suggested poems:

The Prelude by William Wordsworth

Home-thoughts from Abroad by Robert Browning

Poem in October by Dylan Thomas

The Sweetness of England by Elizabeth Barrett Browning

As the Team's Head-brass by Edward Thomas

Beeny Cliff by Thomas Hardy

Binsey Poplars by Gerard Manley Hopkins

Birches by Robert Frost

How Old Mountains Drip with Sunset by Emily Dickinson

Work: 'Work can sometimes seem like drudgery or slavery'. Compare and contrast two poems in the light of this statement.

Suggested poems:

The Chimney Sweeper by William Blake

Working by Tony Harrison

Money by C.H. Sisson

Toads by Philip Larkin

Miners by Wilfred Owen

Toads Revisited by Philip Larkin

Tractor by Ted Hughes

The Blacksmiths by Anon

Dirge by Kenneth Fearing

2 As a class, agree on two poems that compare and contrast well in the light of the given question. Then plan your answer by creating a chart like this:

Poem	Similarities/differences of emphasis	Style and language	Form and structure
A			
B			

3 With a partner, use your entries in column 1 to draft *the first part* of an exam answer. You should:

- make clear statements about the themes and ideas in Poem A
- make comparative comments about the themes and ideas in Poem B
- quote briefly to illustrate each main point you make.

4 In a small group, use your entries in column 2 to draft *the middle part of* an exam answer. You should:

- write about each poet's choice of language (including imagery), use of voice and use of language devices relating to sound (eg alliteration, onomatopoeia, assonance, sibilance)
- relate each poet's language use to their attitude towards the topic
- illustrate your points with quotation
- bring out your comparative points by using discourse markers such as 'Similarly', 'By contrast', 'Whereas', 'On the other hand', 'However', and so on.

5 As a class, use your entries in column 3 to draft *the final part* of an exam answer. You should:

- write about each poet's use of stanza form, line structure, rhyme (if applicable) and rhythm
- relate each poet's use of form and structure to their attitude towards the topic
- illustrate your points with quotation
- bring out your comparative points by using discourse markers.

6 Individually, use your drafts to write a polished answer to the question. Aim to write two to three sides of paper.

Evaluating a sample response

1 As a class, read the two poems below and then the sample response to the following question.

> 'Home is where the heart is'. Compare and contrast at least two poems in the light of this statement.

Piano

Softly, in the dusk, a woman is singing to me;
Taking me back down the vista of years, till I see
A child sitting under the piano, in the boom of the tingling strings
And pressing the small, poised feet of a mother who smiles as she sings.

5   In spite of myself, the insidious mastery of song
Betrays me back, till the heart of me weeps to belong
To the old Sunday evenings at home, with winter outside,
And hymns in the cosy parlour, the tinkling piano our guide.

So now it is vain for the singer to burst into clamour
10 With the great black piano appassionato. The glamour
Of childish days is upon me, my manhood is cast
Down in the flood of remembrance, I weep like a child for the past.

D.H. Lawrence

The House

The house had a dozen bedrooms,
each of them cold, and the wind
battered the windows and blew down
power-lines to leave the house dark.
5   Rats lived in the foundations,
sending scouts under the stairs
for a year or two, and once
a friendly ghost was glimpsed
at the foot of a bed. Downhill
10   half a mile was the Atlantic,
with its ration of the drowned –
one of whom visited the house,
carried there on a door.
It hosted dry corpses, too,
15   with nostrils huge to a child,
but never a murder –
except the lambs bled dry
in the yard outside. Sunlight
never took over the interior,
20   and after dark the cockroaches
came out from under a cupboard
to be eaten by the dog.
Crows were always sitting
on the wires, planning nests
25   in the chimneys, and a shotgun
sometimes blew a few away.
Neighbours never entered
as often as in other houses,
but it did have a piano upstairs.
30   And I did grow up there.

Matthew Sweeney

Writing in the exam

- The question always begins with a general statement. You have to 'compare and contrast … in the light of this statement'. Examiners do not mean you to choose only poems which bear out the statement (eg poems that show 'Home is where the heart is' to be true). Good choices in response to this statement would be a poem about happy times at home and one that shows home in a different light. Good choices in response to the statement about work above would be one poem that shows work to be 'drudgery' and another that shows work in a different light. Remember to focus on the *exact* question and statement given.

- Remember that the key to success in your exam answer is to build up a comparison that is illustrated *in detail* from two or more poems. The highest marks are given for answers that compare the *style* and *structure* of poems, not just their subject matter. You can write about two or more poems to meet the Assessment objectives in full. Top marks are available for the quality of the response whether you write about two or more poems.

2 As a class, discuss the strengths and weaknesses of the answer on the next page. Use the following criteria to evaluate it.

Criteria	Quite well	Very well	Extremely well
Is a clear comparison/contrast established?			
Is a clear comparison/contrast sustained throughout the answer?			
Is comment made on the poems' themes?			
Is comment made on the poems' style and structure?			
Is textual reference and quotation made to support key points?			
Is appropriate use made of literary terms?			

In 'The House', Matthew Sweeney expresses a negative attitude towards home. He disliked growing up there. Although the last line is 'And I did grow up there', it is tacked on as an afterthought, as if he doesn't want to associate his childhood with 'a dozen bedrooms,/each of them cold' and 'cockroaches [which came] from under a cupboard/to be eaten by the dog'. There is no sense in the poem of family warmth. Sweeney makes only a passing reference to his parents and emphasises that 'Neighbours never entered'. It is entitled 'The House' to make the point from the very start that, to him, it was never home. His heart was definitely not there.

By contrast, in 'Piano' D.H. Lawrence sees his home as where 'the heart of me' was when he was a child. Memories of his mother dominate the poem and it is clear that he had a close relationship with her: 'pressing the small, poised feet of a mother who smiles as she sings'.

Whereas Sweeney's home was large and unwelcoming ('the wind/battered the windows'), Lawrence's was small and intimate: 'hymns in the cosy parlour'. The family gathered round the piano to sing. Looking back, Lawrence sees a 'glamour/Of childish days' but all that Sweeney sees is gloom ('Sunlight/Never took over the interior') and a lack of life and cheerfulness: 'but it did have a piano upstairs'.

The language of Sweeney's poem is mainly factual and blunt:
'Downhill/half a mile was the Atlantic' …
'Crows were always sitting/on the wires'.

There is little imagery to soften the effect. Most of the poem is made up of common nouns ('Rats', 'corpses', 'cockroaches', 'Crows') and verbs. The few adjectives are quite stark: 'a dozen bedrooms', 'dry corpses'. These 'corpses' are other humans in the house, a very disparaging view by Sweeney of his family. His voice in the poem is the voice of an adult looking back but time has not mellowed his memories. The sound of words is hard, for example 'battered', 'lambs bled dry', 'a shotgun/sometimes blew a few away'. Sweeney views his home as somewhere he always felt distant from, as he shows by the way he describes it in a list-like way, using an impersonal tone: 'the drowned – /one of whom visited the house,/carried there on a door'. There is an atmosphere of death and decay around the house.

The language, mood and atmosphere of 'Piano' is quite different. Like Sweeney, Lawrence is looking back on childhood but his memories are all of life, warmth and affection: 'A child sitting under the piano', 'with winter outside'. The language is rich and lyrical: 'boom of the tingling strings' 'the tinkling piano our guide'. Lawrence uses strong metaphors like 'the flood of remembrance' to show he is overwhelmed by these happy memories and his 'manhood is cast/Down' as he is reduced to tears. The thoughts of home are so real that he 'weeps' when they return to him. He feels that his life then was better than his life now; this is symbolised by the contrast between 'the great black piano' in the present which sounds ugly and 'the tinkling piano' in the past which sounds cosy.

The form and structure of each poem is well suited to its subject matter. Lawrence's poem is set out in three stanzas which take him from the present to the past and leave him there to 'weep like a child'. He does not want to return to the present because he would rather live in his memories. Sweeney's poem, on the other hand, is all one stanza with a flat, lifeless rhythm showing his lack of feeling for it. There is no development, just a dreary catalogue of how his so-called home was never really a home to him but only 'The House'.

Tackling Section B of the exam

You have to answer one question from a choice of two. You should spend about 50 minutes on it and aim to write two to three sides. Remember that the question asks you to:

- compare poems in the light of a general statement about their topic
- 'compare and contrast': that is, bring out the similarities *and* differences between them
- choose 'at least two poems' for comparison: in other words, you can write about two poems or more than two.

The focus of the question is to *compare and contrast* rather than just comment. It is vital that you base your comparison on the general statement you are given at the start of the question, eg:

Home: 'Home is so sad' (Philip Larkin)

Land: 'Poets sometimes write nostalgically about familiar landscapes.'

Work: 'Work can be a deeply satisfying experience.'

Assessment objectives

To assess your answer on your chosen poems, the examiners use a mark scheme based on three Assessment objectives:

AO1: Articulate creative, informed and relevant responses to literary texts, using appropriate terminology and concepts, and coherent, accurate written expression. (15 marks)

AO2: Demonstrate detailed critical understanding in analysing the ways in which structure, form and language shape meanings in literary texts. (5 marks)

AO3: Explore connections and comparisons between different literary texts, informed by interpretations of other readers. (20 marks)

Activity 18

1   As a class, discuss which of the requirements above you think that at the present time you can meet in full, meet fairly well or not meet at all.

2   Then draw up a personal action plan, designed to turn your current weaknesses into strengths. It could begin like the one below.

Action plan for Section B of the exam	
My biggest problems	How to solve them
Keeping a comparison going throughout my answer	• Try writing consecutive paragraphs about Poem A and Poem B. • Use discourse markers and connectives more: 'By contrast', 'Similarly', 'However,' etc.
Using quotations constructively	• Practise writing single sentences with two or three words from key poems built into them. • Memorise more of my key poems so that the quotations are already there in my head.

Activity 19

1 In a small group, read the question below and then the poems to which it refers.

'Work can sometimes seem like drudgery or slavery.' Compare *The Chimney Sweeper* by William Blake with *Money* by C.H. Sisson in the light of this statement.

The Chimney Sweeper

When my mother died I was very young,
And my father sold me while yet my tongue
Could scarcely cry *'weep 'weep 'weep 'weep*!
So your chimneys I sweep, and in soot I sleep.

5   There's little Tom Dacre, who cried when his head,
That curled like a lamb's back, was shaved; so I said,
'Hush Tom, never mind it, for when your head's bare,
You know that the soot cannot spoil your white hair.'

And so he was quiet, and that very night,
10 As Tom was asleeping he had such a sight –
That thousands of sweepers, Dick, Joe, Ned and Jack,
Were all of them locked up in coffins of black.

And by came an angel, who had a bright key,
And he opened the coffins and set them all free;
15 Then down a green plain leaping, laughing they run,
And wash in a river and shine in the sun.

Then naked and white, all their bags left behind,
They rise upon clouds and sport in the wind.
And the angel told Tom, if he'd be a good boy,
20 He'd have God for his father and never want joy.

And so Tom awoke, and we rose in the dark,
And got with our bags and our brushes to work.
Though the morning was cold, Tom was happy and warm;
So if all do their duty, they need not fear harm.

William Blake

Money

I was led into captivity by the bitch business
Not in love but in what seemed a physical necessity
And now I cannot even watch the spring
The itch for subsistence having become a responsibility.

5   Money the she-devil comes to us under many veils
Tactful at first, calling herself beauty
Tear away this disguise, she proposes paternal solicitude
Assuming the dishonest face of duty.

Suddenly your are in bed with a screeching tear-sheet
10 This is money at last without her night-dress
Clutching you against her fallen udders and sharp bones

In an unscrupulous and deserved embrace.
C.H. Sisson

Writing in the exam

In the exam you are given EITHER one named poem OR allowed a free choice of poems. The question here names two poems for the purpose of the activity only.

2 In your group, read the sample answer below. As you do so, try to remember the Assessment objectives for Section B and mentally assess how well this answer meets them. Focus on:

- how relevant it is to the question
- how well it meets the requirements of AO1
- how well it meets the requirements of AO2
- how well it meets the requirements of AO3.

3 When you have finished, compare your assessments of this answer as a class. Then make a class list of literary terms that helped the writer to make key points.

Blake's 'The Chimney Sweeper' shows how work can be a form of slavery. The speaker is a young boy who has been sold by his father to sweep chimneys: 'So your chimneys I sweep, and in soot I sleep'. He is enslaved along with 'thousands of [other] sweepers', the symbol of this in the poem being 'coffins of black' in which their lives are 'locked up'. Their lives are a form of living death.

C.H. Sisson's poem 'Money' describes a different kind of enslavement to work: 'I was led into captivity by the bitch business'. Through an extended metaphor, love of making money is depicted as a destructive sexual relationship with a 'she-devil' and a 'screaming tear-sheet'. The speaker will never be free but remain locked 'In an unscrupulous and deserved embrace'. The poem describes the progressive stages of this affair. Unlike the chimney sweeper, however, his is a voluntary enslavement which develops into an addiction: 'And now I can not even watch the spring'. The speaker's enslavement is a 'deserved embrace' whereas that of the chimney sweeper is entirely undeserved, his fate being in the hands of the sweep-masters who tell him lies about his 'duty' and its heavenly reward.

The style and language of each poem reflects its speaker. 'The Chimney Sweeper' has the vocabulary and limited range of reference of a boy:

'And so he was quiet, and that very night,
As Tom was asleeping he had such a sight'

The speaker's language is full of common and proper nouns – 'soot', 'bags' and 'brushes', 'Tom Dacre', 'angel', 'God' – and his figures of speech are typical of a child's imagination, made up of a mixture of everyday experience and bible stories: 'curled like a lamb's back', 'an angel, who had a bright key'. The poem is presented as a childlike lyric with a regular stanza structure reminiscent of nursery rhymes and a light, musical rhythm. This reflects the innocence and naivety of the speaker.

In Sisson's poem, the speaker's language is full of revulsion for a 'bitch' he knows has seduced him and from whom there is no escape. The imagery becomes increasingly explicit and sordid as the poem goes on. At first, greed for money is like an 'itch', a mild form of sexual desire. Later, the speaker has to forcibly 'tear away' the 'many veils' of its 'dishonest face' to perceive the corruption beneath. Too late, he sees the 'bitch' as she really is 'without her night-dress': a harridan with deformed breasts ('fallen udders') and a withered body ('sharp bones').

The form and structure of each poem reflects its theme. Blake's lyric is from the sequence 'Songs of Innocence'. There is an incongruity between its nursery rhyme form and the disturbing story of child labour and abuse it tells, since the young speaker remains 'innocent' of the real situation he is caught up in. The middle stanzas describe his vision of heaven:

'Then naked and white, all their bags left behind,
They rise upon clouds and sport in the wind'

The pathos of this stems from the fact that the sweeper believes it completely and sees it as a reward for 'duty', his duty in an industrial society being to sleep in soot and endure a living death. This is what he has been told by the Church and by his exploiters: 'So if all do their duty, they need not fear harm'.

Sisson's poem works more straightforwardly. Each of its three stanzas describes a different stage in the speaker's progress towards complete 'captivity' by the 'itch' to make money. The rhythms, unlike those in 'The Chimney Sweeper', are flat and prosaic: 'Not in love but in what seemed like a physical necessity'. This is the speaking voice confronting an ugly truth. Consequently, the poem's metrical patterns are irregular and the half-rhymes discordant: 'necessity'/'responsibility', 'night-dress'/'embrace'. As the poem goes on, the pronouns change from 'I' in stanza 1 to 'us' in stanza 2 and 'you' in stanza 3, indicating that Sisson is generalising his theme to apply to all of 'us'. His point seems to be that money is a 'she-devil' that destroys everyone in the end, as the last line of the poem confirms.

Writing with the Assessment objectives in mind

Activity 20

1 Look at an exam question from the Edexcel Sample Assessment Materials or devise one yourself. In about 30 minutes, write the first four paragraphs of an answer – paragraphs 1 and 2 about themes and ideas in your chosen poems, paragraphs 3 and 4 about style and language.

2 Exchange your work with a partner. Write comments and advice, reflecting what the examiner would be looking for. Annotate the work by putting 'AO1', 'AO2' and 'AO3' at appropriate points. Then explain and justify your assessments to each other.

3 As a class, discuss how you can show an examiner that you are meeting each requirement for each Assessment objective as you write. Make a class chart, like the one below.

AOs	Indicators to the examiner
AO1: The student can: • sustain a line of argument • use appropriate literary terms.	• Use a short sentence stating the main theme of Poem A in own words. • Use discourse markers. • Use quotations to take the argument a step further. • Round off a paragraph with a comparative reference.

Improving your style and expression

AO1 awards 15 marks for the use of appropriate literary terms and fluent, accurate writing as you build up your answer. The next activity is designed to help you improve your skills in this area.

Activity 21

1 As a class, read aloud the extracts below on poems. They all fall short of the 'fluent and accurate' writing required by AO1. Improve their expression and note down your revised versions.

A
The main subject of the poem is about how home life can be unhappy.

B
The poet puts across to us that work can be boring by his use of a metaphor of a day-dreamer.

C
The next verse says that the woman in the poem died alone because of the 'lonely crochet' reference.

D
This is a comparison between my two poems I have chosen because there is a feeling of grief and loss in each poem.

E
When the poet puts 'Where have they gone, the old familiar faces?' he's not actually talking about faces literally but about people he once knew.

F
The quote 'the wind began to moan' is a metaphor of the wind sort of crying or howling like a person, this is personification.

G
The rhythm is fast and jerky to get across the engine of the tractor bursting into life.

H
'Straws like tame lightnings', this is comparing the shape of a piece of straw to the zig-zag shape of lightening to give us a picture of how it looks.

I
The sound effects of 'The lowest boughs and the brushwood leaf' are very long and drawn out to give an idea to the reader of branches sweeping the ground.

J
Dylan Thomas uses a lot of imagery in his poem 'Poem in October'.

2 In a small group, make a list of single words and phrases you know you always struggle to think of as you are writing about poems. Use essays and other marked work to remind yourself.

3 As a class, share your lists. Make a chart of 'better phrases' you could refer to as you write practice essays for the exam.

4 Individually, read through the examples of comments on imagery (simile, metaphor, personification and symbolism) below. These comments are well expressed, so you can learn from them.

> The poet uses a simile comparing the wind with a stampede of cattle to suggest the way it threatened to demolish everything in its path.

> The metaphorical phrase 'There's daggers in men's smiles' implies that, beneath a mask of friendliness, no one can be trusted.

> The poet uses a metaphor comparing the effect of turbulent winds on the landscape with a wild stampede of cattle creating wholesale destruction.

> The sick rose symbolises the death of young love.

> The twigs are personified as 'aged hands', evoking the impression that, like an old person's fingers, they look gnarled and bony.

> The grinning skull is symbolic of the triumph of death.

> The sun is described metaphorically as 'a fiery disc', indicating both its circular shape and the way it burns fiercely.

> The caged bird is a symbol of the captive imagination.

Section C: Prose

In Section C of the exam, you will write about two novels in the form of an argument. This section, therefore, helps you develop your skills in:

- studying your core novel
- making links between your core novel and a second text.
- using your two novels to build up an argument
- writing your examination response.

Examples of the kind of question you can expect are given in Activity 30 on page 114. Section C is worth 40 marks (40% of the total marks for Unit 1).

Finding links between your novels

For Section C of the exam, you have to study one core novel in detail. You also have to read a second text. In the exam you will refer to this to support your ideas about your core novel.

From the outset, then, you should be looking for links between your novels to provide material for discussion and argument.

Getting started: reading your core novel

There are several ways of getting to grips with your core novel. Here are some suggestions:

- Read the novel all the way through by yourself. Try to experience it as a reader, rather than an exam text. Allow the narrative to take you over.
- Read the first chapter with a friend, a small group or even your whole class and discuss what you expect from the novel. You could also talk about the setting, characters and narrative technique and identify any themes. You can then read the rest of the novel on your own.
- Read the first chapter of your core novel and then the first chapter of your second text. Identify any areas for comparison that strike you before reading the rest of the novels.

Assessment objectives

To assess your answer on your core novel and second text, the examiners use a mark scheme based on two Assessment objectives.

AO1: Articulate creative, informed and relevant responses to literary texts, using appropriate terminology and concepts, and coherent, accurate written expression. (15 marks)

AO2: Demonstrate detailed critical understanding in analysing the ways in which structure, form and language shape meanings in literary texts. (25 marks)

Note that AO3 'Make comparisons …' does *not* apply to Section C. You need to address AO1 (15 marks) including informed and relevant responses to literary texts and AO2 (25 marks) including how structure, form and style shape meaning. You should focus on your core text to establish an argument and refer to your further text to develop your line of argument.

Activity 22

As you read, keep by you a pad of paper and a block of post-it notes. Use them to keep track of your response as a *reader*, not to simply make notes as a student.

1 On your pad, jot down things that aren't completely clear or things that puzzle or surprise you. For example:

2 On your post-it notes, jot down things that seem important about the plot (story), characters and themes. You could use different colours for plot, characters and themes. Leave them stuck in at appropriate pages. For example:

Plot

Heathcliff separated from Cathy by the Lintons: will take his revenge out on Edgar

Characters

Mr Collins – pompous windbag, thinks Eliz will marry him to get status – he's pathetic

Themes

Jane thinks she can't marry Rochester cos of the social gap between them – shows Victorian attitude towards money and class

pages 26–28 I don't see what this bit has got to do with the story – it seems to be jumping around.

pages 49 (Ch7) The story goes into the past here: I wonder why.

pages 110-114 The story is now being told by another character – surprising, but quite interesting to see their point of view on it.

page 156++ I hate the violence here – really nasty and upsetting. Does the story need all this?

page 279 An unusual ending: does the writer believe in ghosts? Different, though – they die rather than get married, as in a lot of novels.

Developing a personal viewpoint

In the exam, it is important that the views you express about your novels are your own. This does not mean they have to be entirely original. It means that you have to have thought out your responses and opinions clearly enough to present a confident viewpoint backed up by the text. The activity below gives you a platform for doing this.

Activity 23

1 Take a large sheet of plain paper. Make a chart to map your first reactions, like the one below.

Plot/story	Characters	Style of writing	Queries
Gripping	Unrealistic	Lots of different voices used to tell the story	Why aren't things presented in chronological order?

Fill in the chart with your honest reactions. You will use it to share your responses to the novel in class, so the entries you make need to be:

- thoughtful and considered
- precise, not general
- tied in to specific examples and particular parts of the book.

2 As a class, exchange reactions to your core novel. Focus your discussion on:

- how convincingly the writer portrays the central character(s) and their relationships
- how realistically the writer depicts the time and place in which the novel is set
- how well the writer creates and maintains suspense
- how well the style and structure of the narrative is matched to its themes
- how much you, as a twenty-first-century reader, enjoyed the nineteenth or twentieth-century novel.

Bringing in your second text: charting links

Read your second text for its own sake, but as you read you should also look for links to your core novel:

- in theme
- between characters and the situation they are in
- between social context (ie the societies and environments in which the stories are set)
- between narrative technique (ie the way each story is told).

Wide Sargasso Sea

Linked to *Jane Eyre* by Rochester and the story of his Creole wife – a less sympathetic view of Rochester, though, and a totally different unEnglish setting.

A Clockwork Orange

Like *Brighton Rock*, portrays gang violence – but a very different style of narration: *Clockwork O* has an unconventional first person narrative voice which uses odd, partly-invented language.

The Shooting Party

At the story's climax there's the killing of a 'lower class' character by a character from the 'upper class', as in *Howards End* – both books deal with class differences and conflicts.

Activity 24

1   As a class, create a diagram like the one below to map the links between your two novels. First fill in the 'Theme' boxes relating to your two novels, then the 'Characters/situation' boxes, and so on. Some ideas for entries have been given in the boxes below to help you get started.

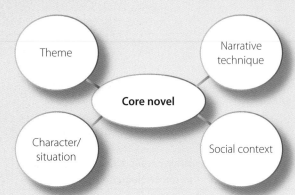
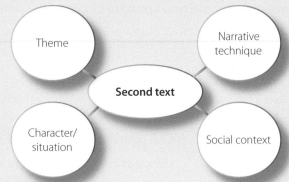

Theme

- Childhood and growing up. Which aspects in particular?
- Good and evil. How do we judge these?
- The experiences of women. Oppression or emancipation?
- Outsiders. Why are some people 'excluded' by society?
- The importance of place and roots. What do we mean by 'home' and 'family'?

Characters/situation

- Characters on a journey to maturity/self-discovery. Failing or succeeding?
- Characters suffering from injustice and cruelty. How do they cope/survive?
- Characters behaving destructively? Motivation? Effect on those around them?
- Characters in search of happiness. Failing or succeeding? Do they change?
- Characters facing tragedy. Victims or heroes?

Social context

- Societies based on wealth and class distinction. Effects on the individual?
- Urban and rural societies. How do they compare and contrast?
- Societies with rigid moral codes. Effects on the individual?
- Societies with prejudiced attitudes or corrupt values. Effects on the individual?
- Societies past and present. How do they compare and contrast?

Narrative technique

- First person narrative throughout. Why this viewpoint?
- Third person narrative throughout. Why this viewpoint?
- A mixture of styles and narrative viewpoints. What effects are achieved by this?
- Frame story with different narrators. How is the reader positioned, and why?
- Effect of different techniques. Why might these have been selected?

2   Look at the typical exam questions below.

'In a male-dominated world, independent women face unhappiness and disappointment.'

Explore the presentation of women in the light of this statement. You should focus on *Pride and Prejudice* to establish your argument and refer to the second text you have read to support and develop your line of argument.

'Families are the moral centre of society.'

Explore the portrayal and importance of a family's values in the light of this statement. You should focus on *Howards End* to establish your argument and refer to the second text you have read to support and develop your line of argument.

Now use your diagram to devise three questions of your own on your two novels. One should be based on themes, one on characters/situation and one on social context. Make sure that each question begins by setting up an argument in the form of a general statement, as above. You will make use of these questions as you work through the activities below.

Writing in the exam

Developing an argument' involves writing 'specifically', not vaguely or generally, about your novels and discussing *how* your novelists write as much as *what* they write about. In other words, most marks in this question are given for your ability to comment on narrative technique. Make sure you do not lose sight of the text itself in your arguments. Everything you say should refer closely back to the texts.

Building up argued viewpoints about your novels

Everything you write in your Section C answer in the exam must take the form of an argument. The activities below support you in:

- exploring your core novel and second text in light of a statement
- choosing suitable argued topics for your two novels
- using your core novel to establish your argument
- using your further novel to develop your argument
- creating a balanced answer which incorporates your two novels.

Practising argument

In your answer in the exam you are required to relate your novels to the general statement at the start of the question. The activity below gives you basic guidance on how to do this. The key is to establish an argued viewpoint at the outset and sustain it to the end.

> ### Writing in the exam
>
> For AO1 you need to demonstrate that you can 'Articulate creative, informed and relevant responses to literary texts, using appropriate terminology and concepts, and coherent, accurate written expression'. So building up viewpoints and developing arguments about your two novels needs to be a central part of your preparation for Section C of the exam.

Activity 25

As a class, look back to your diagram linking your novels on pages 106 and the three exam questions you devised on theme, characters/situation and social context in Activity 24. Use the question on theme to look at the first stage of bringing together your argument.

1. First decide whether your core novel fits the general statement in the question. You could:

   - argue that it fits completely
   - argue that it fits to a certain extent
   - argue that it does not fit at all.

It is the way you explore your core novel and second text in light of the statement that matters – there is no 'right or wrong' answer.

Here is an example of a way to work, based on *Brighton Rock*. A table has been used to explore the statement that 'Violence is not caused by society but by individuals who lack a moral sense' and to consider the way that Greene presents violence in *Brighton Rock* in light of that comment, before moving on to consider the second text.

Viewpoint on *Brighton Rock*	
Violence in the novel: caused by individuals lacking in moral sense rather than by society?	
Agree	**Disagree**
• Pinkie prepared to use violence to become gang leader and maintain his position • Greene refers to him as the Boy, giving the reader a sense of detachment, presenting him as a strange and disturbing figure • Although Pinkie is a Catholic, he embraces the concept of 'Hell, Flames and damnation, torments!' rather than the concept of Heaven • Pinkie describes himself as evil: 'when they christened me, the holy water didn't take' • How the reader is drawn into Rose's plight and her desire to be with Pinkie which overrides any conventional moral sense • Ida has a strong conscience, yet she is portrayed as limited: though she is conventionally 'good' her moral values are not explored in the same depth as Pinkie's and Rose's. Rose says 'you can tell the world's all dandy with her', and her sense of right and wrong is very straightforward: 'right's right, an eye for an eye, when you want to do a thing well, do it yourself	• The description of Rose's family at Nelson Place explains why Rose is so desperate for Pinkie's love and will condone violence • It is not totally true to dismiss Pinkie as having no moral sense. A substantial part of the novel is concerned with examining his thought processes – eg his reaction when Cubitt describes him as 'mean, yellow and scared' • The novel contrasts the shabby with the wealthy – 'the soap-dish, the basin of stale water' in Pinkie's room with the luxury Colleoni enjoys at the Cosmopolitan. Envy and frustration are driving forces behind Pinkie's behaviour • Brighton's 'scarred and shabby side' is presented to us very vividly • Society's expectations of conventional marriage and attitude to sex cause Pinkie dismay and anger: 'was there no escape – anywhere – for anyone? It was worth murdering a world'

Viewpoint on *Brighton Rock*

Violence in the novel: caused by individuals lacking in moral sense rather than by society?

On balance

Graham Greene presents violence in the novel in several ways:

- The backgrounds of Pinkie and Rose are clearly contributory factors in the way they aspire to some sort of 'better life'
- However, the novel does not simply blame society for the violence that ensues. Rose's parents, for example, are presented in quite a comic (and grotesque) way
- The reader is drawn into the individual consciences and thoughts of the characters
- Ida's attempt to save Rose from death is successful, so she succeeds in stopping one act of violence; the ending is not totally happy, however, as Rose remains steadfastly loyal to Pinkie to the end
- The novel presents a conflict between two kinds of morality, that of Pinkie and Rose based on *self-interest* and that of Ida based on *community*.

2 Create a similar chart for your theme-based question on your core novel. As in the example, try to see both sides of the argument and work through to a balanced conclusion.

Writing in the exam

The general statement in the question is meant to provide you with a basis for argument. It is *not* intended to be an accurate or true description of either of your novels. There is no 'right' or 'wrong' answer in the examiners' minds.

Integrating textual evidence

Your next step is to think further about how you will develop your line of argument. You should make reference to events, characters and authorial comment by making statements without direct quotation, and work quotations from the text into your own sentences or set them out, starting on a new line. Here is an example of how to provide evidence in both these ways.

> Pinkie turns to violence partly because it is his only means of achieving status in the gangland of Brighton. Immediately after being warned by the police inspector to clear out of Brighton before the races, he becomes even more determined to use them to take on Colleoni's gang: 'He was going to show the world. They thought because he was only seventeen ...'. The inspector's warning only increases Pinkie's commitment to violence: 'There was poison in his veins. He was ready for more murders'. With Pinkie, the instinct for violence is presented as innate ('in his veins'), not merely the result of social conditioning.

Activity 26

1 Individually, develop how you will use references and quotations in your core novel to support the arguments on your viewpoint chart. You should work on the principle of backing up every main point you make with textual evidence of one kind or another.

2 Using your viewpoint chart as a plan, write the argument it sets out about your core novel.

- Explain the viewpoint you are going to take in the light of the general statement and summarise your main points.
- Introduce two of your main points, supported by references and quotations.
- Introduce one or more further points, supported by references and quotations.

3 At the end of your work, add a list of bullet points identifying the parts of this task you found the most straightforward and those you found the most difficult. Be totally honest. If the second list is longer than the first one, you will be giving your teacher useful feedback about what to concentrate on next.

Constructing an exam answer on your two novels

The activities below give you guidance and practice in building up an argued answer about *both* your novels rather than just one.

Activity 27

1   As a class, look carefully at the sample plan below for writing about *Wuthering Heights* (core novel) and *The Color Purple* (second text). The exam question is:

> 'Social outsiders are often treated in a cruel and unjust way'.
>
> Explore the presentation of 'outsiders' in the light of this statement. You should focus on *Wuthering Heights* to establish your argument and refer to the second text you have read to support and develop your line of argument.

Argued essay plan on my two novels	
Social outsiders: how are they presented as being treated in a cruel and unjust way?	
Core novel: *Wuthering Heights*	**Further novel: *The Color Purple***
	Develop the argument
Nelly calls Heathcliff 'it'	Voice of the victim with no one to turn to in first letters
Readers see Heathcliff more clearly when they hear his own narrative voice, describing Thrushcross Grange from an outsider's point of view	Celie's husband rejects her because poor, ugly and black
Apparent rejection by Catherine – Heathcliff becomes an emotional as well as a social outsider	Empowered by other women, and love of Shug Avery
Reverse situation – the well bred Isabella made a social outsider at Wuthering Heights, told in a letter	Celie develops skills that enable her to become a part of society
Hareton brought from outsider to insider by the younger Catherine	Celie's final letter addressed to an all inclusive world, of which she is a part

2   By yourself, write three paragraphs in answer to the question you devised in Activity 24 on characters/situation in your novels. Use references and quotations to support every main point you make, remembering the guidance in Activity 25. Then add a concluding paragraph that gives an overview of the argument you have presented, making sure it refers to both novels.

Writing in the exam

You should aim to write about two-thirds of your answer about your core novel. This will establish your argument. Examiners expect you to use references to your second text to 'support and develop' this argument. You can do this in two ways:

- write first about your core novel and then introduce your second text

- write each paragraph mainly about your core novel, but make brief comparative references to your second text throughout the answer.

As you write responses that explore the presentation of key issues in linked texts, decide which method works best for you. Examiners do not have a 'preferred structure' for the answer. Either method will allow you to meet the two Assessment objectives for Section C.

In the exam, take a few minutes to draft a plan that will structure your response to best establish your argument with your core text and develop it using your second text.

Tackling Section C of the exam

In Section C of the exam, you have to answer one question from a choice of two. You should spend about 50 minutes on it.

One of the questions refers you to a short extract from your core novel as a starting point for your argument. The other question does not.

Remember that the question asks you to:

- explore an aspect of your two novels, which means present an argued viewpoint
- use a given general statement as the basis for your argued viewpoint
- develop a line of argument based on your core novel and support this by referring to your second text.

Remember that the focus of the question is *argue* and *discuss*, rather than compare.

Making use of the Assessment objectives

Examiners use a mark scheme based on two Assessment objectives to assess your answer. Remember these as you establish and develop your line of argument. In summary, they are:

AO1: You have to make creative, informed and relevant responses to your novels, use appropriate literary terms and concepts, and write clearly and accurately. (15 marks)

AO2: You have to show by close textual analysis how the structure, form and language of your novels convey their meanings. (25 marks)

Activity 28

1 As part of a review of your learning, consider how confident you feel about each of the requirements above.

2 Then draw up a personal action plan designed to improve your skills. It could begin like the one below.

Action plan for the Section C of the exam	
My biggest problems	How to solve them
Telling the story rather than arguing	• Make sure that each paragraph relates to the wording of the question. • If you use narrative words and phrases such as 'when', 'after that', 'at the end of the novel', make sure you have a purpose that is not just telling the story.
Writing enough about my second novel	• Decide where you are going to bring in your second text. • Make card index files with points about novels on them.

Activity 29

Read the sample answer below, developed from the plan in Activity 27 in response to the question:

> 'Social outsiders are often treated in a cruel and unjust way.'
> Explore the presentation of 'outsiders' in the light of this statement.

In your response, you should focus on *Wuthering Heights* to establish your argument and refer to the second text you have read to support and develop your line of argument.

In *Wuthering Heights*, Brontë presents several social outsiders, the most important of whom is Heathcliff. When Nelly first describes his arrival to Wuthering Heights, she refers to him with the personal pronoun 'it'. The cruelty and injustice which follow reinforce the idea that Heathcliff is being considered as something less than human.

He has a companion, however, in Catherine. We are given clear insight into his thinking, and his humanity, in his own account, retold by Nelly, of seeing the inhabitants of Thrushcross Grange for the first time. The reader has a sense of someone who has not only survived physical abuse and lack of formal education but has a natural sense of eloquence and wit. He has seen a world that is totally different from the harshness of Wuthering Heights, 'a splendid place carpeted with crimson'. Heathcliff's account is full of epithets, particularly of colours, told in long eloquent sentences, with the exclamation 'ah! It was beautiful'. Catherine is with him, and they laugh together at the spoilt behaviour of the Linton children, and at this point they are social outsiders together, looking in at how others live. However, this companionship is not to last.

Although Catherine suffers physically, being attacked by Skulker, the Lintons quickly realise their mistake. Catherine is no social outsider. They have seen her at church. She is quickly tended to. Heathcliff, on the other hand, is recognised as 'an out and outer' and chased off the premises. Mr Linton describes him as 'a little Lascar, or an American or Spanish castaway' and Edgar compares him to a fortune-teller's son. There are several references to him as a gypsy. Heathcliff is recognised as an outsider immediately through his appearance, social class and, possibly, race.

The cruelty and injustice suffered by Heathcliff increases during Catherine's absence at Thrushcross Grange, as he is tormented by Hareton. Joseph thrashes him, and Heathcliff is reduced to the status of a field labourer. However worse humiliation follows when Catherine returns, a lady. She is no longer his ally as a social outsider and, in addition to his social exclusion, is his apparent exclusion from love. The tragic irony is that Heathcliff overhears only part of what Catherine later tells Nelly – 'It would degrade me to marry Heathcliff now' – and not her expression of love for him, especially when her language moves into a poetic register, using similes to describe her love for Edgar as the foliage in the woods and for Heathcliff as the eternal rocks beneath. Emotional exclusion combines with social exclusion to make Heathcliff bitter and revengeful, an outsider to humanity and happiness.

A reverse social outsider situation occurs in the case of Isabella, who has been delicately brought up. She is exposed to a harsh and brutal life in her marriage to Heathcliff. Brontë uses the epistolary technique here to capture Isabella's voice in her letter. She begins with a series of rhetorical questions, each one being more hysterical in tone. 'Is Mr Heathcliff a man? If so, is he mad? And if not is he a devil?' The letter gives drama and immediacy to the situation and draws the reader's attention to the cruelty and injustice which Isabella is suffering.

Finally Brontë gives the reader the story of Hareton as a way in which a social outsider can be healed through care, education and, most significantly, love, something which, poignantly, never happens to Heathcliff. Hareton is dismissed as a clown by the unreliable narrator Lockwood at the beginning of the novel because of his lack of social graces. However the novel ends with the younger Catherine teaching him manners and offering him love. This gives a clear structure to the novel, and a sense of closure, as the second generation heals some of the damage done by the first.

In *The Color Purple,* Alice Walker presents the reader with the voice of the social outsider through Celie. The novel opens with Celie's voice, clearly that of a victim, isolated, with no one to turn to, except God. Her writing is demotic, in the historic present, which gives an immediacy to what she says. The ellipses give the language the sound of natural speech – 'My mama dead. She die screaming and cussing'. As with Isabella's letter in *Wuthering Heights*, the epistolary technique works by confronting the reader directly with the horrific situations of abuse she encounters.

The reason Celia is a social outsider is clear. She is told by her husband, 'You black, you pore, you ugly, you a woman. Goddam, you nothing at all'. Each word here is delivered as an insult, growing in intensity, the crowning insult being that she is a woman. Then finally he turns the tables and dismisses her as 'nothing at all.' However, Celie has learnt to answer back. She is able to say 'But I'm here', and this is powerfully confirmed by Shug saying, 'Amen, amen' empowering her words with an almost religious status.

Celie is able to find her own voice in the novel, achieve independence and find love. She is shown to be doing this with the help of Shug, Nettie and Sofia, three role models who help her break free from oppression. Her route to economic independence involves sewing clothes, echoing the importance of stitching and quilting in African-American women's history. Celie finds her place in the world and is a social outsider no more. Her letters reflect this change: in the beginning her stream of consciousness was delivered to God because she was isolated and had no one else to turn to. By the end she sees herself as part of an inclusive world – 'Dear Everything'.

Both novels put emphasis on economic independence. Both novels find love as a powerful force and end with a picture of domestic harmony. In one sense, both novels have happy endings. However, a lasting impression of both novels is a vivid sense of the cruelty and injustice suffered by social outsiders.

2   As a class, use the following criteria to evaluate the sample answer. Provide examples to support your points.

- Is a clear viewpoint established?
- Is a clear argument sustained throughout the answer?
- Is there analysis of the novels' language?
- Is there analysis of the novels' form and structure?
- Is textual reference and quotation made to support key points?
- Are clear links made between the two novels?

1. The development of argument and the structure of the answer.

This is a well-argued response. The idea of 'social outsider' is kept in mind throughout. There is a further development of this idea by considering emotional as well as social exclusion. A rather sympathetic picture of Heathcliff emerges as a result of this (it could be said the cruelty of Heathcliff himself is rather overlooked) but the case is well argued and there is a vision of the novel as ironic and tragic at the turning point where Heathcliff overhears only half of a conversation. This argument is well supported by quotation.

The essay chooses Heathcliff's and Catherine's first glimpse of life at Thrushcross Grange as a very significant episode. This is well handled, noting for the reader that Heathcliff at this point has companionship in being a social outsider. The use of quoted extracts that follow their discovery is especially useful in establishing that Catherine is acceptable because she has been seen at church whereas Heathcliff is definitely an outsider because of his looks. There are some racial and racist suggestions here too – points that could have been developed further had there been more time.

The Color Purple is used effectively to extend this argument. Comparisons with *Wuthering Heights* are not essential in this section of the paper (AO3 is not being assessed) but the link between the epistolary narratives in Celie's letters and Isabella's letter to Nelly makes for a neat, well-rounded argument. The final sentence makes a very effective conclusion by saying that both novels present the reader with a vivid picture of social outsiders.

2. The quality of analysis.

What is particularly impressive in this answer is the fact that it keeps referring to the authors and what they are doing, not simply treating the characters as real people. Although the Wuthering Heights section does read in a character by character way – Heathcliff and Catherine, then Isabella, then Hareton – there are repeated references to what Brontë is actually doing with regard to these characters. For example, the candidate writes, 'Brontë gives the reader the story of Hareton as a way in which a social outsider can be healed through care, education and, most significantly, love, something which, poignantly, never happens to Heathcliff'. In this sentence there is an awareness of how Hareton's story fits into the structure of the novel overall, and how it affects the reader's feelings. We are told that 'poignantly' this never happens to Heathcliff, reinforcing the writer's vision of the novel as an essentially sympathetic portrayal of its central character.

Also impressive is the analysis of language. Catherine's emotional description of her love for Heathcliff is explored well through its use of similes. Celie's stream of consciousness letters are analysed well with reference to ellipsis and the historic present tense.
The essay is very aware of the structure of the novels. It argues that the story of Hareton puts right many of the wrongs in Wuthering Heights, and that Celie's journey is one of self-fulfilment. Both novels, it argues, have happy endings and a sense of closure. Some readers may well disagree with this interpretation of Wuthering Heights and argue that the novel ends with a disturbing picture of ghosts who are not at peace. However, the case is argued well and provides us with a coherent vision of both novels that makes sense in view of the question being asked.

3. The extent to which the answer meets AO1 and AO2.

AO1

- Responds with a sustained argument in an informed and relevant manner.
- Makes sustained and pertinent use of literary terms and concepts to develop a coherent argument.
- Displays accurate and fluent written expression.
- Constructs an original and creative response in a well-developed argument.

AO2

- Provides a sustained analysis of the writers' use and selection of features of structure, form and language, showing a well-developed critical understanding.
- Effectively demonstrates how structure, form and language shape meaning in a clear argument

Activity 30

1   Choose the exam question from those below that applies to your two novels and make a 10-minute plan for answering it.

Jane Eyre with either *Wide Sargasso Sea* or *The Magic Toyshop*

'Relatives should be respected and loved yet in literature they are often presented as cruel and evil.'

Explore the way relatives are presented in the light of this statement. You should focus on *Jane Eyre* to establish your argument and refer to the second text you have read to support and develop your line of argument.

Brighton Rock with either *Lies of Silence* or *A Clockwork Orange*

'Anti-social behaviour is always to be condemned.'

Explore the way in which anti-social behaviour is presented in the light of this statement. You should focus on *Brighton Rock* to establish your argument and refer to the second text you have read to support and develop your line of argument.

Pride and Prejudice with either *The French Lieutenant's Woman* or *The Yellow Wallpaper*

'In novels, female characters are often represented as being at odds with the society in which they live.'

Explore the way female characters are presented in the light of this statement. You should focus on *Pride and Prejudice* to establish your argument and refer to the second text you have read to support and develop your line of argument.

Wuthering Heights with either *The Scarlet Letter* or *The Color Purple*

'In novels, characters who suffer injustice normally provoke the sympathy of the reader.'

Explore the extent to which central characters are presented sympathetically in the light of this statement. You should focus on *Wuthering Heights* to establish your argument and refer to the second text you have read to support and develop your line of argument.

Howards End with either *The Remains of the Day* or *The Shooting Party*

'Class always divides; it never unites'.

Explore the portrayal of class in the light of this statement. You should focus on *Howards End* to establish your argument and refer to the second text you have read to support and develop your line of argument.

Writing in the exam

Remember that one of the alternative questions in Section C of the exam will give you a short passage from your core novel as a starting point for building an argument. You may wish to choose an appropriate passage from your core novel to help you answer the relevant question in the list in Activity 30.

2   By yourself, use your plan to write a full and polished answer to your chosen question. Concentrate on:

- establishing a clear viewpoint about your core novel: make two or three main argued points relevant to the statement in the question
- developing your argument by reference to your second text: spend around one third of your time doing this
- bringing out similarities and/or differences between your two novels in the course of your answer
- illustrating the main points you make with textual reference and quotation.

3   Before handing in your work, put yourself in the role of an examiner and write an assessment of your answer. Model this on the sample comments on page 113. Make sure you take account of the requirements of AO1 (15 marks) and AO2 (25 marks).

How to avoid 'telling the story' in your answer

One of the main challenges of answering the question on your chosen novels is the need to argue and discuss rather than narrate and describe. The activities below gives you guidance on how to ensure you do the former and avoid the latter.

Activity 31

1   Read the two paragraphs below about Sarah Woodruff, the main female character in *The French Lieutenant's Woman*. It does not matter whether this is a novel you are studying.

Paragraph 1

Sarah is known as 'the French Lieutenant's woman' because of the sexual relationship she is rumoured to have had with a sailor, Varguennes. He promised to marry her, but left her in Lyme where she became known as 'the French Lieutenant's whore'. Due to the strict morals of Victorian times, she is looked down on by the community, particularly by older people like her employer Mrs Poultenay who sets a watch on her and tries to educate her out of her immoral ways. However, Sarah continues to walk alone on Ware Common, a meeting-place for lovers, and lays a trail to trap Charles Smithson into having an affair. Charles is engaged to be married, and when he breaks his engagement in order to be with Sarah it causes a major scandal for both of them.

Paragraph 2

Picking up *The French Lieutenant's Woman* for the first time, readers might think they are reading a Victorian novel, not a modern one which was first published in the 1960s. Fowles has used the technique of parody, creating a long novel, with long sentences and an old fashioned vocabulary to create this effect. In the tradition of the Victorian novelists, he treats his reader as 'a person of curiosity', someone who is observing the scene at first hand – 'if you had turned northward and landward in 1867 … your prospect would have been harmonious'. The alert reader's suspicions might be aroused, however, by the description of the central character, Sarah Woodruff. She is described as wearing 'a magenta skirt of an almost daring narrowness – and shortness'. The skirt is so short in fact that it exposes 'two white ankles'. In Sarah, Fowles has created a recognisable modern woman, with modern values and outlook, but placed her in a Victorian framework. We might guess that she is going to be outrageous, and not just in the way she dresses, but in her behaviour too.

---

2   With a partner, compare the two paragraphs as part of an answer to the question about the presentation of female characters on page 114. Consider:

- how much of Paragraph 1 is taken up by narrating and describing. Which aspects of its style show this?

- how much of Paragraph 2 is taken up by presenting an argued viewpoint. Which aspects of its style show this?

3   As a class, share your conclusions from the pair work. Then refer back to AO1 and AO2, and discuss why Paragraph 1 would gain relatively few marks from an examiner whereas Paragraph 2 would score highly. End your discussion by noting down the following golden rules about how to avoid just 'telling the story' in your exam answer.

- The examiner has read your novels and does not need a synopsis of what happens in them.

- All references to the plots of your novels should be made in the course of presenting an argued viewpoint; any sentence that fails to do this will be wasted.

- The statement at the start of the question is a springboard for discussion ('how far and in what ways is this true of my novels?'); it is not an invitation to tell all you know.

> **Writing in the exam**
>
> One paragraph of argument is worth more than three paragraphs of story-telling.

Improving your style and expression

AO1 awards 15 marks for the use of appropriate literary terms and fluent, accurate writing as you build up your answer. The next activity is designed to develop your skills in this area.

Activity 32

1   As a class, read the extracts below on responses to novels. Identify improvements that can be made in use of literary terms and to create fluent and accurate writing.

A
The story of *Howards End* tells us about two families, the Wilcoxes and the Shlegels who stand for different things.

B
In *The Shooting Party*, most of the people are of the upper class.

C
In *A Clockwork Orange*, Anthony Burgess is saying that social conditioning is a bad thing.

D
Jane Eyre is put together in a way that makes us feel sorry for Jane.

E
The main topic of *Pride and Prejudice* is that people can be mistaken in their judgements.

F
In this essay I am going to look at how two books discuss violence.

G
Jean Rhys puts us into the mind of the character Antoinette.

H
The Scarlet Letter contains a lot of symbols and motives.

I
In *The French Lieutenant's Woman*, John Fowles is trying to show us a woman ahead of her time in his character study of Sarah.

J
The time scale of *Wuthering Heights* is disorganised because we get several narrators telling the story.

2   Now relate a recent piece of your own writing about your core novel and a second text. Identify how you could improve appropriate use of literary terms and fluent, accurate writing.

Unit 2

Explorations in Drama

What you will do in the course

This is the coursework unit of Edexcel AS English Literature. In it, you will:

- Read and watch plays from the present and the past
- Read reviews and commentaries on plays and their background
- Study in detail one play from 1300 to 1800
- Read another play from 1300 to 1800
- Write a coursework folder of 2000–2500 words made up of:
  - **explorative study** – an analytical study of both your plays (the second is referred to for purposes of comparison). One play must be by Shakespeare; the other can be, but need not be, by Shakespeare
  - **creative critical response** – a response to your play(s) from a critical standpoint. You will write for a specified purpose and audience: for example, a review of a production for a literary magazine, a scripted talk by a director justifying his/her interpretation for the play's cast, a letter to a newspaper by a theatre-goer criticising a performance.

What you will learn in the course

- The key elements of drama, past and present
- The differences between stage drama and drama on TV or film
- How plays come to be written as they are
- How to study a play from the past
- How audiences and critics have responded to plays over time
- How to write as a critic yourself

How your coursework is assessed

Your coursework folder is assessed by your teacher, using four assessment objectives (AOs). These are:

Assessment objective		What this means in practice
AO1	Articulate creative, informed and relevant responses to literary texts, using appropriate terminology and concepts, and coherent, accurate written expression.	You can use: • ideas relevant to literary study • suitable literary terms • a clear and fluent writing style.
AO2	Demonstrate detailed critical understanding in analysing the ways in which structure, form and language shape meanings in literary texts.	You can show how, in plays and play-related texts: • language conveys meaning • form and structure convey meaning.
AO3	Explore connections and comparisons between different literary texts, informed by interpretations of other readers.	You can: • compare and contrast plays • explain others' interpretations of plays.
AO4	Demonstrate understanding of the significance and influence of the context in which literary texts are written and received.	You can: • put plays into their contexts • show how contexts influence plays • explain audiences' responses to plays.

Your teacher will also look for evidence of:

• original ideas and personal response
• your ability to argue a case in your explorative study
• your ability to write for a specified audience in your creative critical response.

How to succeed in Literature Unit 2

Coursework gives you the chance to plan and write your work over an extended period. In other words, you have more of a say, and more of a responsibility, than you have when preparing for an external exam. You can make the most of this by:

• regularly watching plays in the theatre and on video. This is the single most important way to help yourself to a good coursework grade
• reading a wide range of drama commentaries in books, in the media and on the internet. Collectively, these form the 'illuminator text' you need to refer to in your explorative study.
• develop your own opinions about the plays you see, study and read about. The more independent-minded you become, the better your coursework will be.
• draft and write your two coursework pieces in planned stages over a period of time. Leaving them to the last minute is not an option at A level.

How this book will help you

In this book, Unit 2 is divided into six parts.

Sections A and **B** help you to extend your experience of watching and reading plays, and reading and writing *about* them. They introduce you to a range of drama for TV and the theatre. They also show you some of the ways in which directors, actors and critics write about plays and the different viewpoints they take.

Sections C and **D** help you to prepare your explorative study. They give you guidance on how to relate your two coursework plays together. They also show you how to set your plays in two contexts: the context of the time in which they were written and the context of 'critical reception', i.e. the way in which critics and audiences react to them.

Sections E and **F** support you in writing your explorative study and your creative critical response.

A Responding to drama

1 Introduction

This section provides you with a foundation for both the coursework tasks – your explorative study and your creative critical response. It helps you to explore your current preferences in drama, consider drama from a range of viewpoints, and sample the forms that writing about drama can take.

The focus of this section is on reading and viewing drama critically (your explorative study) in ways that will help you become a critic yourself (your creative critical response). The activities use a broad range of contemporary sources to develop these critical skills.

Bear in mind that your coursework will be based on drama from 1300 to 1800. In this section you will look at a range of dramatic extracts. Not all of these extracts will be from within the prescribed time period, but they will enable you to build up the skills you need to do well in your coursework. As you work through the activities below, you should also be starting to study your main coursework play.

2 Viewing drama: the audience's perspective

Activity 1

1   Choose one TV or film drama and one stage drama to give your opinion about. Then fill in a copy of the chart below.

Myself as an audience: stage and screen	
Drama on screen	**Drama on stage**
Title of the drama seen:	Title of the drama seen:
Liked/disliked it because: • • •	Liked/disliked it because: • • •
Rating 5: (excellent) to 1 (bad):	Rating 5: (excellent) to 1 (bad):

2   Compare your choices and your opinions with a partner's. Are there any patterns of similarity or difference?

3   Share your responses with the class. Then examine your class profile as an audience for drama. What do you conclude about:

- your preferences for stage or screen
- your preferences for dramatic genres (eg comedy, sitcoms, musicals, mysteries etc)
- your expectations when you view live theatre: are these different from your expectations of drama on film or TV?

Activity 2

1 Read aloud the extract below from the TV series *Blackadder Goes Forth*.

During World War I, Blackadder and Baldrick have crashed their plane over Germany and are being held in prison by Baron von Richthoven. They find it more comfortable than the trenches and do not want to be rescued. However, Lieutenant George and Lord Flashheart, the British flying legend, are determined to free them.

BALDRICK: Is it really true, sir? Is the war really over for us?

The question finds BLACKADDER in the best mood of his life.

5 BLACKADDER: Yup! For us, the Great War is finito, a war which would be a damn sight simpler if we just stayed in England and shot fifty thousand of our men in a week! No more mud, 10 death, rats, bombs, shrapnel, whiz bangs, barbed wire and bloody awful songs that have the word 'Whoops!' in the title. Damn, they've left the door open.

15 BALDRICK: Oh, good, we can escape.

BLACKADDER: Are you mad, Baldrick? I'll go and find someone to lock it for us.

There is a knock on the door. BLACKADDER sweeps it open. It is George, also in flying 20 gear.

GEORGE: Shhh! Mum's the word! Not half or what!

BLACKADDER slams the door on him in horror.

BALDRICK: Why did you slam the door on 25 Lieutenant George?

BLACKADDER: I can't believe it. *(He calls out through the door.)* Go away!

GEORGE: It's me — it's me! *(He re-opens the door. GEORGE stands there,* 30 *grinning.)*

BLACKADDER: What the hell are you doing here?

GEORGE: *(very pleased with himself)* Oh, never mind the 'hows' and 'whys'. And the 'do you mind if I don'ts'.

35 BLACKADDER: But it would take a superman to get in here.

GEORGE: Well, funny you should say that, because I did, in fact, have some help from a spiffing fellow. He's 40 taken a break from some top-level shagging.

BLACKADDER: Oh, God.

FLASHHEART swings in through the door on a rope.

45 FLASHHEART: It's me. Hurray!

BALDRICK: Hurray!

FLASHHEART hits BALDRICK.

FLASHHEART: God's potatoes, George! You said noble brother flyers were in the 50 lurch. If I'd known it was only Slack Bladder and the mound of the hound of the Baskervilles, I'd have let them stew in their own juice. And let me tell you, if 55 I ever tried that, I'd probably *drown*!

BALDRICK is up again and laughing. FLASHHEART hits him again.

Still, since I'm here, I might as well doo-o-o it! As the bishop said to the netball team. Come on, 60 chums!

They run away — then look back through the door. BLACKADDER has stayed behind. He sinks to the ground and starts moaning.

Come on. 65

BLACKADDER: Uhm, look, sorry chaps, but I've splintered my pancreas and I've got this awful cough.

He coughs. The coughs sound suspiciously like: Guards! Guards! 70

FLASHHEART: Wait a minute! I may be packing the kind of tackle you'd normally expect to find between the hind legs of a Grand National winner, but I'm not totally stupid — and 75 I've got a feeling you'd rather we hadn't come.

BLACKADDER: No, no, no. I'm really grateful but I'd slow you up.

FLASHHEART: I think I'm beginning to 80 understand.

BLACKADDER: Are you?

FLASHHEART: Just because I can give multiple orgasms to the furniture by sitting on it doesn't mean I'm not 85 sick of this damn war. The blood, the noise, the endless poetry.

FLASHHEART gets out a gun and points it at BLACKADDER.

BLACKADDER: Is that what you really think, 90 Flashheart?

FLASHHEART: Of course … it's not what I think! Now get out that door before I

```
                 redecorate this room in an exciting new colour called
95               Hint of Brain.

    BLACKADDER:  Excellent — nice and clear. In that case, let's get back
                 to that lovely war …

    FLASHHEART:  Woof!

    GEORGE:      Woof!

100 BALDRICK:    Bark!

        But too late! RICHTHOVEN melodramatically appears at the doorway.

    RICHTHOVEN:  Not so fast, Blackadder!

    BLACKADDER:  (with massive relief) Damn — foiled again — what bad
                 luck!

105 RICHTHOVEN:  Ah, and Lord Flashheart, this is indeed an honour.
                 Finally the two greatest gentleman flyers in the world
                 meet. Two men of honour who have jousted together in
                 the cloud-strewn glory of the skies are face to face at
                 last. How often have I rehearsed this moment of destiny
110              in my dreams. The valour we two encapsulate, the unspoken
                 nobility of our comradeship, the …

        And FLASHHEART shoots him — 'bang'. He's dead now.

    FLASHHEART:  What a poof! Let's go!

    ALL:         Hurray!
```

Independent research

Build up a file of online theatre reviews, together with your own comments on them, in preparation for writing your creative critical response.

2 With a partner, explore the comedy of this scene by filling in a copy of the chart below. Justify to one another your entries in column 3.

Blackadder Goes Forth		
Comic device	Example	How effective do you find it?
Physical comedy/slapstick		
Character comedy: caricatures/stereotype figures		
Situation comedy: dramatic irony of Blackadder and Baldrick being safer in prison		
Verbal comedy: puns, jokes, **innuendo**/double entendre		
Satirical comedy: mild mockery of aspects of World War I		

3 Watch an episode from the *Blackadder* series on DVD or an episode from any comedy drama series you enjoy. Then note down and/or discuss:

a how the comedy works, being as specific as you can

b why you think the show has become popular with TV audiences

c whether it would transfer successfully to the stage, saying why or why not.

Key terms
innuendo

satirical (satire)

4 Write two reviews of the comedy episode you watched. Review 1 is your personal response, written for the online *emagazine* aimed at students. Review 2 is in the form of a letter to the *Radio Times* from an adult viewer who disapproves of the programme. Your style for each piece should match your purpose and audience.

Take it further

Read a range of online theatre reviews at the following sites:

- www.arts.guardian.co.uk
- www.arts4schools.com
- www.britishtheatreguide.info
- www.encoretheatremagazine.co.uk
- www.telegraph.co.uk/arts
- www.thestage.co.uk
- www.bbc.co.uk/radio4/arts

3 Performing drama: the actor's and director's perspectives

Activity 3

1 Read aloud the opening of Alan Bennett's play, *Habeas Corpus*, below. The main characters are listed as:

Habeas Corpus (1973)

ARTHUR WICKSTEED: a general practitioner

MURIEL WICKSTEED: his wife

DENNIS WICKSTEED: their son

CONSTANCE WICKSTEED: the doctor's sister

MRS SWABB: a cleaning lady.

There are no notes for the actors and only one stage direction.

ACT ONE

WICKSTEED: Look at him. Just look at that look on his face. Do you know what that means? He wants me to tell him he's not going to die. You're not going to die. He is going to die. Not now, of course, but some time … ten, fifteen years, who knows? I don't. We don't want to lose you, do we? And off he goes. Sentence suspended. Another ten years. Another ten years showing the slides. ('That's Malcolm, Pauline and Baby Jason.') Another ten years for little runs in the car. ('That's us at the Safari Park.') 'So what did the doctor say, dear?' 'Nothing, oh, nothing. It was all imagination.' But it's not all imagination. Sometimes I'm afraid, it actually happens.

5

MRS WICKSTEED'S
VOICE: Arthur! Arthur!

MRS SWABB: It's all in the mind. Me, I've never had a day's illness in my life. No. I tell a lie. I once had my tonsils out. I went in on the Monday; I had it done on the Tuesday; I was putting wallpaper up on the Wednesday. My name is Mrs Swabb (hoover, hoover, hoover) someone who comes in; and in all that passes, I represent ye working classes. Hoover, hoover, hoover. Hoover, hoover, hoover. Now then, let's have a little more light on the proceedings and meet our contestants, the wonderful, wonderful Wicksteed family. Eyes down first for tonight's hero, Dr Arthur Wicksteed, a general practitioner in Brighton's plush, silk stocking district of Hove. Is that right, Doctor?

10

15

WICKSTEED: Hove, that's right, yes.

MRS SWABB: And you are fifty-three years of age.

WICKSTEED: Dear God, am I?

MRS SWABB: I'm afraid that's what I've got down here.

20 WICKSTEED: Fifty-three!

MRS SWABB: Any hobbies?

WICKSTEED: No. No. Our friends, the ladies, of course, but nothing much else.

MRS SWABB: Do you mind telling us what your ambition is?

WICKSTEED: Ambition? No, never had any. Partly the trouble, you see. When you've gone through life stopping at every lamp-post, no time.

25

MRS SWABB: Next we have …

MRS WICKSTEED:	I can manage thank you. Elocution was always my strong point. Speak clearly, speak firmly, speak now. Name: Wicksteed, Muriel Jane. Age? Well, if you said fifty you'd be in the target area. Wife to the said Arthur Wicksteed and golly, don't I know it. Still potty about him though, the dirty dog. Oh, shut up, Muriel.
MRS SWABB:	And now … this is Dennis, only son of Arthur and Muriel Wicksteed. And what do you do, Dennis?
DENNIS:	Nothing very much. I think I've got lockjaw.
MRS SWABB:	Really? Whereabouts?
DENNIS:	All over.
MRS SWABB:	Are you interested in girls at all?
DENNIS:	If they're clean.
MRS SWABB:	That goes without saying. You don't want a dirty girl, do you?
DENNIS:	In a way, I do, yes.
MRS WICKSTEED:	Dennis!
MRS SWABB:	And now we have the doctor's sister, Miss Constance Wicksteed. Connie is a thirty-three-year-old spinster …
CONNIE:	I am not a spinster. I am unmarried.
MRS SWABB:	And to go with her mud-coloured cardigan Connie has chosen a fetching number in form-fitting cretonne. Have you any boyfriends, dear?
CONNIE:	No.
MRS SWABB:	Connie, you big story! What about Canon Throbbing, our thrusting young vicar? Why! That sounds like his Biretta now.
	THROBBING *crosses on his power-assisted bicycle.*
	Now, Connie, would you like to tell the audience what your ambition is? Go on, just whisper.
CONNIE:	I'd like a big bust.
MRS SWABB:	And what would you do with it when you'd got it?
CONNIE:	Flaunt it.
MRS WICKSTEED:	Connie!

(Line numbers: 30, 35, 40, 45, 50)

2   In a group, plan a performance of this opening. Share the task between you. You need to decide about:

   a   The staging – Should there be a bare stage, a setting defined by scenery, moves and interaction between characters, costumes and props?

   b   The genre (the kind of play) – Should it be light comedy, a **thriller**, a **farce**, a **murder mystery**?

   c   The production style – Should it be realistic (as in soaps), comedy routine (as in *Blackadder*), documentary (as in *The Office*, for example), a skit (or parody)?

3   Then EITHER give your own performance, rehearsing it to the point where you need the book only as a prompt, OR write rehearsal notes from the director about aspects of this scene that would be important in performance.

4   Evaluate the performances OR compare your rehearsal notes. Can you agree on and justify an acting style that suits this drama best?

Independent research

Find a selection of contemporary plays from libraries, bookshops and the internet. Read them yourself, then bring some into class to read extracts as you proceed with your course. Try these publishers' lists: Faber & Faber, Nick Hearn Books, Longman, Eyre/Methuen, Samuel French. Playwrights might include: Caryl Churchill, David Hare, Alan Bennett, Timberlake Wertenbaker, Tom Stoppard.

Key terms
thriller
farce
murder mystery

4 Reviewing drama: the critic's perspective

Activity 4

Read the two reviews below. Review **A** is of a stage musical posted on the internet. Review **B** is of a TV drama and was printed in a quality newspaper.

Review A:

Joseph and the Amazing Technicolor Dreamcoat

Adelphi Theatre

After all the hype, feverishly stoked up by the BBC's search-for-a-star series 'Any Dream Will Do', *Joseph* arrives breathlessly on the West End stage with packed houses guaranteed. A cool £10 million has already been taken at the box office. Lord Lloyd-Webber is nothing if not a multi-millionaire.

5   Does this money-making monster breathe new life into a show that has packed 'em in at (surely) every school hall in the country? Well, in a word, yes and no. The set looks as if it could have been borrowed from St Saviour's Juniors. Are we in Canaan, Egypt or on the beach at Skyathos? Hard to tell, really. Not much of a clue in the second-hand-shop costumes either.

    The tunes are catchy, of course. Even after all these years it's hard not to hum along to 'Any

10 Dream Will Do', the Benjamin Calypso and 'One More Angel in Heaven'. There are some delicious moments of musical pastiche too, reminders that Lloyd-Webber was a truly versatile composer before his love affair with romantic schmaltz set in about the time of 'Phantom of the Opera'. And Tim Rice's witty lyrics, with their outrageous rhyming of 'farmers' and 'pyjamas' and 'greatest man since Noah, only goes to showah', can still raise a laugh in the

15 dress circle.

    But this production isn't for the dress circle. It's for the screaming, stand-up-if-you-love-Lee-in-his-loincloth, hordes of pre-teen girls who swarm all over the stalls and know his big numbers off by heart. Just as well, really, since the singing is amplified to migraine proportions. They voted for him on the telly, and they worship Lee Meads in the flesh. So, is

20 he the new Donny Osmond?

    Smile-wise, certainly. When not in Potiphar's prison, he grins inanely throughout. Voice-wise? Much better than Donny: this guy can sing, and 'Close Every Door to Me' came close to being moving. Acting-wise? Well, Donny didn't do acting and Lee is right up there with him. None of this matters much, of course. A star is born. The TV and theatre moguls have willed

25 it.

    The supporting cast is a major disappointment. Preeya Kalidas (not a name to take lightly) plays the female narrator as if she has arrived late for the auditions – lacking expression, lacking vocal range, lacking harmony with the chorus of on-stage kids. As Elvis-Pharoah, Dean Collinson gives it plenty of welly and is funny for three minutes. He wears off quickly,

30 though: a one-trick pony. The dancers jig, wiggle and shimmy with a minimum of conviction and a maximum of repetition.

    Be in no doubt, though. It will be a long time before the light is dimming on this retro revival for the i-pod generation. It's written in the star – and in his contract.

Carly Phelps

Review B:

The Sunday Times

The Cheap Laughs

Rod Liddle

I keep dreaming that I'm driving a racing car and Death, dressed in an off-the-peg chador, is waving a chequered flag at me. That's a sign, I reckon, of old age approaching, of the grave beckoning to me from the middle distance.

5　But that's not the worst of it. My favourite television programme these days is *Midsomer Murders*. I actually want to be Chief Inspector Barnaby and talk in those weary, clipped tones,
10　in the manner of someone who wrote an exultant letter to *The Daily Telegraph* about Margaret Thatcher in 1979 and for whom everything has been downhill ever since. Obviously, one would have
15　to be in the latter stages of Alzheimer's to find *Midsomer Murders* anything but ludicrous. I'm not quite there yet, but accepting the programme's bizarre conceits is the first step on the way to
20　gentle senility. I know all this, but it doesn't bother me any more. I even got a boxed set of *Midsomer* DVDs for my last birthday. I used to get leather jackets and Jack Daniel's and footballs
25　and so on.

　　So bear all this in mind, please, while I tell you how good *Outnumbered* (Tuesday, BBC1) is. An exquisitely middle-class, middle-aged domestic
30　situation comedy set in North London – maybe Crouch End or Tufnell Park – and starring one of those bloody stand-up comics who now festoons every network, it really should be hated
35　before it is even seen. Start liking this sort of programme and you are an ace away from enjoying Terry and June and having a house that smells faintly of weak tea, Murray Mints and urine.
40　So, maybe it's just me, but *Outnumbered* is very funny indeed: the BBC still knows how to make people laugh. Comedy may be the very last thing the corporation does well.
45　　The knack, I suppose, is in the writing: Andy Hamilton and Guy Jenkins's script is beautifully observed and understated. The first episode was built entirely around a harassed
50　husband and wife trying to get their children ready for school in the morning. It really doesn't sound promising, does it? We've seen that stuff before, after all. And there are
55　familiar tropes – the prepubescent offspring who is more knowledgeable than his hapless dad at high-tech stuff, the humorously knowing three-year-old girl and so on. But somehow it
60　works. More surprisingly, the children are not like the sort of children you usually see in sitcoms, the ones you want to smash over the head with a mallet and drag down to the river in
65　a hessian sack. They are instead both likeable and hilarious.

　　There is a nicely cluttered, claustrophobic feel to the drama too, and the intimation of something dark
70　and destructive lurking just around the corner, just to let you know all is not well. And the whole thing is handled with that rarest of sitcom devices: subtlety. Quite how the directors got
75　the kids to act so naturally is a mystery to me – presumably they beat them or threatened them with never seeing their parents again or pinched them really hard on the arm. My favourite
80　moment came when the three-year-old girl presented her mum with a picture she'd drawn at school. 'It's very nice,' said Mum. 'What is it?' And the child replied: 'It's a cow. A cow, killing
85　people because it doesn't want to be made into food'. Maybe getting old makes me find stuff like that funny.

Independent research

Begin building up a collection of theatre reviews from daily and Sunday newspapers and arts magazines. These will prove invaluable in preparing for your creative critical response.

National and regional theatres will be keen to send you free promotional material. Theatre programmes are also a good source for different perspectives on drama in production. Add these to your collection of theatre reviews.

Activity 5

1   Use information from Reviews **A** and **B** to fill in a copy of the chart below.

Review of *Joseph*	Review of *Outnumbered*
Aspects of the musical which show it was created for the theatre: • • •	Aspects of the programme which show it was created for TV: • • •
What the reviewer liked/disliked:	What the reviewer liked/disliked:

2   Compare your chart with a partner's. Then discuss whether the two reviewers had different expectations of the shows because of their contexts – one recorded, one live. If so, did this influence their judgement, and in what ways?

Activity 6

Reviews give information and opinions.

1   Look carefully at Review **A**. Identify points in it where Carly Phelps uses language to make a personal judgement and/or persuade the reader to share her opinions.

Do you think her opinions are expressed fairly, or do they just reflect her own tastes in stage drama? Discuss whether you trust her judgement, and why.

2   Look carefully at Review **B**. Discuss and/or make notes about:

   a   the purpose and effect of the first two paragraphs, where Rod Liddle says nothing about the TV programme under review

   b   the use of emotive language to express opinion in paragraph 3

   c   the strongly personal style of paragraphs 4 and 5.

Do you think Rod Liddle's opinions are expressed fairly or do they just reflect his own tastes in TV drama? Discuss whether you trust his judgement, and why.

3   Compare the style and tone of Reviews **A** and **B**. Which do you prefer?

Activity 7

1   Give your opinions about reviews in general. Draw on your experience of reading reviews of music, films and books as well as of drama to say:

   a   what you see as the main purpose of a review

   b   what features of a review attract you to it and whether these are linked to the context in which it appears (eg on the internet, in a newspaper, in a teenage magazine, etc)

   c   what kind of review writing appeals to you most (eg highly personal, mainly factual, humorous, serious, idiosyncratic, etc).

2   Imagine you are a professional TV critic. Watch a drama or a drama documentary and review it for the adult readership of a quality newspaper. Annotate your writing to show what your purposes were and how your choices of style and language helped you to achieve them.

5 Commenting on drama: voices from inside and outside the theatre

This section introduces you to reviews of, and commentaries on, drama in a range of formats. The activities will help you to investigate the breadth and scope of 'critical response', examine some style models which will prove useful when you come to decide on your own creative critical writing, and write in some of these formats yourself.

Assessment objectives

Your creative critical response is assessed by: AO1: Articulate creative, informed and relevant responses to literary texts, using appropriate terminology and concepts, and coherent, accurate written expression (6 marks)

AO2: Demonstrare understanding of the significance and influence of the contexts in which literary texts are written and received (12 marks)

Text A: promotional leaflet for *The Importance of Being Earnest* by Oscar Wilde

PENELOPE KEITH stars in THE IMPORTANCE OF BEING EARNEST

Oscar Wilde's *The Importance of Being Earnest* is one of the most popular plays ever written. Subtitled 'A trivial comedy for serious people', it is bursting with hilarious lines and extraordinary twists of fate and sparkles with the witty dialogue of its genteel **protagonists**.

Prim-and-proper Jack Worthington is in love with the equally prim-and-proper Gwendolyn Fairfax. His friend, Algernon Moncrieff, is in love with Cecily Cardew. But both Gwendolyn and Cecily are in love with Earnest. Add the magnificently imposing Lady Bracknell, a nanny with a dubious story about a handbag, and the result is a delightful entertainment as fresh and funny as when it was first performed in 1895.

Penelope Keith, one of Britain's best-loved actresses, was born to play Lady Bracknell. Her many previous theatre appearances include *Time and the Conways, Blithe Spirit, Entertaining Angels* and *Relatively Speaking*. Her numerous television series include the hugely successful *The Good Life* and *To the Manor Born*.

Text B: online message board for a Radio 4 production of *Arcadia* by Tom Stoppard

Message 1 posted by **DogCrusoe**, 30 June 2007

Phew – what a complicated play! The reviewers hailed this as an outstanding production but I needed to read up on the **synopsis** and the science before I began to appreciate the complexities of the story. Did Radio 4 take on too much, since the stage plays action took place on the same set, making the switch from present to past and back again easier to understand and less open to confusion? Nevertheless, an engaging production for a wet afternoon. Thank you.

Message 2 posted by **LucyLocket**, 30 June 2007

The best thing Radio 4 has done for ages! I really enjoyed it and hopefully will be able to have another go at it on *Listen Again* to help with the complexities. Oh for more of this sort of thing on Radio 4 – just like the old days! At the moment they are doing the 15-minute *Hamlet*.

Message 3 posted by **Kumara**, 1 July 2007

I agree LucyLocket, it was a great production. I saw it years ago with Felicity Kendal, Rufus Sewell and Bill Nighy as the unscrupulous academic. I so admire (and envy) Stoppard's ability to grasp a huge subject – here the complexity of lots of aspects of Romanticism – and make challenging comment and criticism.

Independent research

Begin a collection of critical responses to drama from different sources. Start with promotional literature, theatre programmes and message boards. As you work through the rest of this section, find your own examples of types of response like Texts C–F on pages 128–130.

In a group, talk and/or make notes about:

a   the different contexts and purposes of Texts **A** and **B** on page 127

b   the way in which the style and structure of each text is matched to its audience.

Focus on:

Key terms
protagonist
synopsis

- the deliberately exaggerated language of Text **A**. Look closely at two or three examples and say whether you find them effective or merely clichéd
- the way in which the contributors to Text **B** write. Look closely at how they express their opinions and say whether you find them persuasive or merely gushing.

Text C: blog review of *Equus* by Peter Shaffer on the West End Whingers website

20 March 2007

Wild horses couldn't drag Andrew to Peter Shaffer's *Equus*. Being of a somewhat sensitive and nervous disposition, the idea of horses having their eyes poked out proved a little too much for him. Phil tried to convince him that 'it's just a play' and 'they're only acting' but Andrew dug in his substantial heels and stayed curled up on his sofa watching the much less upsetting *Snakes on a Plane*, while Phil was left alone to witness
5 the most talked about snake on the London stage – Daniel Radcliffe's, to be precise. Harry Potter himself was required to get his kit off on his debut on the professional stage.

But the audience is here for one reason, Harry Potter himself, subtle, but slightly subdued, and
   Well, Phil can report that he found the wonderful Richard Griffiths subtle, but slightly subdued, and struggling to control a cough. He needn't have worried; there was an elegant sufficiency of far less restrained coughing from the audience in the lengthy first act. Yes, Andrew, there were an awful lot of words; you couldn't
10 have coped.

   But the audience is here for one reason, Harry Potter himself. This has to be the most hyped appearance in the West End since Madonna wearied this Whinger in *Up for Grabs*. And although doing healthy business, unlike Madonna, he's not selling out. Radcliffe has to be applauded for taking on such a difficult role for a stage debut. He's perfectly fine, but not much more, has reasonable stage presence, remembers his lines, speaks
15 clearly, and if there were furniture to bump into he'd surely acquit himself nicely there too. But convincing as an intense, repressed and guilty 17 year old? Well, Phil certainly believed he was 17. And in that scene? You have to wait until the last 15 minutes of the play for it – no leaving at the interval here. Phil's wizened heart went out to poor Danny boy as 900 pairs of eyes concentrated on one small area of the stage. As he dropped his drawers, the focus of the play became very different indeed. All coughing stopped as one special
20 cast member took the spotlight. The Whingers are too polite to comment further, but, as one couple cruelly remarked leaving the Gielgud, 'You'd need binoculars for that one'.

Text D: part of a panel discussion of Shakespeare's *Henry V* at the National Theatre broadcast on *Newsnight Review* on BBC2

TIM LOTT: It's a real people's production. Almost an Andy McNab influence coming in here! You got the sense you were in there, there's armoured vehicles coming on. Lots of bangs and crashes. It really is a very dynamic and energetic performance. It's not a play I have been fond of before. I find all the history plays rather dull. But I was entranced throughout. I didn't think Adrian Lester's performance was perfect. It lost
5 a lot of its internal life and it was an exterior performance, in a way. It had terrific charisma. There are some very long, boring sections in this play, and he dealt with that terribly well, I felt.

BONNIE GREER: I think this is easily the first great Shakespearean production of the twenty-first century. This is gorgeous. Nick Hytner [the director] could have done something very, very simple – made an anti-war play. He doesn't. He puts war on the stage. You walk out of there with what you want to take out of it. If you
10 never understood why this was Shakespeare's first great hit, you will when you see this. It has everything. The jokes. The little foreign stuff going on. The only thing I don't agree with you about is that I think Adrian Lester's performance is magnificent. It's a very anti-Henry performance. We usually see very romantic Henrys or people who play the verse. He plays him metallically, very coldly. He has a job to do and he sets out to do it. It's a wonderful performance.

15 KIRSTY WARK: On the killing business, when he puts the gun to the head of the looter and kills him, you know it's coming but you still feel …

BONNIE GREER: There are atrocities on both sides. People are invoking God on both sides. It is a play about the reality of war. If you are for war, you will love it. If you are against war, you will love it.

Compare the way Texts **C** and **D** target particular audiences. Consider:

a the intended audience for the blog. On the evidence of its style and language, what kind of reader does the 'West End Whinger' have in mind?

b the intended audience for *Newsnight Review*. On the evidence of the discussion, what kind of viewer is the programme aimed at?

c the personal tone and register of each review. Which is more successful in engaging *you*, and why?

Activity 10

Imagine you are the publicity officer for the National Theatre's production of *Henry V* OR a play of your choice. Write a promotional flyer or leaflet for it like the one advertising *The Importance of Being Earnest* (page 127). Your task is to make the production sound appealing to young adults. Use heightened language, a suitable tone and register and any other stylistic techniques you wish in order to achieve this.

Text E: diary entries of Peter Hall who directed *Volpone* by Ben Jonson at the National Theatre in 1977; the National opened in 1976 with Hall as its director

Tuesday, 26 April

Very nervous all day because of Volpone opening this evening. John Goodwin gave me comfort by pointing out how the launch of the new theatre had succeeded despite so much being against us:
5 the swing against institutions, against large buildings and modern architecture, against nationalised art or industry of any kind, against expensive cultural enterprises at a time of recession. I tried to watch Volpone but couldn't and was in my office most of the evening. It is unusual for me not to have the guts to sit out a
10 first night. I gather the play went well, certainly the reception was good. Quick backstage congratulations: Paul [Scofield, who played the lead] relaxed; it seems he gave his greatest performance in the play so far.

Wednesday, 27 April

15 The press for Volpone is good. Michael Billington [The Guardian drama critic] finds my approach too academic, not social enough; and he writes that the monstrosity in the play is not venal enough. But I think he ought to listen to the prologue. Jonson's satire is healthy, not sick. It is lusty, full of juice, not the misanthropic
20 mood of the middle plays of Shakespeare. I am mightily relieved this morning, though.

Independent research

Theatre directors and actors publish their diaries and other accounts of productions. Build up a library of these. Some good starting points are: *Diaries*, Peter Hall; *National Service*, Richard Eyre; *Will and Me*, Dominic Dromgoole; *Being an Actor*, Simon Callow; *Beside Myself* and *The Year of the King*, Antony Sher; *Players of Shakespeare* (6 volumes), edited by Robert Smallwood. The last title is indispensable for actors' accounts of Royal Shakespeare Company productions.

Writing your coursework

For detailed guidance on planning and writing your creative critical response, see Section F, pages 179–182.

Refer back to the reviews and commentaries in this Section when you are considering a suitable format for your creative critical response.

Activity 11

1 As a class, use Text **E** to discuss the role of a director in bringing plays to an audience. Apart from working with the actors in rehearsal, what other aspects of production does the director make decisions about?

2 Look at the reviews of two productions of Shakespeare (pages 171 and 172). Read and compare them. How do they show that directors can interpret the same play in radically different ways?

1 Read the production credits below, which will help you clarify your ideas about a director's role. It comes from a Royal Shakespeare Company programme for *The Tempest*, performed in 1998.

Directed by Adrian Noble

Music director Richard Brown

Designed by Anthony Ward

Assistant director Rebecca Gatward

Lighting designed by Howard Harrison

Company voice work by Andrew Wade, Lyn Darley and Cicely Berry

Music by Stephen Warbeck

Movement by Ian Spink

Costume supervisor Christine Rowland

Sound by Paul Arditti

Stage manager Eric Lumsden

2 Speculate about the job specification of each member of the production team. How might they have contributed individually to realising on stage the director's interpretation of the play? How might they have *combined* to do so?

Text F: press reviews of a production of *Antony and Cleopatra* by the Royal Shakespeare Company

Gregory Doran's magnificent production … he brings piercing intelligence to the central relationship … Patrick Stewart's superb Antony … Harriet Walter's mesmerising Cleopatra … supremely revealing … the real triumph of the production lies in allowing us to see Shakespeare's gaudy epic with fresh unclouded eyes

The *Guardian*

Gregory Doran's new production makes you see the play in a fresh and fascinating light … Patrick Stewart's remarkable performance … I cannot remember seeing an Antony so deep in melancholia or self-disgust … Harriet Walter captures the Queen's blazing theatricality, vulnerability and joie de vivre … Doran manages the lovers' stoic suicides with a spectacular élan

Evening Standard

An absolutely storming *Antony and Cleopatra* … you have never seen such high testosterone Shakespeare

… there are so many superb performances and potent stage presences here … especially from Ariyon Bakare as Pompey, Joe Alessi as Philo and David Rubin as a swaggering piratical Menas … also exceptional are John Hopkins as Octavius and Ken Bones as Enobarbus … superb costume design from Kandis Cook

Sunday Times

Activity 13

1 Look back over all the eight reviews and commentaries on pages 127–130 and the ones you have written yourself. Use them to make a chart like this:

Formats for critical response to drama		
Kind of text	**Viewpoint and intended audience**	**Main features of style and language**
Promotional flyers and leaflets		
Online message boards		

2 Choose one format from the chart that you find appealing as a reader. If you can visit a local theatre, review the current production or. Alternatively, review a play on DVD in your chosen format.

B Analysing key elements of drama

1 Introduction

This section introduces you to the basic elements of stage drama. Whatever the topic of your explorative study, these will be central to it. The texts used to illustrate them are drawn from twentieth-century theatre as well as the theatre of 1300–1800. This is to help you use your experience of modern plays to engage with plays from the past. It will also show you that, while the language of older plays may seem unfamiliar at first, you can find common approaches by playwrights from different times to such elements of drama as scene setting, characterisation, staging and plot construction.

As you work through this section, continue thinking of drama as a *live* medium written for the stage rather than for the page. An important focus of your coursework will be the *audience's* expectations of, and responses to, drama. The basic needs of an audience in 1600 were not greatly different from those of an audience in 2000, although the plays they saw were.

The activities below are designed to support you during your study of your coursework plays.

Assessment objectives

There are 14 marks available in total for your explorative study are given for writing coherently about your play texts, using critical terminology (AO1) and analysing how structure, form and language shape meaning in drama texts (AO2). You need to understand the key elements of drama in order to meet these AOs

2 How dramatists set the scene

Activity 14

1   Read aloud the opening of the play below (*Teechers*). It was written by John Godber for the Hull Truck Theatre Company in 1988. There are three characters, Salty (male), Gail and Hobby (female).

A comprehensive school hall.

A wooden stage. There are two double desks upstage. Upstage right is an old locker with a school broom leaning against it. Downstage centre is a chair; left and right two single desks and chairs angled downstage, and three bags. A satchel, plastic bags and sports bags are near the chairs and desks. They belong to SALTY, GAIL and HOBBY respectively.

Some music plays and SALTY, GAIL and HOBBY enter, recline on the chairs and desks and look at the audience for a moment before speaking.

SALTY: No more school for us, so you can knackers!

GAIL: Salty, you nutter.

SALTY: What?

GAIL: Swearing.

5   HOBBY: Shurrup.

SALTY: So what?

HOBBY: You daft gett.

SALTY: It's true.

GAIL: Just get on with it.

10   SALTY: Nobody can do us.

HOBBY: We've not left yet.

SALTY:	*(shouts loudly)* Knackers!	
GAIL:	Oh God, he's cracked.	
HOBBY:	Shurrup.	
15 SALTY:	I've always wanted to be on this stage. I've always wanted to come up here and say 'knackers'. I bet you all have. Whenever I see Mrs Hudson come up on this stage to talk about litter or being a good samaritan or corn dollies or sit down first year stand up second year I think about that word. Cos really Mrs Hudson would like to come up here and say, 'knackers school'. She would.	
GAIL:	Are we doing this play or what?	
20 SALTY:	It's like when she gets you in her office, all neat and smelling of perfume, and she says, 'You don't come to school to fool around, Ian, to waste your time. We treat you like young adults and we expect you to behave accordingly. I don't think that writing on a wall is a mature thing to do.'	
GAIL:	Let's start, Salty.	
HOBBY:	I never thought I'd be doing this. I hated drama, only took it for a doss about.	
25 SALTY:	Right, don't forget to keep in character, and, Hobby, always face the front.	
HOBBY:	I will do.	
SALTY:	A lot of the stuff in the play was told to us by our drama teacher, Mr Harrison –	
GAIL:	And even though you might not believe it, everything what happens in this play is based on truth.	
HOBBY:	But the names and the faces have been changed.	
30 SALTY:	To protect the innocent.	
GAIL:	We're going to take you to Whitewall High School. It's a comprehensive school somewhere in England … And they're expecting a new teacher to arrive.	
HOBBY:	There's fifteen hundred kids at Whitewall and it's a Special Priority Area which means that it's got its fair share of problems …	
35 SALTY:	All we want you to do is use your imagination because there's only three of us, and we all have to play different characters …	
HOBBY:	And narrators …	
SALTY:	And narrators.	
HOBBY:	So you'll have to concentrate …	
40 SALTY:	Oh, yeh, you'll have to concentrate …	
GAIL:	Title …	
SALTY:	Oh, shit, yeh … And it's called *Teechers*.	

A sudden burst of music. They become teachers, with briefcases and files, walking about a number of corridors.

Key terms
plot
exposition

2 Discuss with a partner:

    a whether this is an effective opening to a play in the theatre. Why or why not?

    b how well it meets the needs of an audience. What are these needs?

3 Copy and complete the chart below. It will record your own ideas about how a dramatist writing for the theatre can set the scene.

Setting the scene for a play in the theatre: my suggestions on how to …			
Establish the setting, mood and atmosphere	Introduce characters	Get the **plot** under way	Let the audience know what kind of play this is, eg whodunit, farce, serious social drama.

4 Read the opening scene or two of the main plays from 1300 to 1800 you are studying for coursework. Use the chart you created above to make three or four different points about how the dramatist stages the **exposition** and how well you think it works.

Activity 15

1 Read the following extract. It is the Prologue to Shakespeare's *Henry V*. The play dramatises the war between England and France in the fifteenth century. The action moves between the two countries and reaches a climax at the Battle of Agincourt.

Enter CHORUS.
CHORUS:

O for a Muse of fire, that would ascend	Muse: poetic inspiration
The brightest heaven of invention,	invention: imagination
A kingdom for a stage, princes to act,	
And monarchs to behold the swelling scene!	
5 Then should the warlike Harry, like himself,	Harry: King Henry V
Assume the port of Mars; and at his heels,	Mars: Roman god of war
Leash'd in like hounds, should famine, sword, and fire,	
Crouch for employment. But pardon, gentles all,	gentles: men and women in the audience
The flat unraisèd spirits that hath dar'd	unraisèd spirits: humble actors
10 On this unworthy scaffold to bring forth	scaffold: stage
So great an object. Can this cockpit hold	cockpit: theatre
The vasty fields of France? Or may we cram	
Within this wooden O the very casques	wooden O: Globe Theatre
That did affright the air at Agincourt?	
15 O, pardon! Since a crooked figure may	
Attest in little space a million;	
And let us, ciphers to this great accompt,	ciphers: small figures accompt: account
On your imaginary forces work.	
Suppose within the girdle of these walls	
20 Are now confin'd two mighty monarchies,	
Whose high uprearèd and abutting fronts	
The perilous narrow ocean parts asunder.	
Piece out our imperfections with your thoughts:	imperfections: bad acting
Into a thousand parts divide one man,	
25 And make imaginary puissance;	puissance: prancing horses
Think, when we talk of horses, that you see them	
Printing their proud hooves i' th' receiving earth;	
For 'tis your thoughts that now must deck our kings,	deck: dress, costume
Carry them here and there, jumping o'er times,	
30 Turning th' accomplishment of many years	
Into an hour-glass; for the which supply,	
Admit me Chorus to this history;	
Who prologue-like, your humble patience pray	
Gently to hear, kindly to judge, our play.	

Henry V was first performed in 1599. Shakespeare's Globe Theatre had a bare stage and an open roof. No scenery was used, although props were. Performances took place in daylight. All the actors were male.

2 Look carefully at what the Chorus says to the audience. With a partner, talk about what part Shakespeare asks them to play in the performance and the reasons why he may have chosen to begin the play in this way.

3 Is the idea that members of the audience are part of the performance one you have considered before? Why is this not true of television and film drama? Share your ideas with the class.

Activity 16

Take it further

Read the first scene of *Hamlet* and the first scene of *The Tempest*. Write a short comparison of how Shakespeare sets the scene and establishes mood and atmosphere.

Key term

monologue

Writing your coursework

Remember that you have to write in detail about one play from 1300 to 1800 and use a further play from the same period for purposes of comparison. You cannot write about a modern play.

1   Compare the opening of *Henry V* with the extract from *Teechers* (pages 131–132) and your main coursework play. Fill in a copy of the chart below as you make your responses.

Comparing openings			
Key considerations	*Henry V*	*Teechers*	Main coursework play
Setting How it is created?			
Characters What do we find out about them?			
Plot development How far does the action progress?			
Dialogue/ monologue What does this achieve?			
Language How does this signal the play's period and social context?			
Genre What kind of play is this going to be? How can we tell?			
Role of the audience What relationship is created between audience and play?			

2   Use the headings on the chart to write an account of the way your main coursework play opens. This will prove valuable in getting to grips with the text and in becoming familiar with the terms and concepts used in studying drama. It could also feed directly into your explorative study. If you wish, use the extracts from *Teechers* and *Henry V* as points of reference and comparison.

3 How dramatists develop the characters

The activities below help you to understand characterisation in stage drama. Characterisation means the way a dramatist creates and presents characters, not what their personalities are like. In your explorative study you will have to write about this, the commonest element in all drama, although not necessarily in the form of a character study.

Activity 17

1 Read aloud the extract below from Willy Russell's play, *Educating Rita*, first performed in 1980.

A room on the first floor of a Victorian-built university in the north of England. There is a large bay window with a desk placed in front of it and another desk covered with various papers and books. The walls are lined with books and on one wall hangs a good print of a nude religious scene.

FRANK who is in his early fifties, is standing holding an empty mug. He goes to the bookcases and starts taking
5 *books from the shelves, hurriedly replacing them before moving on to another section.*

FRANK: *(looking along the shelves)* Where the hell ...? Eliot? *(He pulls out some books and looks into the bookshelf)*. 'E' *(He thinks for a moment)*. 'E', 'e', 'e' ... *(Suddenly he remembers.)* Dickens. *(Jubilantly he moves to the Dickens section and pulls out a pile of books to reveal a bottle of whisky. He takes the bottle from the shelf and goes to the small table by the door and pours himself a large*
10 *slug into the mug in his hand.)*

The telephone rings and startles him slightly. He manages a gulp at the whisky before he picks up the receiver and, although his speech is not slurred, we should recognise the voice of a man who shifts a lot of booze.

FRANK: Yes? ... Of course I'm still here ... Because I've got this Open University woman coming, haven't I? ... Tch ... Of course I told you ... But darling, you shouldn't have prepared dinner should you?
15 Because I said, I distinctly remember saying that I would be late ... Yes. Yes, I probably shall go to the pub afterwards, I shall need to go to the pub afterwards, I shall need to wash away the memory of some silly woman's attempts to get into the mind of Henry James or whoever it is we're supposed to study on this course ... Oh God, why did I take this on? ... Yes ... Yes I suppose I did take it on to pay for the drink ... Oh, for God's sake, what is it? ... Yes, well – erm – leave it in the oven ...
20 Look if you're trying to induce some feeling of guilt in me over the prospect of a burned dinner, you should have prepared something other than lamb and ratatouille ... Because, darling, I like my lamb done to the point of abuse and even I know that ratatouille cannot be burned ... Darling, you could incinerate ratatouille and still it wouldn't burn ... What do you mean am I determined to go to the pub? I don't need determination to get me into a pub ...

25 *There is a knock at the door.*

Look, I'll have to go ... There's someone at the door ... Yes, yes, I promise ... Just a couple of pints ... Four ...

There is another knock at the door.

FRANK: *(calling in the direction of the door)* Come in! *(He continues on the telephone.)* Yes ... All right ...
30 yes ... Bye, bye ... *(He replaces the receiver.)* Yes, that's it, you just pop off and put your head in the oven. *(shouting)* Come in! Come in!

The door swings open revealing RITA.

RITA: *(from the doorway)* I'm comin' in, aren't I? It's that stupid bleedin' handle on the door. You wanna get it fixed!

35 *She comes into the room.*

FRANK: *(staring, slightly confused)* Erm – yes, I suppose I always mean to ...

RITA: *(going to the chair by the desk and dumping her bag)* Well, that's no good always meanin' to, is it? Y'should get on with it; one of these days you'll be shoutin' 'Come in' an' it'll go on forever because the poor sod on the other side won't be able to get in. An' you won't be able to get out.

40 FRANK *stares at* RITA *who stands by the desk.*

2 With a partner, talk about how the dramatist characterises Frank. Use the chart below to focus your discussion. Fill in a copy of it as you make your decisions.

3 Share your findings with the class.

Willy Russell's characterisation of Frank: how is it achieved?		
Dramatic technique	**Example**	**How this helps establish Frank's character**
Dramatist's notes to the director/actors		
Stage directions		
Monologue		
Dialogue on the telephone		
Dialogue with Rita		
Actions on stage		
Choice of language		

4 Look carefully at what you have noted down about Frank's choice of language or diction. Make suggestions about:

 a why he calls his wife 'darling' when he really wants her to 'put your head in the oven'

 b what his language shows about his attitude to teaching

 c his vocabulary in 'I like my lamb done to the point of abuse' and 'you could incinerate ratatouille'

 d his joke about determination and going to the pub.

5 Compare Rita's diction with Frank's. How much can you tell about her from her five lines of dialogue?

6 Continue this dialogue for the next 20 lines or so. Rita, who has never been inside a university before, but is not overawed, inspects Frank's room. Frank searches his papers for Rita's details; he is not sure she really is the Open University student he has been expecting. See how closely you can reproduce the two characters' speech styles or idiolects. If you use stage directions, keep them brief.

Activity 18

1 Read aloud the extract below from Marlowe's *Doctor Faustus*, written about 1594.

Doctor Faustus is about a university teacher who sells himself to the devil, called Lucifer in the play. The bargain is that Lucifer, a fallen angel with supernatural powers, will give Faustus 24 years of boundless 'pleasure and delight' on earth in return for his soul. Faustus is also promised knowledge of heaven, hell and the secrets of the universe.

In this extract, Mephostophilis, the servant Lucifer has assigned to Faustus, comes from hell to seal the bargain with 'a deed of gift'. This is to be signed in blood.

Enter MEPHOSTOPHILIS.

	FAUSTUS:	Now tell me: what saieth Lucifer thy lord?	
	MEPHOSTOPHILIS:	That I shall wait on Faustus whilst he lives, So he will buy my service with his soul.	
	FAUSTUS:	Already Faustus hath hazarded that for thee.	
5	MEPHOSTOPHILIS:	But now thou must bequeath it solemnly And write a deed of gift with thine own blood, For that security craves Lucifer. If thou deny it, I must back to hell.	
10	FAUSTUS:	Stay, Mephostophilis, and tell me what good Will my soul do thy lord?	
	MEPHOSTOPHILIS:	Enlarge his kingdom.	
	FAUSTUS:	Is that the reason why he tempts us thus?	
	MEPHOSTOPHILIS:	*Solamen miseris socios habuisse doloris.*	*Solamen miseris socios habuisse doloris:* the unhappy find comfort in others' misfortunes
	FAUSTUS:	Why, have you any pain that torture others?	
15	MEPHOSTOPHILIS:	As great as have the human souls of men. But tell me, Faustus, shall I have thy soul? And I will be thy slave and wait on thee And give thee more than thou hast wit to ask.	
	FAUSTUS:	Ay, Mephostophilis, I'll give it him.	
20	MEPHOSTOPHILIS:	Then, Faustus, stab thy arm courageously, And bind thy soul, that at some certain day Great Lucifer may claim it as his own; And then be thou as great as Lucifer.	
25	FAUSTUS:	Lo, Mephostophilis, for love of thee Faustus hath cut his arm, and with his proper blood Assures his soul to be great Lucifer's, Chief lord and regent of perpetual night. View here this blood that trickles from mine arm, And let it be propitious for my wish.	proper: own
30	MEPHOSTOPHILIS:	But, Faustus, Write it in manner of a deed of gift.	
	FAUSTUS:	Ay, so I do. But, Mephostophilis, My blood congeals, and I can write no more.	
	MEPHOSTOPHILIS:	I'll fetch thee fire to dissolve it straight. (*Exit*)	
35	FAUSTUS:	What might the staying of my blood portend? Is it unwilling I should write this bill? Why streams it not, that I may write afresh? 'Faustus gives to thee his soul': O, there it stay'd. Why shouldst thou not? is not thy soul thine own?	portend: signify
40		Then write again: 'Faustus gives to thee his soul'.	

Enter MEPHOSTOPHILIS with the chafer of fire. chafer: cauldron

Take it further

Read the first and last
scenes of *Dr Faustus*.
Use the knowledge of
the play you already
have to speculate about
what happens in the
course of it.

MEPHOSTOPHILIS:		See, Faustus, here is fire; set it on.
FAUSTUS:		So, now the blood begins to clear again
		Now will I make an end immediately.
45 MEPHOSTOPHILIS:	*[Aside]*	What will not I do to obtain his soul!

2 With a partner, talk about understanding the dialogue. How well could you follow it? Where there were difficulties, what caused them?

3 With your partner, talk about the dramatic appeal of the dialogue. Do you think it would work well on stage? Why, or why not?

Activity 19

1 In a group, look carefully at the diagram below.

What the dialogue shows about how each character sees himself

- A daring risk-taker
- A heroic figure greater than other men
- A servant with a job to do
- A fallen angel in torment

Faustus

Mephostophilis

- A man on a level with Lucifer
- In control of the situation
- A subordinate to Lucifer
- In control of the situation

2 Find quotations in the dialogue to illustrate each point in the diagram. Then discuss how each character sees the other. What is the effect of showing two characters who perceive the situation here in totally different ways?

3 Share your findings with the class. Then, looking closely at the passage, discuss:

a the frequent use of the words 'soul' and 'blood' in the dialogue. What do you think Marlowe's purpose is in creating this **verbal patterning**?

b how Marlowe's choice of blank verse for this dialogue (a lot of the play is in prose) helps the characterisation. Think about the seriousness and formality of the situation and about the way the line structure and the rhythm emphasise key words and phrases

c the short **soliloquy** Faustus speaks in lines 35–40. What do you think Marlowe's purpose is in taking us inside Faustus's mind here? Does it affect your attitude towards him?

Key terms
verbal patterning
soliloquy

Activity 20

1 Choose a passage of dialogue from your main coursework play which you think illustrates the characters and the dramatist's techniques of characterising them particularly well. It is best to choose a passage with only two speakers.

2 Write two or three paragaphs on the following topic, using close textual reference and drawing on all the work you have done in this sub-section.

> How does this passage illustrate the characters of the speakers? Comment in detail on the dramatist's techniques of characterisation.

4 How dramatists use language and verse form

Many plays between 1300 and 1800 were written partly or mainly in blank verse. In your explorative study, you are likely to have to comment on this to show how a dramatist's style and language conveys character, creates mood and atmosphere and develops key themes. The activities below provide you with a toolkit for reading the language and verse of plays from the past.

Activity 21

1   Read the opening lines of Shakespeare's *The Merchant of Venice*. Antonio, a wealthy businessman, is telling two friends that he feels unaccountably depressed.

> ANTONIO: In sooth, I know not why I am so sad,
>   It wearies me, you say it wearies you;
>   But how I caught it, found it, or came by it,
>   What stuff 'tis made of, whereof 'tis born,
> 5   I am to learn:
>   And such a want-wit sadness makes of me,
>   That I have much ado to know myself.

2   This speech was written to be spoken, not read silently. Now read it aloud to a partner.

Rules for reading blank verse

1   Read it aloud or aloud inside your head.

2   Don't pause at the end of every line. Do pause for about one second when you reach a semi-colon, colon, full stop or other strong punctuation mark, wherever it comes.

3   Get used to following the basic rhythm of a blank verse line. This is called an iambic pentameter and usually has five stresses or strong beats:

   di Dum / di Dum /di Dum /di Dum /di Dum /di Dum.

The Merchant of Venice (RSC, 1981)

Activity 22

1 Read aloud to a partner the following blank verse speech from *The Merchant of Venice*. It is spoken to Antonio by one of his friends, Bassanio. Bassanio is attracted to a rich heiress, Portia.

> BASSANIO: In Belmont is a lady richly left,
> And she is fair, and (fairer than that word),
> Of wondrous virtues. Sometimes from her eyes
> I did receive fair speechless messages:
> 5 Her name is Portia, nothing undervalu'd
> To Cato's daughter, Brutus' Portia,
> Nor is the wide world ignorant of her worth,
> For the four winds blow in from every coast
> Renowned suitors, and her sunny locks
> 10 Hang on her temples like a golden fleece,
> Which makes her seat of Belmont Colcho's strond,
> And many Jasons come in quest of her.

2 On a copy of the extract, put a vertical stroke | just after each strong pause.

> Of wondrous virtues. | Sometimes from her eyes
> I did receive fair speechless messages: |
> Her name is Portia …

3 Read the speech aloud again. Where there is no strong pause or 'end-stop' at the end of a line, read straight on. Base your reading on the di Dum, di Dum, di Dum, di Dum, di Dum rhythm.

Rules for reading blank verse

4 'Feeling' the iambic pentametre beat of blank verse as you read helps you understand the gist of what is being said.

5 Because blank verse is a form of poetry, the full meaning is often quite compressed. So be content to get the general gist at first, then fill in the details later. Don't give up.

4 With your partner, look at the second half of Bassanio's speech (from line 8). It is full of comparisons – similes and metaphors. You have got the idea that Bassanio thinks Portia is beautiful and rich. Use the information below, from a footnote in the text, to work out the details of what he is saying about her.

The Roman hero, Brutus, had a wife named Portia. She was celebrated for her virtue and her devotion to her husband.

In Greek mythology, Jason and the Argonauts searched for the Golden Fleece. They found it at Colchos.

Talk about why you think Bassanio uses these two comparisons to describe Portia in Belmont. Does he seem to want her for her money, her beauty, her suitablity as a wife – or for all of these?

Rules for reading blank verse

6 Use footnotes to fill in the gaps in your understanding. Even the most knowledgeable readers find footnotes useful.

7 When you have filled in the gaps, read the speech again. You will be struck by how much of the meaning depends on imagery (i.e. simile and metaphor) and how much more sense it makes now. Imagery, along with the blank verse form, is the most distinctive feature of the language of older plays.

8 Ask questions about what the imagery is telling you, now you have understood it. You will almost always be able to come up with your own answers. For example:

- Why do you think Bassanio describes Portia's hair as 'sunny'?
- What impression does he give of her by saying her hair is 'like a golden fleece'?
- Why do you think he says her hair 'hangs on her temples'? (He might have said 'shoulders').

Activity 23

1 Read the extract below from later on in *The Merchant of Venice*.

Antonio has provided Bassanio with money to travel to Belmont to win Portia. This money was borrowed in the form of a 'bond' from Shylock, a Jewish money-lender. The bond stated that, if Antonio could not repay him by a set date, Shylock could claim a pound of his flesh as a forfeit.

Antonio's merchant ships are all lost at sea. He cannot repay Shylock and is imprisoned pending trial. Deaf to pleas to show mercy, here Shylock meets Antonio on his way from prison to the court. (There is long-standing hatred in Venice between Christians and Jews.)

Enter SHYLOCK, ANTONIO *in chains and the* GAOLER.

SHYLOCK:	Gaoler, look to him – tell me not of mercy, –	
	This is the fool that lent out money gratis.	gratis: without charging interest
	Gaoler, look to him.	
ANTONIO:	Hear me yet, good Shylock.	
5 SHYLOCK:	I'll have my bond, speak not against my bond,	
	I have sworn an oath, that I will have my bond:	
	Thou call'dst me dog before thou hadst a cause,	
	But since I am a dog, beware my fangs, –	
	The duke shall grant me justice.	duke: head of the judiciary
10 ANTONIO:	I pray thee hear me speak.	
SHYLOCK:	I'll have my bond. I will not hear thee speak,	
	I'll have my bond, and therefore speak no more.	
	I'll not be made a soft and dull-ey'd fool,	
	To shake the head, relent, and sigh, and yield	
15	To Christian intercessors: follow not, –	intercessors: pleaders
	I'll have no speaking, I will have my bond.	

2 With a partner, read through this dialogue as if you were a theatre director preparing notes for the actors on how to speak the verse. On a copy of the extract, underline the words and phrases you want them to emphasise. Make brief notes on the tone of voice you want them to use and on any patterns of speech you want to stand out in performance, (eg Shylock's repetition of 'I'll have my bond' and his pounding emphasis on 'I'.)

3 Now read the dialogue aloud following your own instructions.

Rules for reading blank verse

9 Read it as if you are an actor or a director, for the stage rather than on the page.

10 Look for patterns in the verse, for example repetitions, contrasts, balanced phrases, pauses, climaxes.

11 Verse patterns will often be built up through the sound of words. These sounds are an important part of the meaning. Identify them and think about their effect in performance. For example:

- How many of Shylock's words in this extract *sound* harsh and fierce, as if he is spitting them out?
- How many of these words are given extra emphasis by coming immediately before a heavy stop and/or at the end of a line?
- How would you describe the rhythms of Shylock's speeches here? (A good definition of rhythm is 'a pattern of sounds').

12 Try to identify the pace or speed of the lines in a blank verse speech. Is the pace fast (if so, why)? Is the pace slow and drawn out (if so, why)? Is the pace uneven and irregular (if so, why)? The answers you come up with will reflect the characters' mood and feelings as they speak.

This sub-section has given you basic guidance on how to read blank verse and make it comprehensible. Apply what you have learned to your coursework plays, but bear in mind that:

- the meaning of many words and expressions has changed over time – there is no substitute for looking them up in footnotes
- meaning depends strongly on context – as you become familiar with the whole verbal, social and cultural context of your plays, understanding will come more quickly and naturally.

5 How dramatists advance the plot

Most plays, including those written between 1300 and 1800, have an episode where events reach a critical turning point or **crisis**. This means that from there on the action is set on a new or changed course which leads directly, and often swiftly, to the play's **dénouement** (closing sequence).

In your explorative study, you are likely to write about this aspect of dramatic structure. The activities below give you guidance in doing so. Both exemplar plays are from 1300 to 1800.

Activity 24

1 Read the extract below from *The Revenger's Tragedy*, written by either Thomas Middleton or Cyril Tourneur (scholars have not yet made up their minds). It was first performed in 1607.

Vindice (Vin-deechée: the Italian name means 'revenger') wants to murder the Duke. Now an old man, the Duke raped and poisoned Vindice's fiancée, Gloriana, nine years before. Vindice carries around her skull to focus his mind on revenge. He has disguised himself as Piato, a pimp who supplies young girls to the Duke for sexual pleasure.

In this scene, Vindice has attached Gloriana's skull to a broomstick and dressed her up as a country girl. The Duke believes he is coming to have sex with her in a private place outside the palace. The extract begins with Vindice showing his brother, Hippolito, how he has planned the Duke's murder.

VINDICE:	Look you, brother,	
	I have not fashioned this only for show	
	And useless property; no, it shall bear a part	
	Even in its own revenge. This very skull,	
5	Whose mistress the Duke poisoned, with this drug,	drug: arsenic
	The mortal curse of the earth, shall be revenged	mortal: deadly
	In the like strain, and kiss his lips to death.	
HIPPOLITO:	Brother, I do applaud thy constant vengeance.	

VINDICE puts poison on the lips of the skull.

10	VINDICE:	So, 'tis laid on. Now come, and welcome, Duke.

VINDICE puts a mask on the skull.

	Hide thy face now, for shame, thou hadst need have a mask now;	
	'Tis vain when beauty flows, but when it fleets	fleets: withers
	This would become graves better than streets.	become: suit
15	HIPPOLITO:	You have my voice in that. Hark, the Duke's come.
	VINDICE:	Peace, let's observe what company he brings,
		And how he does absent 'em, for you know	absent: send away
		He'll wish all private. Brother, fall you back
		A little with the bony lady.
20	HIPPOLITO:	That I will.
	VINDICE:	So, so –
		Now nine years' vengeance crowds into a minute!

They step aside as the DUKE *enters, with some* GENTLEMEN.

	DUKE:	You shall have leave to leave us, with this charge,	charge: command
25		Upon your lives: if we be missed by th' Duchess,
		Or any of the nobles, to give out
		We're privately rid forth.
	VINDICE:	*aside* O happiness!
	DUKE:	With some few honourable gentlemen, you may say;
30		You may name those that are away from court.
	GENTLEMEN:	Your will and pleasure shall be done, my lord.
		[*Exit* GENTLEMEN.]
	VINDICE:	[*aside*] 'Privately rid forth';
		He strives to make sure work of it!
35		[*to the* DUKE] Your good grace.
	DUKE:	Piato, well done. Hast brought her? What lady is 't?

	VINDICE:	Faith, my lord, a country lady, a little bashful at first, as most of them are; but after the first kiss, my lord, the worst is past with them. Your grace knows now what you have to do. She has somewhat a grave look with her, but –	
40	DUKE:	I love that best; conduct her.	conduct: bring
	VINDICE:	[aside] Have at all! Back with the torch; brother, raise the perfumes.	raise: waft about
	DUKE:	How sweet can a Duke breathe? Age has no fault. Pleasure should meet in a perfumèd mist.	

45 *The* DUKE *approaches the skull.*

> Lady, sweetly encountered; I came from court,
> I must be bold with you.

[*The* DUKE *kisses the skull.*] O, what's this? O!

	VINDICE:	Royal villain, white devil!	
50	DUKE:	O!	
	VINDICE:	Brother – Place the torch here, that his affrighted eyeballs May start into those hollows. Duke, dost know Yon dreadful vizard? View it well; 'tis the skull Of Gloriana, whom thou poisonedst last.	hollows: eye-sockets vizard: mask
55			
	DUKE:	O, it has poisoned me. What are you two?	
	VINDICE:	Villains, all three! The very ragged bone Has been sufficiently revenged,	
	DUKE:	O, Hippolito! Call treason.	
60	HIPPOLITO:	Yes, my good lord; treason, treason, treason [*stamping on him*]	
	DUKE:	Then I'm betrayed … Is it thou, villain? Nay, then –	
	VINDICE:	'Tis I, 'tis Vindice, 'tis I.	

2 In a small group, act out this scene, books in hands. Appoint one person to direct it. They should plan the moves carefully and pay particular attention to where characters speak 'aside'.

3 As a class, discuss what you learned from your performances about the dramatist's:

a stagecraft

b characterisation of Vindice and the Duke

c use of language in a play that is 400 years old.

What do you think would be the effect of this scene on a modern audience in the professional theatre?

4 With a partner, examine the aspects of diction and verse form listed below.

a The five uses of the word 'revenge' or 'vengeance'. This establishes a verbal pattern in the passage. What do you think is the dramatist's purpose?

b Images of poisoning and kissing, bones and body parts, and beauty and masks/disguises. These establish a pattern of imagery in the passage. What do you think is the dramatist's purpose?

c The blank verse. Compare it with the blank verse in *Doctor Faustus* (pages 137 and 138). How are its rhythms much closer to natural live speech than Marlowe's? What do you think is the dramatist's purpose?

Activity 25

1 Choose a passage from your main coursework play where events reach a crisis which advances the plot. Analyse its dramatic and linguistic effects by focusing on:

   a stagecraft: how does the staging direct the audience's response to character?

   b diction and imagery: how do these underline key themes?

   c **verse form** (or prose style): how does this work to express character and create dramatic tension?

Activity 26

1 Read aloud the extract below from Shakespeare's *Othello*, first performed in 1604.

Othello, an army general in Venice, has begun to suspect that his wife, Desdemona has been 'disloyal' to him with Michael Cassio. His ensign, Iago, has deliberately planted this suspicion in Othello's mind while outwardly playing the part of his devoted friend.

In this extract, Iago continues to poison Othello's mind.

	OTHELLO:	Give me a living reason that she's disloyal.	living: convincing
	IAGO:	I do not like the office,	office: task
		But sith I am enter'd into this cause so far,	sith: since
		Prick'd to't by foolish honesty and love,	prick'd: prompted
5		I will go on: I lay with Cassio lately,	
		And being troubled with a raging tooth,	
		I could not sleep.	
		There are a kind of men so loose of soul	
		That in their sleeps will mutter their affairs,	
10		One of this kind is Cassio:	
		In sleep I heard him say 'Sweet Desdemona,	
		Let us be wary, let us hide our loves'.	
		And then, sir, would he gripe and wring my hand,	
		Cry out, 'Sweet creature!' and then kiss me hard,	
15		As if he pluck'd up kisses by the roots,	
		That grew upon my lips, then laid his leg	
		Over my thigh, and sigh'd, and kiss'd, and then	
		Cried 'Cursed fate, that gave thee to the Moor!'	the Moor: Othello
	OTHELLO:	O monstrous, monstrous!	
20	IAGO:	Nay, this was but his dream.	
	OTHELLO:	But this denoted a foregone conclusion.	foregone conclusion: previous liaison
	IAGO:	'Tis a shrewd doubt, though it be but a dream,	
		And this may help to thicken other proofs	thicken: stengthen
		That do demonstrate thinly.	
25	OTHELLO:	I'll tear her all in pieces.	
	IAGO:	Nay, but be wise, yet we see nothing done,	
		She may be honest yet; tell me but this,	
		Have you not sometimes seen a handkerchief,	
		Spotted with strawberries, in your wife's hand.	
30	OTHELLO:	I gave her such a one, 'twas my first gift.	
	IAGO:	I know not that, but such a handkerchief –	
		I am sure it was your wife's – did I today	
		See Cassio wipe his beard with.	
	OTHELLO:	If't be that –	

35	IAGO:	If it be that, or any that was hers, It speaks against her, with the other proofs,	
	OTHELLO:	O that the slave had forty thousand lives! One is too poor, too weak for my revenge: Now do I see 'tis true; look here, Iago,	
40		All my fond love thus do I blow to heaven – 'Tis gone. Arise, black vengeance, from thy hollow cell, Yield up, O love, thy crown, and hearted throne, To tyrannous hate; swell, bosom, with thy fraught,	
45		For 'tis of aspics' tongues! [*He kneels.*]	aspics: snakes
	IAGO:	Pray be content.	
	OTHELLO:	O blood, Iago, blood!	
	IAGO:	Patience, I say, your mind perhaps may change.	
	OTHELLO:	Never, Iago. My bloody thoughts, with violent pace	
50		Shall ne'er look back, ne'er ebb to humble love, Till that a capable and wide revenge Swallow them up. Now by yond marble heaven, In the due reverence of a sacred vow,	
		I here engage my words.	engage: pledge
55	IAGO:	Do not rise yet. IAGO [*kneels.*] Witness, you ever-burning lights above, You elements that clip us round about, Witness that here Iago doth give up The excellency of his wit, hand, heart,	
60		To wrong'd Othello's service: let him command, And to obey shall be in me remorse, What bloody work so ever. [*They rise.*]	
	OTHELLO:	I greet thy love; Not with vain thanks, but with acceptance bounteous,	
65		And will upon the instant put thee to't:	put thee to't: set you a task
		Within these three days, let me hear thee say That Cassio's not alive.	
	IAGO:	My friend is dead: 'Tis done as you request; but let her live.	dead: as good as dead already
70	OTHELLO:	Damn her, lewd minx: O damn her! Come go with me apart, I will withdraw To furnish me with some swift means of death, For the fair devil: now art thou my lieutenant.	
	IAGO:	I am your own for ever. [*Exeunt.*]	

2 With a partner, discuss how Iago makes Othello believe that Desdemona is having an affair and that he, Iago, has Othello's best interests at heart. Focus on the way Iago presents:

  a his account of Cassio talking in his sleep

  b his story about the handkerchief

  c himself as an embodiment of 'honesty and love'.

Look carefully at Iago's language. How does the dramatist make you aware of both its text (to Othello: 'I'm telling you this in all honesty for your own good') and its sub-text (to the audience: 'I'm leading him by the nose to his destruction')? Share your ideas with the class.

3 Then look carefully at Othello's lines in this passage. Fill in a copy of the chart on the following page to show how his language reveals his character.

Take it further

Watch a performance of *Othello* on DVD. Write your personal response to his tragedy. Do you feel any sympathy for him?

Examples of Othello's language	Comment on his language choice	What this shows about him
'I'll tear her all in pieces'		
'All my fond love thus do I blow to heaven –/'Tis gone'		
'Arise, black vengeance'		
'some swift means of death/For the fair devil'		

4 Why do you think Othello 'kneels' half-way through this passage and Iago kneels shortly after? What will be the effect on the audience of this **stage emblem**?

Activity 27

Your explorative study may include commentary on the production aspects of your two plays. This activity gives you practice in exploring drama from a director's viewpoint.

Choose either the extract from *The Revenger's Tragedy* (pages 142–143) or the extract from *Othello* (pages 144–145).

Imagine you are a director in the professional theatre. Make detailed production notes on your chosen scene, using the following headings. (You need not include notes about costume, lighting, props and sound.)

- An explanation of how you interpret the scene.
- General comments to the actors about the effects you want to create for the audience.
- Instructions about how to stage the scene: moves, key moments in the action and how to highlight them, use of physical gesture, pauses, etc.
- Instructions on how to speak the lines and establish relationships between the characters.

Key terms
crisis
dénouement
stagecraft
verse form
stage emblem

6 How dramatists construct an ending

The dénouement of a play shows the outcome of the plot and the situation in which the main characters end up. In comedy, the dénouement centres on events that signal personal happiness and social harmony: reunion, forgiveness, reconciliation, celebration, marriage. In tragedy, the dénouement dramatises the consequences of the main character's actions in the course of the play. It is sometimes termed the **catastrophe** because these consequences invariably prove fatal. Tragedies typically end with suffering and death – separation, murder, suicide, revenge – and the society in which the hero lived is left in a state of fracture or total ruin.

Both exemplar plays in this section are tragedies. Either or both of the plays you discuss in your explorative study could be tragedies. The activities below help you to explore this dramatic genre, particularly common from 1580 to 1620, by focusing on its most striking aspect: the tragic **resolution**.

Activity 28

1 Read aloud the extract below from Arthur Miller's *The Crucible*, first performed in 1954.

The play is set in a puritan community in Salem, New England in 1692. Accused of witchcraft and devil worship, a group of girls try to pass the blame to adults in the village. A court is set up by Judge Danforth to try them. John Proctor is among the accused. He has, wrongly, been found guilty, but Danforth rules that if he makes a public confession he will be spared hanging.

At the end of the play, Proctor has a difficult choice. He can lie and have his life, or he can continue to speak the truth and die. He has a wife, Elizabeth, and three young children. He has already 'confessed' verbally. Now Danforth demands 'good and legal proof' in writing.

DANFORTH:	Mr Proctor, I must have good and legal proof that you –
PROCTOR:	You are the high court, your word is good enough! Tell them I confessed myself; say Proctor broke his knees and wept like a woman; say what you will, but my name cannot –
DANFORTH:	[*with suspicion*]: It is the same, is it not? If I report it or if you sign it?
5 PROCTOR:	No, it is not the same! What others say and what I sign to is not the same!
DANFORTH:	Why? Do you mean to deny this confession when you are free?
PROCTOR:	I mean to deny nothing!
DANFORTH:	Then explain to me, Mr Proctor, why you will not let –
PROCTOR:	[*with a cry of his soul*] Because it is my name! Because I cannot have another in my life! Because I 10 lie and sign myself to lies! Because I am not worth the dust on the feet of them that hang! How may I live without my name! I have given you my soul; leave me my name!
DANFORTH:	[*pointing at the confession in Proctor's hand*] Is that document a lie? If it is a lie, I will not accept it! What say you? I will not deal in lies, Mister! [PROCTOR *is motionless*]. You will give me your honest confession in my hand, or I cannot keep you from the rope. [PROCTOR *does not reply*]. 15 Which way do you go, Mister?

His breast heaving, his eyes staring, PROCTOR *tears the paper and crumples it, and he is weeping in fury, but erect.*

DANFORTH:	Marshal!
REVEREND HALE:	Man, you will hang! You cannot!
PROCTOR:	[*his eyes full of tears*] I can. And there's your first marvel, that I can. You have made your magic now, 20 for now I do think I see some shred of goodness in John Proctor. Not enough to weave a banner with, but white enough to keep it from such dogs.

ELIZABETH, *in a burst of terror, rushes to him and weeps against his hand.*

Give them no tears! Tears pleasure them! Show honour now, show a stony heart and sink them with it. [*He has lifted her, and kisses her now with great passion*].

25 DANFORTH:	Hang them high over the town! Who weeps for these, weeps for corruption. [*He sweeps out past them.*]
MARSHAL HERRICK:	Come, man …

HERRICK *escorts them out.* ELIZABETH *stands staring at the empty doorway.*

REVEREND HALE:	Woman, plead with him! Woman! It is pride, it is vanity.

30 *She avoids his eyes and moves to the window. He drops to his knees.*

Be his helper! – What profit him to bleed? Shall the dust praise him? Shall the worms declare his truth? Go to him, take his shame away!

ELIZABETH:	[*grips the bars of the window, and with a cry*] He have his goodness now. God forbid I take it from him!

35 *The final drumroll crashes, then heightens violently.* HALE *weeps in frantic prayer, and the new sun is pouring in upon her face, and the drums rattle like bones in the morning air.*

2 With a partner, talk about how the dramatist presents John Proctor, the play's tragic hero in this passage, which ends the play. Focus on:

   a why he is so concerned about his 'name'

   b how the dramatist arouses our sympathy and admiration for him (look at the characterisation of Danforth and Elizabeth as well as Proctor)

   c how the stage directions guide the actor playing him.

   Share your ideas with the class.

3 Look carefully at the language of the passage. Compare Proctor's idiolect with Danforth's. Fill in a copy of the chart below to help you reach your conclusions.

Danforth's idiolect		Proctor's idiolect	
Language feature	Example	Language feature	Example
Repeated questions (interrogatives) in first half		Repeated exclamations and **declarative** statements in first half	
Imperative sentences in second half		Sentences structured around 'Because', 'name' and 'I'	
Inflexible legal language throughout		Mixture of colloquial speech and figurative language	
Stern, aggressive tone throughout		Varied tone: anguished at first, then quietly assured, then defiant/triumphant	

4 The key moment in this passage is enacted, not spoken. What is it, and why is it key?

5 Use the work you have done above to write a commentary on the dramatist's presentation of the tragic hero in this passage.

Activity 29

Re-read the ending of your main coursework play and the comments introducing this sub-section (page 146). Use the comments as a starting point to examine in detail how your dramatist constructs the resolution to the play whether it is a tragedy, a comedy or some other genre.

Activity 30

1 Read the extract from near the end of Shakespeare's *Antony and Cleopatra*, first performed in 1608.

> Mark Antony, a consul of Rome, has died, bringing to an end his love affair with Queen Cleopatra of Egypt, which has plunged two empires into turmoil. The Roman army under Octavius Caesar has invaded Egypt. Cleopatra knows that, if she lives, she will be overthrown and taken captive. In this passage, she arranges her own death. Her servants are Charmian and Iras. The setting is Cleopatra's palace.

Enter CHARMIAN

CLEOPATRA: Now Charmian.
             Show me, my women, like a Queen. Go fetch
             My best attires. I am again for Cydnus,   Cydnus: where Anthony and Cleopatra first met
             To meet Mark Antony. Sirrah Iras, go.   sirrah: servant of either sex
5   Now, noble Charmian, we'll dispatch indeed,   dispatch: die
             And when thou hast done this chare, I'll give thee leave   chare: task
             To play till doomsday. Bring our crown and all.

Exit IRAS. *A noise within.*

             Wherefore's this noise?

10   *Enter a* GUARDSMAN.

GUARDSMAN: Here is a rural fellow
That will not be denied your highness' presence.
He brings you figs.

15 CLEOPATRA: Let him come in. [*Exit* GUARDSMAN.]
What poor an instrument
May do a noble deed! He brings me liberty.
My resolution's placed, and I have nothing
Of woman in me. Now from head to foot
I am marble-constant; now the fleeting moon
20 No planet is of mine.

Enter CLOWN.

Hast thou the pretty worm of Nilus there,   worm: snake, asp   Nilus: River Nile
That kills and pains not?

CLOWN: Truly I have him; but I would not be the party that
25 should desire you to touch him, for his biting is
immortal; those that do die of it seldom or never recover.

CLEOPATRA: Remember'st thou any that have died on't?

CLOWN: Very many, men and women too. I heard of one of them
no longer than yesterday, a very honest woman, but
30 something given to lie, as women should not do, but
in the way of honesty, how she died of the biting of it,
what pain she felt. Truly, she makes a very good report
o'th'worm. But he that will believe all that they say shall
never be saved by half they that do. But this is most
35 fallible, the worm's an odd worm.

CLEOPATRA: Get thee hence, farewell …

CLOWN: I wish you all joy of the worm.

CLEOPATRA: Farewell. [*Exit* CLOWN.]

Enter CHARMIAN *and* IRAS *with a robe and a crown.*

40 CLEOPATRA: Give me my robe, put on my crown, I have
Immortal longings in me. Now no more
The juice of Egypt's grape shall moist this lip.
Yare, yare, good Iras; quick. Methinks I hear   yare: make haste
Antony call; I see him rouse himself
45 To praise my noble act, I hear him mock
The luck of Caesar, which the gods give men
To excuse their after wrath. Husband, I come.
Now to that name my courage prove my title.
I am fire and air; my other elements
50 I give to baser life. So, have you done?
Come, then, and take the last warmth of my lips.
Farewell kind Charmian; Iras, long farewell.

She kisses them. IRAS *falls and dies.*

Have I the aspic in my lips? Dost fall?   aspic: snake's venom
55 If thou and nature can so gently part,
The stroke of death is as a lover's pinch,
Which hurts, and is desired. Dost thou lie still?
If thus thou vanishest, thou tell'st the world
It is not worth leave-taking.

60 CHARMIAN: Dissolve, thick cloud and rain, that I may say
The gods themselves do weep.

CLEOPATRA:	This proves me base.	
	If she first meet the curlèd Antony,	curlèd: curly-haired
	He'll make demand of her, and spend that kiss	
65	Which is my heaven to have. Come thou mortal wretch	mortal: deadly

She applies the asp to her breast.

	With thy sharp teeth this knot instrinsicate	instrinsicate: inmost
	Of life at once untie. Poor venemous fool,	
	Be angry and dispatch. O couldst thou speak,	
70	That I may hear thee call great Caesar 'Ass,	
	Unpolicied!'	unpolicied: disempowered
CHARMIAN:	O eastern star!	
CLEOPATRA:	Peace, peace!	
	Dost thou not see my baby at my breast,	
75	That sucks the nurse asleep?	
CHARMIAN:	O break! O break!	
CLEOPATRA:	As sweet as balm, as soft as air, as gentle –	
	O Antony! Nay, I will take thee too.	

Applies another asp to her arm.

80	What should I stay. [*She dies*].	
CHARMIAN:	In this vile world? So fare thee well.	
	Now boast thee death, in thy possession lies	
	A lass unparalled. Downy windows, close;	
	And golden Phoebus never be beheld	Phoebus: the sun
85	Of eyes so royal! Your crown's awry,	
	I'll mend it, and then play –	

Take it further

Read accounts by actors in *Players of Shakespeare* of performing in *Othello* and *Antony and Cleopatra*. What impressions of the plays do they give?

Key terms
catastrophe
resolution
imperative
declarative

2 Fill in a copy of the chart below. Work with a partner or in a group.

Examples of Cleopatra's use of language in this passage			
Sounds poetic	**Sounds down-to-earth**	**Sounds like an actress**	**Sounds sad**

3 Share your responses with the class. Then talk about:

a anything that surprises you about how the play's tragic heroine faces death

b why you think Shakespeare chose to include three minor characters (two serving women and a clown) at this point in the play

c whether this death scene strikes you as 'tragic'.

Activity 31

1   Read the following comments about this scene by Frances de la Tour, an actress who played Cleopatra for the Royal Shakespeare Company.

> The death-scene itself begins with the audience anticipating something solemn: 'Now from head to foot/I am marble constant', she says, and this is where we expect the aria, the big speech that is going to make her a legend, an icon. And just as the handkerchiefs are coming out in preparation, Shakespeare wrong-foots us all again, and on comes the clown to take
> 5   over the scene with his smutty jokes … Even after this, and after the solemn dressing-up for death, we aren't allowed to settle into an anticipated moment of solemnity, for Iras's death sends Cleopatra off into a fit of jealous anxiety: 'If she first meet the curlèd Antony/He'll make demand of her, and spend that kiss/Which is my heaven to have'. Our laughter (and it's inevitable) at this moment is even more extraordinary than our earlier laughter at the clown;
> 10   and then, just ten lines later, we are again invited to laugh – and *at* her rather than with her – as she desperately grabs the asp to catch up with Iras: 'Come, thou mortal wretch/With thy sharp teeth this knot intrinsicate/Of life at once untie'. This is brilliant writing. Of course, Shakespeare could have conducted the audience through a vale of tears to a predictable conclusion; but the manipulation is much cleverer than that with the audience, wrong-footed,
> 15   being swung between emotional extremes all the way to the end.

With a partner, discuss whether you agree with her. Read aloud particular passages in the text to help you make up your mind.

2   Look at Cleopatra's speech beginning 'Give me my robe' down to 'my other elements/I give to baser life'. Write out the speech as one prose paragraph, keeping Shakespeare's sentences and punctuation. Read this aloud to a partner. Discuss what has been lost. Focus on:

   a   pauses and emphases

   b   the pace and rhythms of the lines

   c   patterns of language.

Activity 32

1   Choose a key speech from the dénouement of one of your coursework plays that is written in blank verse. Write a commentary on what the dramatist achieves that would have been achieved less effectively in prose.

2   Read and compare the dénouements of your two coursework plays. Use the work you have done in this sub-section to:

   a   analyse the way they reach a resolution

   b   comment on how the hero, or heroine, is presented at the end of the play compared with how they were presented at the beginning

   c   describe the contribution to their effectiveness made by the dramatist's stagecraft and use a blank verse, or prose.

C Comparing plays in their context

1 Introduction

This section gives you detailed guidance on how to find links and make connections between your main coursework play and your further play. You will also learn what is meant by 'context', how to use 'illuminator' texts to search for contextual material, and how to apply your knowledge of context to your two chosen plays in the ways examiners expect.

2 Exemplar assignments for the explorative study

Here are three examples of assignments you could choose for your explorative study from the wide range of possibilities you could agree with your teacher. Each would lead to an essay of between 1000 words (the minimum recommended) and 2000 words (the maximum recommended).

Assignment 1

Compare and contrast the presentation of Marlowe's *Dr Faustus* and Shakespeare's *Hamlet* as tragic heroes. Your study should refer to relevant contextual material and also include appropriate readings of the plays by other critics.

Assignment 2

Compare and contrast the satirising of greed and avarice in Shakespeare's *The Merchant of Venice* and Gay's *The Beggar's Opera*. Your study should refer to relevant contextual material and also include appropriate readings of the plays by other critics.

Assignment 3

Here are two quotations from *A Midsummer Night's Dream*.

'Reason and love keep little company together nowadays' (Bottom)

'Shall we their fond pageant see?
Lord, what fools these mortals be!' (Puck)

Compare and contrast the presentation of love's folly in Shakespeare's *Twelfth Night* and either *A Midsummer Night's Dream* or *Antony and Cleopatra*. Your study should refer to relevant contextual material and also include appropriate readings of the plays by other critics.

Writing your coursework

For your explorative study, you will study one drama text in some depth and use a further drama text, perhaps studied in less depth, to provide contrast, comparison or illumination. You should also use another text, which represents critical or cultural comment. Make sure your explorative study shows connections and comparisons between different texts and the significance of the contexts in which texts are written and received.

3 Spotting links, finding connections: how to get started

Assessment objectives

Nearly two-thirds of the marks for your explorative study are given for comparing two plays from 1300 to 1800. You have to 'explore connections and comparisons between different literary texts, informed by interpretations of other readers' (AO3).

Activity 33

Take an overview of the main coursework play you have studied from 1300 to 1800 and the further play from the same period that you are using for comparison.

With a partner, talk about possible areas of comparison, which will allow you to write about what you find most interesting in the plays. Then draw up a list of provisional titles for your explorative study. These could be based on:

- common themes in the plays
- the dramatists' techniques of characterisation
- the dramatists' use of setting and staging
- the structure and style of the plays
- the ways in which the plays appeal to an audience.

Make sure that your choice of topic is one you feel confident and enthusiastic about.

4 Making a plan

Activity 34

1   Take 15 minutes to make an outline plan for your provisional topic, using the model below. Think in fairly broad terms. Your purpose is to see whether your provisional topic has the potential to be extended into an essay of the required length and content.

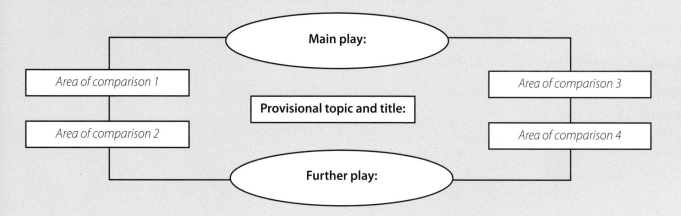

Main play:

Area of comparison 1

Area of comparison 2

Provisional topic and title:

Area of comparison 3

Area of comparison 4

Further play:

2 Compare your outline plan with a partner's. Explain to each other:

   a how and why you chose your areas of comparison

   b which areas you feel confident about developing further and which you feel less confident about

   c whether, on reflection, one or more areas might merge into others.

3 Redraft your outline plan. Ask your partner to comment constructively on the result. Do the same for them.

Activity 35

1 Look back to Assignment 1 on page 152. Here is an outline plan for the *first half* of it, leaving aside 'contextual factors'. Read it carefully.

Presentation of the tragic hero by Marlowe and Shakespeare

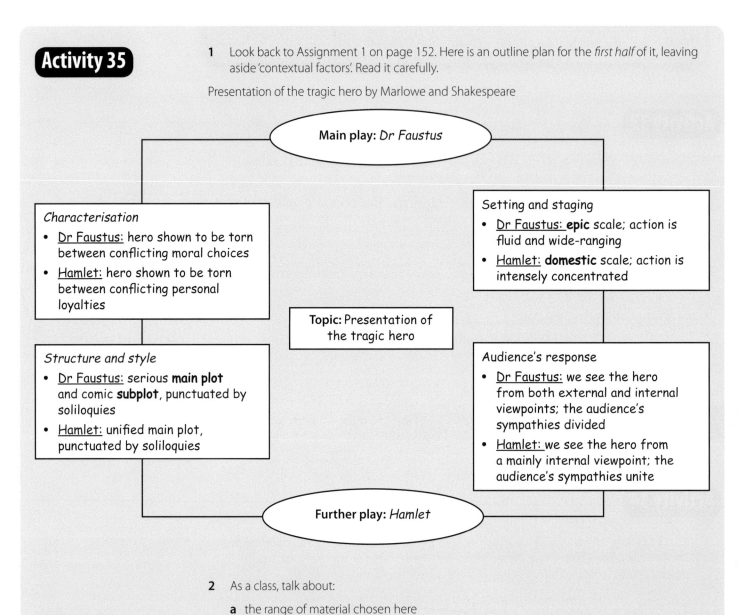

Main play: *Dr Faustus*

Characterisation
- Dr Faustus: hero shown to be torn between conflicting moral choices
- Hamlet: hero shown to be torn between conflicting personal loyalties

Setting and staging
- Dr Faustus: **epic** scale; action is fluid and wide-ranging
- Hamlet: **domestic** scale; action is intensely concentrated

Topic: Presentation of the tragic hero

Structure and style
- Dr Faustus: serious **main plot** and comic **subplot**, punctuated by soliloquies
- Hamlet: unified main plot, punctuated by soliloquies

Audience's response
- Dr Faustus: we see the hero from both external and internal viewpoints; the audience's sympathies divided
- Hamlet: we see the hero from a mainly internal viewpoint; the audience's sympathies unite

Further play: *Hamlet*

2 As a class, talk about:

   a the range of material chosen here

   b the relevance of the material to the essay title

   c what the writer needs to do next.

Key terms
main plot
subplot
epic
domestic

5 Developing connections and comparisons

At this stage, your outline plan does not include material on context. This is appropriate for now. Your next task is to develop connections between the content of your two plays, using the areas of comparison you have chosen.

Activity 36

1   The person who planned to compare the presentation of the tragic hero in *Dr Faustus* and *Hamlet* went on to write a first draft for 'Area of Comparison 1: characterisation'. Read the part of this shown below, referring back to the relevant box in the plan (page 154).

Both Faustus and Hamlet are presented as being torn between opposing courses of action. At the end of his first soliloquy, Faustus is resolved to reject Christianity ('What will be, shall be. Divinity, adieu!') and commit himself to the black arts in order to win 'a world of profit and delight':

> A sound magician is a demi-god.
> Here tire, my brains, to get a deity!

Similarly, when Hamlet is commanded by his father's ghost to 'Revenge his foul and most unnatural murder', he does not hesitate to accept the task:

> Haste me to know it, that I with wings as swift
> As meditation or the thoughts of love,
> May sweep to my revenge!

Like Faustus, he determines to 'wipe away all trivial fond records/All saws of books, all forms, all pressures past' and pursue one object single-mindedly. For Faustus, the object is to gain power and knowledge; for Hamlet, the object is to gain revenge.

However, shortly after making these apparently firm resolutions, each hero is shown to have doubts that cause them to hesitate. The difficulty for Faustus is his conscience, symbolised by the conflicting voices of the GOOD and BAD ANGELS:

> GOOD ANGEL: O, Faustus, lay that damnèd book aside
>   And gaze not on it lest it tempt thy soul …

> BAD ANGEL: Go forward, Faustus, in that famous art
>   Wherein all nature's treasury is contained

The diffculty for Hamlet is also within himself. The ghost has hardly departed in Act 1, Scene 5 when we see him beginning to waver:

> The time is out of joint. O cursèd spite
> That ever I was born to set it right!

For a long time after this, Hamlet finds himself unable to 'sweep' to revenge or even focus his mind on the task:

> Yet I,
> A dull and muddy-mettled rascal, peak
> Like John-a-dreams, unpregnant of my cause,
> And can do nothing.

The audience observes his inaction, but, like Hamlet himself, is unsure exactly what causes it.

In these ways, the tragic course of each main character is prepared …

---

2   The draft continued. At the end, the writer added several questions:

   a   Is this sufficiently focused on characterisation?

   b   Am I linking the two plays together enough?

   c   I'm planning to move on to 'Structure and style' next and compare Faustus's and Hamlet's soliloquies. Would this make a smooth link from what I've written?

As a class, discuss and answer the writer's questions.

3 Talk about what you can learn from this draft. Focus on three aspects of it in particular:

    a is it answering the question about the *presentation* of the tragic hero?

    b is the paragraph structure helpful to the reader?

    c are quotations being used for a purpose or are they just being 'offered'?

4 Write a first draft of 'Area of Comparison 1' in your own explorative study. Ask a number of questions at the end to which you genuinely want answers from your teacher.

6 Identifying contexts for your plays

Writing your coursework

Remember that you need to refer in your explorative study to one or more 'illuminator' texts to show the sources of your research.

Assessment objectives

12 marks out of 62 for your explorative study are given for examining the *context* of two plays from 1300 to 1800. You have to 'demonstrate understanding of the significance and influence of the contexts in which literary texts are written and received' (AO4).

Writing about the context of your plays is an important part of the explorative study. This sub-section, therefore, shows you what 'context' means and the kinds of context examiners have in mind. It also shows you how to use illuminator text(s) to find contextual material and how to incorporate this material into your explorative study.

Activity 37

1 Read through the table below at least twice.

Contextual influences on drama 1300–1800		
'Context' refers to the factors that influence:	These contextual factors can be grouped into headings:	These headings relate specifically to:
The dramatist's choice of plot, characters and theme	Literary	• the dramatist's use of their reading
	Social and political	• events and attitudes of the time
	Theatrical	• the tastes of the audience
		• the theatres where drama was performed
The dramatist's choice of genre, style and language	Literary	• the conventions of drama of the time
		• the conventions of drama from the past
	Theatrical	• the tastes of the audience
		• the theatres where drama was performed
The dramatist's way of thinking about life	Literary	• the dramatist's use of their reading
	Social and political	• events and attitudes of the time
	Cultural	• **philosophical** ideas of the time
		• **theological** views and beliefs of the time
The staging of the play	Literary	• the conventions of drama of the time
	Theatrical	• the tastes of the audience
		• the theatres where drama was performed

Note: A dramatist's own life and experience, the personal context, is clearly an important influence on their writing. It is not included in this table because the precise ways in which life influences literature can be speculated about but never ascertained and because relatively little is known for sure about the lives of most dramatists writing between 1300 and 1650, including Shakespeare's.

2 As a class, talk about:

a the headings in the central column (make sure you can differentiate between them)

b the notes in the left- and right-hand columns (make sure you can see how they link to the headings in the central column).

This table provides you with a structure for planning and writing about the context of your main and further plays. Refer to it regularly as you build up your explorative study.

7 Relating your plays to their context: an example

This section explains how to develop a knowledge of context so that you can apply it to your plays. It shows you that contextual factors influence both the way a play is written and the audience's response to it. For this reason, your own interpretation of your coursework plays must take contextual factors into account.

The exemplar play used in this section is Shakespeare's *Macbeth*. Watch a performance of the play on DVD before working on the activities below.

Macbeth (RSC, 2007)

Activity 38

1 Consider the literary contextual factors that influenced *Macbeth*. Use the information below.

Shakespeare's sources

The plot of *Macbeth* is derived from other literature. This was Shakespeare's common practice, as it was with almost all Elizabethan and Jacobean dramatists: they had a different way of thinking about 'originality' from our own model of 'make it up yourself'.

The main source for Macbeth is *Chronicles of England, Scotland and Ireland* compiled by Raphael Holinshed in 1587 (when Shakespeare was 23). Its historical narrative describes how King Duff of Scotland became stricken with a strange illness, which was blamed on a group of witches in the town of Forres. Donwald, captain of the castle of Forres and loyal to the King, broke into the witches' house and found them casting spells against King Duff. The witches were executed and the King cured.

The previously loyal Donwald mounted a rebellion against King Duff and murdered him. Donwald was, in turn, put to death.

King Duncan ascended the Scottish throne. His generals, Macbeth and Banquo defeated an invasion attempt by King Canute of England. Then Macbeth murdered Duncan and took the throne himself, beginning a reign of terror in Scotland that lasted nearly 20 years. Earlier, three witches had prophesied that Macbeth would never be slain by 'one of woman born'. Macduff, loyal to Duncan's son, Malcolm, led an insurrection against Macbeth and killed him in his castle at Dunsinane. Apparently, Macduff had been born by Caesarian section.

---

2 As a class, discuss how Shakespeare makes use of Holinshed's *Chronicle*. Focus on:

a how he adapts events

b how he deliberately changes and merges together some parts of the **chronology**

c why he may have chosen to dramatise the story of Macbeth rather than King Duff and Donwald (Lady Macbeth is a minor figure in Holinshed's *Chronicle*.)

Activity 39

1 Consider some of the social and political contextual factors that influenced *Macbeth*. Use the information below.

King James I

James I of England (James VI of Scotland), a direct descendent of Banquo, succeeded Queen Elizabeth I in 1603. The Act of Union joined the two kingdoms. Elizabeth had not produced a male heir and James's right to the English throne was disputed.

Macbeth was written in 1605 or 1606. James I was a keen **patron** of drama. He gave a royal charter to Shakespeare's theatre company, which took the title of The King's Men in 1603. They performed regularly at court.

James I wrote several treatises on kingship, notably the *Basilicon Doran*, published in 1599. This contains a long section contrasting a good king with a usurping **tyrant**. James I believed firmly that kings were appointed by God and that regicide, the killing of a king, was blasphemy against the natural order of God's world.

James I also had a particular interest in witchcraft. He wrote repeatedly about it, most extensively in his treatise on *Demonology*, published in 1597. Many elements of **demonology** are common to James's writings on the subject and Shakespeare's play: the supernatural powers of witches, their capacity to become invisible and to change shape, their allegiance to the devil, the ingredients of their magic brews.

The Gunpowder Plot failed, but very nearly succeeded, in November 1605. Catholic loyalists tried to blow up King James and his parliament. The Plot was followed by a series of arrests and executions.

---

2 As a class, discuss:

> **Key terms**
> patron
> tyrant
> demonology

   a which events and ideas in *Macbeth* James I would have recognised

   b which political themes would strike a chord with James I's views about, and experiences of, kingship up to 1606

   c whether you agree with those scholars who argue that *Macbeth* was written as a compliment to James I.

Activity 40

1 Consider some of the theatrical contextual factors that influenced *Macbeth*. Use the information below.

Macbeth was acted at the Globe Playhouse, the theatre where The King's Men normally performed. The Globe had a platform stage with a trapdoor, frequently used as a 'hellmouth' (through which demonic characters made entrances and exits). There was no stage lighting and no fixed scenery. Performances took place in the open during the afternoon. In Shakespeare's time, there was a convention for fluid movement between one scene and the next. The actors utilised a large store of 'props', which were used and re-used for two or three different productions a week.

The audiences at the Globe crossed social barriers. They ranged from ordinary workmen and women to highly educated professional people and minor nobility. Between them they had a particular taste for horror, violence and bloodshed; the supernatural, particularly ghosts and witches; battles; colourful spectacle; broad comedy and obscenity; British history (many members of the audience were illiterate and could not read about this); political themes; and debate about philosophical and religious matters.

> **Take it further**
>
> Watch two feature film versions of *Macbeth*: the Japanese *Throne of Blood* and version. Compare these very different Macbeths with the previous performance you watched. What kind of interpretation of the play does each of them make?

2 As a class, discuss:

   a any two scenes from the play: how do you visualise them being performed at the Globe?

   b how well you think *Macbeth* is suited to its contemporary audience

   c how the performance of *Macbeth* you watched was, or was not, comparable in production style to a performance at the Globe in the early 1600s.

8 Building material on context into your explorative study

The contextual influences you highlight in your explorative study will depend on your particular plays. Choose relevant contextual factors from below.

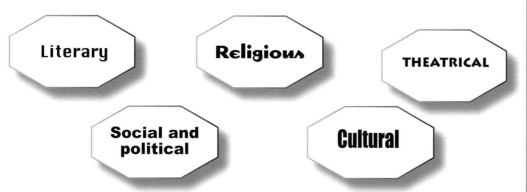

Take it further

Watch a production of *King Lear* on DVD. Use your knowledge of the Jacobean political context to assess how far it reflects the events of its time. Useful contextual comments on this play and many others are made by Emma Smith in *The Cambridge Introduction to Shakespeare*.

The next step is to make an 'Areas of comparison' plan identical to that for the content of your plays (page 153), except for its title. This time create an outline plan entitled 'Contextual factors influencing … (the topic of your explorative study)'.

Activity 41

1 Study the example below of an outline plan for context. It applies to the second half of Assignment 1 on the presentation of the tragic hero in *Dr Faustus* and *Hamlet*.

Contextual factors influencing the presentation of the tragic hero in Dr Faustus and Hamlet

Literary context (1)
Theatrical genres
- <u>Dr Faustus</u>: links with medieval Morality Plays
- <u>Hamlet</u>: links with Elizabethan Revenge Plays

Main play: *Dr Faustus*

Topic: Presentation of the tragic hero

Literary context (2)
Dramatic genre of tragedy
- <u>Dr Faustus</u>: tragic hero's fatal flaw = pride, ambition
- <u>Hamlet</u>: tragic hero's fatal flaw = indecision, inaction (arguably)

Further play: *Hamlet*

Religious context of Christian belief
- <u>Dr Faustus</u>: damnation awaits if man challenges God's supremacy
- <u>Hamlet</u>: damnation awaits if man commits murder

Cultural context of Renaissance philosophy
- <u>Dr Faustus</u>: idea of man in charge of his own destiny
- <u>Hamlet</u>: idea of man in charge of his own destiny

Independent research

Make a study of the acting conditions and the audiences at the Globe between 1599 and 1610. Among the useful sources are Glynne Wickham, *Early English Stages*; de Gracia and Wells, *The Cambridge Companion to Shakespeare*; Stanley Wells, *Shakespeare for All Time*; James Shapiro, *1599: A Year in the Life of William Shakespeare*.

2 Follow this model to make a provisional outline plan for context on your own topic.

9 Writing about context

Activity 42

Independent research

Research in detail one contextual influence (cultural, religious or theatrical) of your main play. You might choose sources from the reading list printed on page 167.

1 Read part of an explorative study comparing *King Lear* and *Macbeth* as fatally flawed kings. The writer chose to write about social and political contextual factors.

> Both 'King Lear' (1605–6) and 'Macbeth' (1605–8) were written at a time when kingship and the role of the monarch in a well-ordered society were of great concern to Jacobean audiences. James I ascended the throne in 1603, thus nominally uniting England and Scotland. But a period of political instability followed. James I was a Protestant king and the Catholic-led Gunpowder Plot of 1605 was one of several insurrections showing there was strong opposition to his rule. Emma Smith writes in 'The Cambridge Introduction to Shakespeare' (2007): 'The political buzzwords of 1605 were "unification of the kingdoms", just in the way that "weapons of mass destruction" and "I did not have sexual relations with that woman, Miss Lewinsky" have become the political buzzwords of our own day'.
>
> This political background to the new king's accession shaped Shakespeare's presentation of 'King Lear'. Almost the first words of the play refer to 'the division of the kingdom' of ancient Britain and the Earl of Gloucester, an experienced diplomat, clearly disapproves of Lear's plans to parcel it out to his three daughters and the husbands he has arranged for them:
>
>> but now, in the division of the kingdom, it appears not which of the Dukes he values most; for equalities are so weigh'd that curiosity in neither can make choice of either's moiety.
>
> When Lear enters, he immediately calls for a map, something that would have struck a strong chord with contemporary audiences:
>
>> Meantime, we shall express our darker purpose.
>> Give me the map there. Know that we have divided
>> In three our kingdom …
>
> James I justified his plan for uniting England and Scotland by commissioning maps of ancient Britain, the period in which 'King Lear' is set, to show that one monarch could successfully rule both kingdoms.

2 As a class, discuss what you can learn from this extract about how to take account of contextual factors. Focus on:

a its relevance to the topic – Shakespeare's presentation of fatally flawed kings

b the way research into context is combined with analysis of the text

c how effective you think the style is.

3 Make a final version of your outline plan for context. Then use it to draft two or three paragraphs of your explorative study.

Writing your coursework

For your explorative study, remember to

- settle on a topic you are interested in and confident about
- plan the 'Areas of comparison' thoroughly before you begin to write
- draw comparisons between the two plays (do not write about each in isolation)
- integrate material on context into your comparative analysis
- plan how to use your illuminator text
- make full use of the opportunity to write over a period of time (not in a rush); plan and redraft, maintain a dialogue with your teacher and polish your writing style.

10 The history of English drama, 1300–1800

This chart will help you to 'place' your two coursework plays and identify some of the contextual factors that influenced them.

The history of English drama, 1300–1800 – an outline

Main features of drama	Main plays and playwrights	Contexts
Medieval and Tudor (1300–1558)		
• Mainly religious, based on stories from the Bible • Mystery Plays performed by ordinary people belonging to **craft guilds** • Mystery Plays performed in cycles of 10 to 20+ episodes or 'pageants' • Tudor **Interludes** performed at country houses and Inns of Court in London	• Mystery Plays: originated in church services when parts were read by priests and congregation • York, Chester, Wakefield and Coventry *Mystery Play Cycles*: anonymous • Morality Plays represented **vices** and **virtues** as **stock characters** – *Everyman, The Castle of Perseverance,* anonymous	• A largely illiterate population • The Black Death • The Hundred Years' War • The Peasants' Revolt (1381) • *The Canterbury Tales*, Geoffrey Chaucer (1387) • Caxton's Printing Press (1470s)
Elizabethan (1558–1603)		
• Drama becoming increasingly popular and commercial • Many public theatres built in London from 1570 onwards: open roofs, platform stages • Professional acting companies formed: male actors only • A variety of genres: histories, comedies, tragedies, satires	• *The Spanish Tragedy*, Thomas Kyd (1558–94) • *Tamburlaine the Great, Dr Faustus,* Christopher Marlowe (1564-93) • William Shakespeare (1564–1616) • *Volpone, The Alchemist,* Ben Jonson (1572–1637)	• Elizabeth I (1558–1603) • Sir Francis Drake circumnavigates the globe (1577–80) • *Chronicles*, Raphael Holinshed (1577) • Thomas North's translation of Plutarch's *Great Lives* (1579) • *Essays*, Sir Francis Bacon (1597)
Jacobean (1603–25)		
• Indoor theatres established in London (eg Blackfriars): boys' acting companies • Strong Puritan opposition to public theatres • Court **masques** and civic pageants: elaborate scenic effects • Revenge Tragedy and City Comedy increasingly popular	• *The Duchess of Malfi, The White Devil,* John Webster (1580?–1625?) • *The Revenger's Tragedy,* Middleton/Tourneur • *The Changeling,* Middleton/Rowley • *'Tis Pity She's a Whore,* John Ford (1586–1640)	• James I (1603–25) • Rise of Puritan influence • Pilgrim Fathers sail for America (1620) • English Civil War (1642–1651) • All theatres closed by law (1642)
Restoration (1660–1700)		
• Prohibition of public drama lifted: theatres re-opened • New theatre building in London and the provinces: **proscenium arch** stages • Lavish scenery and lighting effects • Comedy of Manners popular: themes of sexual intrigue and 'town versus country' in witty prose dramas • Women allowed to act by law for the first time	• *The Man of Mode,* George Etheredge (1635–92) • *The Rover,* Aphra Behn (1640–89) • *The Country Wife, The Plain Dealer,* William Wycherley (1640–1716) • *Love for Love, The Way of the World,* William Congreve (1670–1729)	• Restoration of the monarchy • Charles II (1660–85) • Samuel Pepys's *Diary* (1660–9) • *Paradise Lost*, John Milton (1667) • John Locke's *Essay on Human Understanding* (1690) • Satirical poems by John Dryden, John Wilmot, Earl of Rochester and others

Main features of drama	Main plays and playwrights	Contexts
Eighteenth century (1700–1800)		
• Sentimental Comedy a popular dramatic genre • Increase in the range of genres: pantomime, ballad opera, heroic tragedy • New theatres built in London and major towns and cities: elaborate architecture matched by elaborate stage scenery and costumes • Professional actor-managers (e.g Garrick at Drury Lane)	• *The Beggar's Opera*, John Gay (1695–1732) • *She Stoops To Conquer*, Oliver Goldsmith (1730–74) • *The Rivals, The School for Scandal*, Richard Brinsley Sheridan (1751–1816) • *The Enchanted Isle*, an operatic version of Shakespeare's *The Tempest* performed frequently	• The Age of Enlightenment: belief in rationalism, scientific progress and high culture • Stage Licensing Act (1737) • Dr Johnson's *Dictionary* published in 1755 • The rise of the novel (Defoe, Richardson, Fielding) and the educated middle class • *The Dunciad, The Rape of the Lock*, Alexander Pope (1688–1744) – social and political satires

Key terms

craft guilds

vice

virtue

stock characters

Interlude

masque

proscenium arch

D Exploring others' reactions to plays

1 Introduction

In your explorative study you need to take account of how other readers have interpreted your chosen plays *over time*, i.e. from when the plays were first performed to the present day.

This section shows you how to trace and make use of others' interpretations in your explorative study. Take 'other readers' to mean: theatre directors, actors and dramatists; literary critics and academic commentators; audiences and theatre critics. Use the general term **critical reception** to refer to the reactions and interpretations of these three groups.

Assessment objectives

AO3 states that 'the interpretations of other readers' must 'inform' the way you analyse and compare your plays. This means using your knowledge of other texts to develop your line of argument, which can include analysing their interpretations in a critical way.

2 The range of critical reception: an example

You need to watch a stage production of Shakespeare's *The Tempest* OR a production of the play on DVD OR the DVD of Derek Jarman's film, *Tempest* (1980) before working on the activities below.

Activity 43

1 Read the synopsis of the play below. The synopsis was written by Kathy Elgin in the programme for a Royal Shakespeare Company production in 1998.

The play

Twelve years ago Prospero, the Duke of Milan, was usurped by his brother Antonio, with the help of Alonso, King of Naples, and the King's brother Sebastian. Cast adrift in a boat with his baby daughter Miranda, Prospero landed on an island where ever since, by the use of his magic art, he has ruled over the spirit Ariel and the savage Caliban. Now he uses his powers to raise a storm that will shipwreck his enemies and work his revenge.

On the island the shipwrecked travellers are separated. The King of Naples searches for his son Ferdinand, although believing him drowned: Sebastian, the King's brother, plots to kill him and usurp the crown: the drunken butler, Stephano, and the jester, Trinculo, are persuaded by Caliban to kill Prospero so that they can rule the island.

Ferdinand meets Miranda and they fall in love. Prospero sets heavy tasks to test Ferdinand, and then presents the young couple with a betrothal masque celebrating chastity and the blessings of marriage. With his enemies finally brought before him, Prospero forgives them. He grants Ariel his freedom and prepares to leave the island.

2 With a partner, talk about:

a which aspects of the play's plot the production you watched brought out particularly strongly

b your reaction to the way Caliban and Ariel were portrayed. Did either or both of them arouse your sympathy?

c how the video portrayed Prospero. As a magician with awesome powers; loving father; bullying tyrant; wise ruler; or broken man?

d how the production made use of visual spectacle and music.

Activity 44

1 Read the following summary of the stage history of *The Tempest* in the seventeenth and eighteenth centuries.

Seventeenth- and eighteenth-century reception of *The Tempest*

The Tempest, the last play Shakespeare wrote unassisted by other dramatists, was first performed in 1611. It must have been popular with audiences at Blackfriars, the indoor playhouse where The King's Men performed, and at the Globe, since it was placed first in the Shakespeare *Folio*, a collection of his plays brought out by two surviving members of his company in 1623. (Shakespeare died in 1616.)

Public theatres in England were closed down by an act of parliament in 1642. After they reopened, John Dryden and William Davenant, who claimed to be Shakespeare's illegitimate son, staged a production of *The Tempest* in 1667. They sub-titled it *The Enchanted Isle* and substantially rewrote it. Miranda was given a sister, Dorinda, and Ferdinand a brother, Hippolito, who was played by a woman. Dryden noted that his co-dramatist 'designed the adaptation to Shakespeare's plot, namely that of a man who had never seen a woman, [so] that these two characters of innocence and love might the more illustrate and commend each other'. Visual spectacle and music were central to the performance.

The diarist Samuel Pepys saw this production. He noted appreciatively in November 1667: 'The [play]house mighty full, the king [Charles I] and the Court there, and the most innocent play that I ever saw, and a curious piece of Musique in an Echo of half-sentences, the Echo repeating the former half while the man goes on to the latter, which is mighty pretty. The play no great wit, but yet good, above ordinary plays'.

The Dryden-Davenant *The Tempest* was used by the poet laureate, Thomas Shadwell for a further adaptation in 1674, this time into a spectacular opera with music by the English composer, Henry Purcell. This was the version of the play audiences saw until the later eighteenth century. There were no others. A play bill of 1838 shows that Dorinda and Hippolito were still leading characters.

---

2 Refer to the production you watched to discuss with a partner why *The Tempest* might have appealed as an opera to seventeenth- and eighteenth-century audiences.

3 As a class, talk about the possible reasons why seventeenth- and eighteenth-century dramatists 'adapted' Shakespeare so freely. Use what you know of the historical and cultural context to consider these factors:

a the acting facilities in their theatres

b a desire to please audiences with entertainment suited to the taste of the times

c the repeal of the law prohibiting women from acting on stage

d a different view of human life and society from that current in Jacobean times.

Activity 45

1 Read the information below about the critical reception of *The Tempest* in the nineteenth century.

Nineteenth-century reception of *The Tempest*

In 1838, the theatre director, William Macready was the first to stage *The Tempest* in something like its original form.

Nineteenth-century critics and commentators generally saw *The Tempest* as 'a specimen of the Romantic drama: i.e. a drama which arises from its fitness to that faculty of our nature, the imagination, which gives no allegiance to time and place' (Samuel Taylor Coleridge, 1812). Willam Hazlitt considered the play to be 'a fantastic creation of [Shakespeare's] mind which haunts the imagination with a sense of truth … the real characters and events partake of the wildness of a dream' (*The Characters of Shakespear's Plays*, 1817). He meant this as high praise. Nineteenth-century Romanticism celebrated the power of the imagination to transcend the limits of ordinary life, transforming it through vision and symbol into 'something rich and strange', as Ferdinand says in the play. Prospero thus became, for Romantic critics, a myth-maker, an exemplar of the creative imagination, who has the power through his 'most potent art' to reorder the world.

Late nineteenth-century critics tended to read all of Shakespeare's plays 'in terms of a psycho-biography that could be recovered from the texts' (Trevor Griffiths, *The Shakespeare Handbook*, 2007). Prospero was seen as a Shakespeare figure and *The Tempest* as his farewell to the stage. Edward Dowden wrote in 1901: 'We identify Prospero in some measure with Shakespeare himself … because the temper of Prospero, the grave harmony of his character, his sensitiveness to wrong, his unfaltering justice, a certain remoteness from the common joys and sorrows of the world, are characteristic of Shakespeare as discovered to us in all his latest plays' (Edward Dowden, *Shakespeare: A Critical Study of his Mind and Art*, 1901).

This search for Shakespeare-the-man in *The Tempest* was extended by other nineteenth-century critics well beyond Prospero. Ariel represented his spiritual instincts, Caliban his bodily ones, Antonio and Sebastian his potential for sin, Gonzalo his potential for goodness. The island setting became a projection of Shakespeare's fertile imagination, his abandonment of it at the end of the play a symbol of his retirement from the theatre. (In 1610, he left London to live with his family in Stratford on Avon):

> But this rough magic
> I here abjure …
> I'll break my staff,
> Bury it certain fathoms in the earth,
> And deeper than did ever plummet sound
> I'll drown my book' *(solemn music)*

---

2 Look back over the critical material you have read so far. Use it to make brief notes about:

   a the different perspectives of critics/commentators from the seventeenth to the nineteenth centuries

   b the way in which critics/commentators find in *The Tempest* a reflection of their own day and age.

Then share your findings with the class.

Begin to research information about the critical reception of your main coursework play over a period of 100 years. Make notes on everything you find that relates clearly to the topic of your explorative study. There is a list of reference books you might use and websites you might visit on page 167.

Activity 47

Take it further

Read the comments of John Dryden, William Hazlitt and S.T. Coleridge on your Shakespeare play(s). How do their accounts reflect what you know of their day and age?

Assessment objectives

AO3: 'Explore connections and comparisons between texts, *informed by the interpretations of other readers'.*

1   Read the information below about the critical reception of *The Tempest* in the twentieth-century.

Twentieth-century reception of *The Tempest*

At the start of the twentieth century, when the foundations of the British Empire began to weaken, critical interest in *The Tempest* focused on its colonial theme. Caliban was seen variously as a slave, a black man or a proletarian; Prospero as an oppressor, a white colonist or a capitalist.

Literary criticism became a profession in the mid-twentieth century after English Literature was admitted into the university curriculum. Influential academic critics such as G. Wilson-Knight saw *The Tempest* less as a stage play than as a 'dramatic poem'. The method of 'practical criticism', close reading of the text, led him and others to find 'a harmony of metaphorical design' in the play, 'linked through almost inexhaustible analogies'. 'Key metaphors' were discovered in the dramatist's use of imagery, which highlighted, according to Reuben A. Brower, 'six main continuities: strange-wondrous, sleep-and-dream, sea-tempest, music-and-noise, earth-air, slavery-freedom' (*Fields of Light*, 1951). Through such metaphorical patterning 'key themes' emerged which carried the play's meaning.

Recent literary criticism of *The Tempest* has explored historical factors which may have influenced the play. So-called New Historicist commentators such as Stephen Greenblatt see the play as Shakespeare's 'American Fable', depicting the way colonists (like Prospero) reacted to the wild, uncivilised Americas discovered during Elizabethan times by Sir Francis Drake and others.

Feminist criticism of *The Tempest* has been prolific, despite the fact that only one of its characters is female. Silvia Frederici's study *Caliban and the Witch: Women, the Body and Primitive Accommodation* (2004), claims that Sycorax the witch, Caliban's mother, is 'the embodiment of those female subjects that capitalism had to destroy: the heretic, the healer, the disobedient wife, the woman who dared to live alone, the obeah woman who poisoned the master's food and inspired the slaves to revolt'. The influence on such a reading of anthropology, increasingly studied at university, is clear.

---

2   As a class, look back over the critical material you have read in this sub-section. Talk and make notes about:

   a the different kinds of 'critical reception' likely to be relevant to your plays

   b what uses you might make of these in the course of your study

   c how you can use them to meet the requirements of AO3.

Activity 48

Now you need to add to the research you have begun. Search for critical reception relating to the topic of your explorative study in these four sources.

- The Introductions and Notes to the editions of the plays you are using. These will, at the very least, point you in the right direction. For critical reception of Shakespeare, the Arden editions are excellent, as are the New Mermaids and The Revels Plays series for Jacobean, Restoration and eighteenth-century plays.
- The theatrical history of your plays. (See the suggested Reading List below)
- Works by academic critics and commentators. (See the suggested Reading List below)
- The internet. (See the suggested list of websites on page below)

The golden rules for this research task are:

- be thorough: don't rely on only one source
- be focused: before you start to research: clarify the topic of your explorative study and only collect material that is strictly relevant to it
- be selective: don't allow yourself to become overwhelmed with material you will not need.

Suggested reading

The following sources are likely to be helpful to your search for critical reception.

Aughterson, K – *The English Renaissance: An Anthology of Sources and Documents*

Bate, J – *The Genius of Shakespeare*

Belsey, C – *The Subject of Tragedy*

Bradley, AC – *Shakespearean Tragedy*

Brooke, N – *Horrid Laughter in Jacobean Tragedy*

Chambers, EK – *The Elizabethan Stage*

Cotton, N – *Women Playwrights in England*

de Gracia, M and Wells, S – *The Cambridge Companion to Shakespeare*

Duffy, M – *The Passionate Shepherdess: Aphra Behn*

George, DM – *London Life in the Eighteenth Century*

Greenblatt, S – *Will in the World*

Griswold, W – *City Comedy and Revenge Tragedy in the London Theatre: 1576–1980*

Hogan, CB – *The London Stage 1776–1800*

Hunter, GK – *John Webster: A Critical Anthology*

Jacoby, S – *Wild Justice: the Acting of Revenge*

Kermode, F – *Shakespeare's Language*

Knights, LC – *Explorations*

Kott, J – *Shakespeare Our Contemporary*

Levin, H – *Marlowe the Overreacher*

Maguire, L – *A Feminist Companion to Shakespeare*

Palfrey, S – *Doing Shakespeare*

Rice, P and Waugh, P – *Modern Literary Theory*

Rossiter, AP – *English Drama from Early Times to the Elizabethans*

Shapiro, J – *1599: A Year in the Life of William Shakespeare*

Smith, E – *The Cambridge Introduction to Shakespeare*

Spurgeon, C – *Shakespeare's Imagery and What It Tells Us*

Wells, S – *Shakespeare: an Oxford Guide*

Wickham, G – *Early English Stages 1300–1660*

Suggested websites

The following sites are likely to be helpful in your search for critical reception.

www.rsc.org.uk

www.nationaltheatre.org.uk

www.shakespeare.org.uk/main/3/339

www.shakespeares-globe.org

www.shakespeareswords.com/

www.propeller.org.uk

4 Including critical reception in your explorative study

The main focus of your explorative study is *comparison*. The secondary focus is *context*. Your comments on critical reception should be introduced at points *where they help you to compare your plays in their contexts*.

Activity 49

1 Read the example below of the use of critical reception. It is taken from an explorative study comparing Prospero's use of magic power in *The Tempest* with Faustus's in *Dr Faustus*.

The Tempest (RSC, 1982)

> The consensus of critical opinion is that Prospero uses his magic powers creatively for the common good, whereas Faustus uses his magic powers transgressively and solely for his own ends. At the crisis of 'The Tempest', Prospero has to resolve a deep inner conflict between using 'my most potent art' to punish his enemies or forgive them:
>
>> Though with their high wrongs I am struck to th'quick,
>> Yet with my nobler reason 'gainst my fury
>> Do I take part: the rarer action is
>> In virtue than in vengeance.
>
> The temptation to punish others for the wrongs they did him in the past is strong: 'Most cruelly/Didst thou, Alonso, use me and my daughter.' Yet he does forgive even Antonio, 'who to call brother would even infect my mouth': 'I do forgive thee,/ Unnatural as thou art'.
>   Not all critics, however, see Prospero as a compassionate, selfless ruler. According to Robert Wilson,
>
>> Prospero has played God: 'graves at my command/Have waked their sleepers, oped, and let them forth/By my so potent art.' It is a blatant assumption of divine power, a meddling with life and death. Prospero is caught up in a sort of inflated admiration for his own power.'
>
> Such an interpretation makes Prospero seem remarkably like Faustus: 'A sound magician is a demi-god'.
>   Although most commentators see Faustus as being unheroic, unlike Prospero, the atheist critic, J.D. Pandowski takes a different line. To him, Faustus is a humanist hero whose use of magic simply reflects all men's desire to know what Christianity forbids. 'Which is better,' asks Pandowski, 'to submit meekly to an outdated religious doctrine based on punishment and repression or to reach exhilaratingly for the stars?'
>   My own view of these two magicians falls between Wilson's and Pandowski's ...

Dr Faustus (Minerva Theatre, 2004)

2 As a class, discuss how well critical reception is used to develop his own ideas. Focus on:

a the way other readers' interpretations are introduced

b the purpose for which they are introduced

c what you think you can learn from this example.

5 Using critical reception by theatre professionals in your explorative study

Some of the most illuminating critical responses to plays come from the professionals of the theatre – directors, actors and theatre critics. This section shows you how to track down their comments and then select from and integrate them into your explorative study. You can also add them to your collection of 'formats for writing about drama' to use as possible models for your creative critical response.

Activity 50

1 Read the following comments by theatre directors.

Text A:

Sir Peter Hall directed Marlowe's *Tamburlaine the Great* (1587) at the National Theatre in 1976. His *Diaries* describe some early rehearsals.

Friday, 18 June

Big inquest this afternoon with the full Tamburlaine Company. I tried to explain what we'd found in the last weeks. The actors must represent a character rather than being it. They should present the narrative and the emotion to the audience, and ask for a judgement from them, support or denial. This doesn't mean they shouldn't feel; they must. But they need a powerful sense of narrative, plus emotion. They are all also, in a sense, opera singers. They have specific little solos which have to be fully taken. The play is an intricate mosaic of extreme emotions and there is no bridge from one to another. It is the break from one mood to another which gives the play its vitality. We have seven weeks before the first dress rehearsal, and a great deal of work to do.

Sunday, 20 June

Something further to note about Tamburlaine. I have never worked on an Elizabethan text with a more precise structure, in its scenes, its writing, and its people. I now believe that no scholar has properly understood what is going on. It is very calculated. Not primitive.

Tuesday, 3 August

On to the outside terraces where we did about an hour of Tamburlaine. Revelation. Dennis Quilley immediately started talking to bystanders, and his performance became free, open and necessary. It's a curious thing to me that there have been many attempts to recreate the Elizabethan stage, but has anybody understood that the basic thing about Elizabethan theatre is that it was played in daylight? The actor saw the eyes of the audience.

Another interesting thing about Tamburlaine: it has to be high, astounding and unsubtle because it was designed to interest and excite a noisy and unsophisticated audience. It's a bit like the great epics of early silent movies. It works in broad ways.

Text B:

When Max Stafford-Clark directed George Farquahar's play, *The Recruiting Officer* (1702), his notes took the form of letters to the dramatist. They are published in *Letters to George* (1989).

Thursday, 14 July 1988

Dear George,

Today I learned to love the last scene. Of course, the play is a romantic comedy that ends with two marriages. I think I told you that we don't have plays like that any more. In fact, this is the first play I've directed that has romance as the mainspring of its plot. And it's very moving.

Your predecessors, the Jacobeans, were more concerned with lust than romance, which is why their plays were deemed crude and unsuitable by eighteenth-century theatre managers, who, I'm sure, were assessing their market correctly. Meanwhile, here at the latter end of the twentieth century, we currently have a grim pleasure in doom. Most plays now end pessimistically. The hero does not get the loot or the girl. This is the Eighties.

As the Left has failed to unite and present a coherent critical voice against Mrs Thatcher and Thatcherism, responsibility for the voice of opposition has been taken up by theatre and television.

Your situation was very different, George, and although your plays are critical of aspects of the society you lived in, they are, on the whole, plays of celebration. They celebrate an England in harmony with itself. You, Vanbrugh and Mrs Centlivre were the three most successful writers in the early eighteenth century, and you were all Whigs supporting a Whig government who had just won a famous Whig victory. To place a serving officer as a hero of a play, as you do in *The Recruiting Officer*, would have been inconceivable to a Tory writer like Dryden or Swift. In 1710 a Tory ministry came to power again. It was three years after your death. I'm sorry we never got to see your plays of opposition.

2 As a class, talk about:

a how you might use Peter Hall's comments about *Tamburlaine the Great* and its Elizabethan audience if you were writing an explorative study of it

b how you might use Max Stafford-Clark's comments about the eighteenth- and twentieth-century contexts of The Recruiting Officer if you were writing an explorative study of it.

3 Then consider what insights theatre directors give you into critical reception that literary critics and academics do not.

Activity 51

1 Read the following comments by actors.

Richard III (RSC, 1984)

Text A:

Antony Sher played the lead in Shakespeare's *Richard III* for the Royal Shakespeare Company in 1984. This extract from his diary describes a rehearsal five weeks before the production opened.

Wednesday, 9 May

A bad day.

Queen Margaret scene. This morning Bill [Alexander, the director] comes in and talks to the cast about finding more tribal / animal behaviour. Getting away from the stiff formality of history-play acting.

Bill has always been open about how uncomfortable he feels with improvisations, workshops and exercises. Unfortunately, for something like this, it's the only way. Instead Bill suggests running the scene 'trying to be more bestial'.

The result is a disaster. Behaviour not from the animal world but the world of pantomime. Cackling laughter. Food being thrown around, sinewy 'wicked' acting. Although I'm participating and probably responsible for some of the worst excesses, I can hardly bear to watch the others. In one fell swoop there is a vision of how ludicrous this play can be if we don't get it right. The endless suffering, squabbling and cursing.

The rehearsal ends with extreme dishonesty. We all mutter the usual bullshit ('Well, we've got a basic shape to work from') instead of sitting down and saying 'That was terrible, that was embarrassing, we must never be so bad again'.

Text B:

David Troughton played *Richard III* for the Royal Shakespeare Company in 1995. This extract from his essay about the production describes how he approached acting Richard's disability.

'Deformed, unfinished, sent before my time
Into this breathing world scarce half made up …'

Shakespeare tells us that Richard 'halts', has a 'crook-back' and a 'blasted sapling' of a withered arm. There is no getting away from this, so addressing the problem early was of the utmost importance. What is the nature of the deformity and how to display it comfortably and with complete safety?

According to history, Richard had come into the world feet first, a breach birth – his mother speaks of a horrendous delivery. Having experimented for a few days with deformed feet and various limps, I decided to talk to Steve Young, an orthopaedic surgeon and a friend of mine. I asked him how this difficult entry into the world might have affected the baby. He was very exact in his reply: hip dislocation. As Richard grew up, because of the pain of walking, a severe limp would develop, forcing his spine to grow crooked, giving the appearance of one shoulder being higher than the other. His arm could also have been deformed at birth or through an illness such as polio.

In pain all his life? What an insight into a character. Here was one very simple explanation of Richard's malevolence.

2   With a partner, talk about:

   a   the different aspects of *Richard III* these actors were exploring

   b   what insights you get from their accounts of the process of building up a performance

   c   how you might use their comments if you were writing about the critical reception of *Richard III* in your explorative study.

3   Research accounts by actors of performing in one or both of your coursework plays. Some fruitful sources are listed in the independent research box.

Independent research

The six-volume *Players of Shakespeare* series (Cambridge University Press) contains actors' essays on almost all the main parts in Shakespeare's plays.

For productions of plays by other dramatists, try the following sources:
www.arts.guardian.co.uk
www.bbc.co.uk/radio4/arts

www.telegraph.co.uk/arts
www.encoretheatremagazine.co.uk
www.arts4schools.com
www.britishteatreguide.org.uk
www.thestage.co.uk

Activity 52

1   Read the following reviews by theatre critics.

These two newspaper reviews are of productions of Shakespeare's *Twelfth Night*. The first describes a Royal Shakespeare Company production in 2007.

Text A:

Twelfth Night: Not sexy, just self-indulgent

You might have thought there was plenty of sexual ambiguity and gender confusion in *Twelfth Night* already, but there clearly isn't for that most subtly subversive of gay directors, Neil Bartlett.

Viola, perhaps the most beguiling heroine in Shakespearean comedy, is here played by a male actor rather than a young woman. It's true that Viola spends most of the play disguised as a boy, Cesario, and that in Shakespeare's time all female parts were played by boys. But that was the convention of the age, and I think that we have the advantage over Shakespeare's audiences in watching women played by women.

Put simply, it seems to me to be funnier, sexier and more emotionally complex to watch a woman pretending to be a man than watching a young man pretending to be a woman.

The fascinating sexual ambiguity of the play – in which both Orsino and Olivia find themselves besotted with the same ambiguous youth – here becomes little more than an explicitly gay reading of this most haunting and bittersweet of comedies. Olivia loves a young man, but he cannot return her affection because he is besotted by Orsino, who also comes to realise that he has fallen for someone of the same sex.

It seems a trite, reductive reading, and in Chris New's performance, apart from an opening sequence in unconvincing drag, there is no attempt to capture Viola's femininity. He just comes over as a strangely charmless, somewhat priggish gay young man.

Ingenious though it is, the production often feels like a directorial commentary on the play, rather than a genuine attempt to penetrate the mysterious heart of Shakespeare's drama.

Charles Spencer, *The Daily Telegraph*

Text B is a review of a Royal Shakespeare Company Production of *Twelfth Night* in 1955.

At Stratford-upon-Avon Sir John Gielgud's production of *Twelfth Night* trod softly but sternly on the dream that Shakespearean comedy was a world of gaiety and refreshment. An astringent frost nipped the play, leaving bleakness behind it and an impression for which the polite word would be 'formal' and the exact word 'mechanical'. A frigid charm was sought and achieved, in pursuance of which Sir John muted the clowns, so that we got no more than a whisper of Maria from Miss Angela Baddeley, and from Mr Alan Webb no Sir Toby at all. The comics were clearly warned to be on their best behaviour, on pain of expulsion from the soirée. Carousing is frowned upon; and the warmth normally generated by even the worst performance of the play is shunned as a corrupting plague.

In applying his novocaine injections Sir John finds an ideal accomplice in Miss Vivien Leigh, who buries her stock-in-trade, brittle vivacity beneath a dazzling vocal monotony, unchanging in pace, pitch, tone or emphasis. This Viola does not, as she promises, speak 'in many sorts of music'; she commands but one sort, a music recognisable to sheltering wayfarers as that of steady rain on corrugated tin roofing. No trace of ardour disturbs this small tranquillity.

Remains Sir Laurence Olivier, whose sun peeped through the chintz curtains of this production and might, with any help, have blazed. Hints abounded of a wholly original Malvolio; a self-made snob, aspiring to consonance with the quality but betrayed by vowels from Golders Green. Malvolio was seen from his own point of view instead of (as usually) Sir Toby's. Yet the sketch remained an outline; a diverting exercise, but scarcely the substance of Sir Laurence's vocation.

Kenneth Tynan, *The Observer*

Take it further

Watch productions of *Twelfth Night* and *Richard III* on DVD. Write reviews of them in which you show how they develop your thinking about the differences between comedy and tragedy.

2 With a partner, talk about:

  a what each critic dislikes about the production

  b whether the critics' judgements are based mainly on the performances or on their view of the play

  c which critic's style of writing makes the greater impact on you, and why.

3 Share your ideas with the class.

6 Summing up this section

This section has shown you the importance to your explorative study of reading a range of critical reception relating to your plays *and* to performances of them; using critical reception to help develop your own view of your play; and integrating comments on critical reception into your comparative analysis

Refer frequently to the material in this section when you are planning, drafting and writing your explorative study.

Writing your coursework

The texts used in this sub-section provide you with further style models to consider when deciding on your creative critical response.

Assessment objectives

Both AO3 and AO4, two of the four Assessment objectives applied to your explorative study, test your knowledge and use of critical reception. You cannot afford to 'overlook' it.

E Writing your explorative study

This section helps you to produce the final version of your explorative study by drawing together the advice for planning and drafting your study given in Sections C and D. It gives you further guidance on how to write in the way examiners will reward, based on the Assessment objectives used to assess your work.

1 Meeting the Assessment objectives

Assessment objectives

The criteria you need to meet for your explorative study are expressed by the examiners like this:

AO1 (6 marks): Articulate creative, informed and relevant responses to literary texts, using appropriate terminology and concepts, and coherent, accurate written expression.

AO2 (8 marks): Demonstrate detailed critical understanding in analysing the ways in which structure, form and language shape meanings in literary texts.

AO3 (36 marks): Explore connections and comparisons between different literary texts, informed by interpretations of other readers.

AO4 (12 marks): Demonstrate understanding of the significance and influence of the context in which literary texts are written and received.

The Assessment objectives can be summarised as follows:

1   Compare your two plays with a sense of purpose.
2   Show how contextual factors influenced the way your plays were written and performed.
3   Show how your plays have been interpreted by readers over time.
4   Show how your plays have been received by audiences over time.
5   Write in the form of an argument, not just a description.

All five of these points are important, but points **1** and **2** are vital. Comparing your plays in their contexts is the key to a successful explorative study. The majority of marks are given for this.

You can use your further play chiefly to bring out points about your main one. However, the comparative method remains fundamental to the way you write the whole explorative study. Use your 'illuminator' text(s) to introduce comments on context. Make sure you specify your sources either in the body of your study or in the bibliography.

The typical word count of an explorative study is between 1500 and 2000 words.

Remember, the maximum word count for your *whole* coursework folder is 2500 words including quotations.

2 Making sure you compare: some strategies

By now you will have decided which is your main play and your further play, and chosen the illuminator text(s) you are going to use for context. You will have made an 'areas of comparison' plan (pages 153 and 154) and written at least a partial draft based on your plan.

The following suggestions will help you ensure that you make comparisons and connections throughout your explorative study. Remember that comparison means bringing out the similarities and differences, not just the differences.

1   Use two highlighters as you go through your plan and draft: one colour for your main play, one for your further play. This will show you at a glance the degree of attention you have paid to each play and any parts of your plan or draft where you are not comparing, or not comparing enough.

2   The two most effective ways of showing that you are comparing are to make comparisons within each paragraph or to use alternate paragraphs to bring out comparisons – the first paragraph about your main play, the following one about your further play.

Look back at the examples of writing on pages 155 and 160 to see both these methods in practice. They are used well.

3   Remember that you should write most about your main play and use your further play to bring out comparisons and connections. However, it is inadvisable to devote the main bulk of your explorative study to one play and a separate section near the end to your other play. If you do this, you run the risk that your comparison will get 'lost' in the gap and you will fall into writing description rather than argument.

4   Precise paragraphing is vital. It shows the reader whether or not your explorative study has a clear structure and how well it has been planned. Spend time getting it right.

5   Signpost the fact that you are comparing by using discourse markers, familiar from your argued writing at GCSE, such as 'However …', 'On the other hand …', 'Similarly …', 'By contrast …', 'Whereas …' and so on. However, use discourse markers judiciously. Over-using them can make your writing style seem mechanical rather than fluent.

6   Make sure you write a *comparative conclusion* to your explorative study. Pick out the two or three key points of comparison you have developed throughout the essay. Then summarise them in a final paragraph. Refer to both plays and make final comments on the key points you have established.

3 Making sure you argue: some strategies

Activity 53

1 As a class, look at these three titles for explorative studies.

> **a** Compare Shakespeare's presentation of women in *The Taming of the Shrew* with Aphra Behn's presentation of women in *The Rover*.

> **b** It has been suggested that both Middleton in *The Changeling* and Shakespeare in *The Winter's Tale* explore obsessive-compulsive behaviour. Compare the ways in which they do so.

> **c** In *As You Like It* Shakespeare uses comedy to celebrate romantic love; in *She Stoops to Conquer* Goldsmith uses comedy to mock it. Compare the dramatists' use of comedy to achieve their different purposes.

Bear in mind that 'argue' means 'present and sustain a point of view'. It does *not* mean 'say which is right and which is wrong' – as you might do, for example, if you were giving your opinion about abortion or lowering the age for voting. The title of your explorative study should reflect the fact that you are presenting a viewpoint. This will help you to avoid just describing what happens.

In the light of this, talk about how any or all of the titles above might give rise to an *argued* study. It does not matter whether or not you know the plays.

2 By yourself, go over the plan and/or draft for your own explorative study. Make sure that you are 'presenting and sustaining a point of view' that is relevant to your title all the way through.

3 In a small group, talk about how the reader is going to be persuaded that you are arguing throughout your explorative study. Make a checklist of Dos and Don'ts, starting with:

- write to the title: don't get sidetracked onto another topic
- write an introductory paragraph setting out the viewpoint you will take
- end paragraphs and sections with a reference back to the title: show the reader 'I'm still on track'.

4 Making sure you quote: some strategies

Remember that you must not generalise in a literature essay: you need to support and illustrate points from the text. However, there are better and worse ways of doing this.

Activity 54

1 As a class, read the following extracts from three explorative studies.

> **Extract 1:**
>
> In 'King Lear', Shakespeare draws frequent analogies between physical blindness and a lack of moral understanding:
>
> GLOUCESTER: I have no way, and therefore want no eyes:
> I stumbled when I saw.
>
> Only when Gloucester becomes blind can he achieve insight into 'how this world goes' and recognise his former short-sightedness in putting his trust in Edmund. He now sees his illegitimate son as 'villain' and his legitimate son Edgar as the 'loyal and natural boy' he really is.

> **Extract 2:**
>
> In 'The Merchant of Venice' Shylock is presented in an ambivalent way. At times, he alienates the audience by showing vengeful malice: 'Let him prepare his bosom for the knife'. At other times, he arouses the audience's sympathy: 'What's his reason? I am a Jew. Hath not a Jew hands, eyes, passions, organs, dimensions? If you prick us, do we not bleed?' Thus Shylock is an ambivalent figure in the play, whereas Volpone is not.

> **Extract 3:**
>
> Hamlet is a thinker, Macbeth is a doer:
>
> HAMLET: Thinking too precisely on th'event.
>
> MACBETH: The very firstlings of my thought shall be
> The firstlings of my hand.
>
> These quotations really bring out the differences between the two characters.

2 Put yourselves in the place of an examiner. Give each extract a mark out of 3 for its use of quotation: 1 out of 3 is poor – doesn't make purposeful use of quotation; 2 out of 3 is fair – quotations show knowledge of the plays; 3 out of 3 is good – quotations develop the argument of the explorative study.

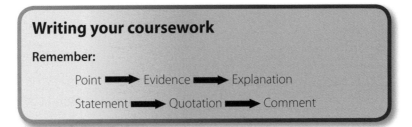

Writing your coursework

Remember:

Point ➡ Evidence ➡ Explanation

Statement ➡ Quotation ➡ Comment

It is a good strategy to integrate short quotations into your own sentences. When you use 'blocks' of quotation, never quote more than two or three lines at the most. Always comment on quotations to show why you have used them: they will not speak for themselves.

5 Making sure you express yourself well: some strategies

Activity 55

1 In a small group, read these three extracts from explorative studies.

Extract 1:

Thus we see that 'The Alchemist' and 'Much Ado About Nothing' compare well, Subtle and Face get off scot free and Claudio does not have to be killed as Beatrice told Benedick to do to him. Another comparison is the comedy of the plays, because in comedies people live happily ever after and in 'The Alchemist' and 'Much Ado' most people do, except of course Sir Epicure Mammon in 'The Alchemist' who says 'I will go mount a turnip-cart'. But this is comedy as well since he had such big dreams for himself earlier on and the idea of him on a turnip cart brings him down to earth with a bump.

Extract 2:

As Harriet Walter, who played Cleopatra for the Royal Shakespeare Company, says: 'She is a great actress; it is part of her "infinite variety" as a woman'. This is apparent at many points in the play, both in what she says herself and in what others say about her. Enobarbus, for example, captures Cleopatra's capacity for self-dramatisation in his almost rapturous speech describing her on her barge:

> The barge she sat in, like a burnished throne,
> Burned on the water: the poop was beaten gold.

Extract 3:

Richard III is presented as a villain; Henry V is presented as a hero. This contrast is brought out well in the way they behave on the night before battle. Richard has bad dreams and is 'visited' by the spirits of those he has wronged and put to death. Henry, by contrast, mingles quietly with his soldiers, boosting their morale and showing that he cares about them as individuals: 'A little touch of Harry in the night'.

2 Give an overall mark out of 5 to each extract for:

   • fluency   • conciseness   • coherence   • accuracy.

   A mark of 5 means 'excellent'; a mark of 1 means 'very poor'.

3 As a class, compare your conclusions from the group work. If there are differences of opinion, resolve them through analysis and argument rather than personal preference.

4 Then draw up two class lists of 'Good features' and 'Bad features' of style and expression in explorative studies.

The more critical commentaries you read and learn from, the more assured your own written style is likely to be.

6 Getting it right

1 Before you hand in your final version, check with your teacher that you are within the word limit agreed. Remember that the maximum word count for your *whole* coursework folder including your creative critical response is 2500 words. This includes quotations.

2 Check that you have correctly attributed all quotations from critics and other commentators. A bibliography at the end should be set out in a consistent format, like this:

Sher, A – *The Year of the King* (Methuen, 1985)

Smith, E – *The Cambridge Introduction to Shakespeare* (Cambridge, 2007)

Tynan, K – *Theatre Writings* (Nick Hearn Books, 2007)

3 If you have word-processed your explorative study, carefully proofread a print out as well as on screen.

4 Make sure you use a font that is easy to read.

F Writing your creative critical response

This section helps you to write your creative critical response. It does this by drawing together the examples of 'formats for writing about drama' in Sections A and D (pages 119–130 and pages 163–172) and giving you guidance on choosing a suitable topic and a suitable format to cater to your skills as a writer, basing on AO1 and AO4, used to assess your creative critical response.

1 Choosing your topic

The key to success in your creative critical response is to write on a topic which expresses a clear viewpoint, has a real purpose and a defined audience, and is linked to one or both plays in your explorative study. It must also meet AO1 and AO4.

You need to strike a sensible balance between being 'creative' and being 'critical'. If you are happy with a conventional theatre review (the sort you find in a quality newspaper) settle on that. If you want to try something more experimental, do so – but be sure it allows you to meet the two Assessment objectives.

Activity 56

1   Read these four examples of creative critical response topics, which have led to successful writing.

a Watch a performance of one of your plays. Read reviews about it by others from the past and/or the present. Then write your own review of the performance, giving your opinion and responding to what others say. (Word count: 500 words)

c Write an outline pitch for the BBC's 'Shakespeare Re-told' series, using the Shakespeare play you have studied. Describe how you would re-tell it for a twenty-first-century viewing audience of teenagers. Explain your reasoning. (Word count: 500 words)

b Script a talk to your class on two very different interpretations of your main play. Comment on the differences and make clear how *you* see the play. (Word count: 500 words)

d Imagine you are directing a difficult scene from one of your plays. Script a talk to give to the actors involved outlining the challenges posed by the scene and how you plan to explore them in rehearsal. (Word count: 500 words)

2   Look through these topics carefully. In a group, talk about:

   a what demands they make on the writer's knowledge of the play(s)

   b the different styles they would need to be written in

   c which, if any, appeals to you as a topic for your own writing.

3   With a partner, discuss possible topics for your own creative critical response. Focus on:

   a how interesting they would be to a reader and how interesting *you* find them

   b what implications there would be for using your illuminator text(s)

   c whether they would meet AO1 and A04.

2 Choosing your format

Your choice of format is critical to the quality of your creative critical response. Give it careful thought and use trial-and-error.

Activity 57

1 Carefully reread the examples of creative critical response formats (pages 127–130 and 169–172).

2 With a partner, discuss which formats would suit your topic and which would not.

Suggest other formats you might try. For example:

- an exchange of letters in the *Times Literary Supplement* between two directors who interpret your main play differently

- extracts from an actor's autobiography giving an account of how they interpreted a lead part in one of your plays and brought this out on stage

- an online post for young people new to Shakespeare, giving them advice about what to look for in a performance of your main play

- a section in a National Theatre programme for a production of one of your plays, persuading the audience that it has important things to say about the modern world.

3 Choose a format for your topic. Make sure that it has a specified purpose and audience and that you have a clear idea of the style in which it requires you to write. It must also allow you to 'demonstrate detailed critical understanding' (AO2) of your play(s).

Don't worry if your 'creative' critical response does not seem terribly original. Marks are given for matching your style to purpose and audience, and for writing coherently, fluently and accurately. As long as your creative critical response topic and format allows you to meet these objectives, it is 'creative' enough.

3 Planning and drafting

Clarify with your teacher the approximate word count of your creative critical response. This will partly depend upon how many words you have used for your explorative study but your aim should be to use no more than 500. The maximum word count for your *whole* coursework folder is 2500 words.

Activity 58

1 Make a 'beginning–middle–end' plan. Here is an example. The writer has imagined she is a theatre director. She is planning the script of a talk to her cast about how to perform the witches in *Macbeth*.

> Beginning: Must avoid caricatures of witches – no pointed hats or broomsticks, etc – will only work if the audience is genuinely frightened – the witches are evil, not Hallowe'en creepies
>
> Middle: Base characterisation on what we know about 'real' Elizabethan witches – use my research here into their rituals, their spells, their links with the devil, the way they were tortured and put to death in Elizabethan times, etc.
>
> End: Must make witches relevant to present day. Who are our modern equivalents, our 'bogey men/women'? Who embodies 'evil' for us nowadays? Start workshop/improvisation into this ...

a their interest value to a reader

b appropriate writing styles for them

c how well they meet AO1 and AO4.

3 Turn your plan into a full-length draft. Ensure that it has a real purpose and targets a specific audience.

Coursework gives you the opportunity to draft your creative critical response and then try it out on 'consumers' – classmates, members of a real theatre audience, online subscribers – and then refine it in the light of their feedback

4 Writing appropriately

Activity 59

1 Read the partly-completed creative critical response draft below.

> **Topic:** An exchange of letters in *The Guardian* Arts section between two directors who have different views about *Measure for Measure*.

Dear Boyd,

I'd like to start by suggesting that *Measure for Measure* isn't at all the 'problem play' you take it to be. It's very clear and unambiguous, in fact, although it does address itself to a moral problem. It's a play about sin and redemption, with the emphasis on redemption. Angelo trespasses against his own strict moral code by his sexual bargain with Isabella: 'Lay down your body to my lust', he says, 'and I'll reprieve your brother'. But the Duke doesn't let it happen, of course. Instead, he acts in the play as a God-figure, guiding Angelo – the fallen 'angel' – towards an awareness of his sin. And, crucially, offering him the chance to repent rather than seek the easy way out through death, which is what Angelo wants.

    I take your point that at times the Duke seems to be presented as a fallible human being rather than as God-like. Yes, as you say, his best-laid plans go wrong. Your observation that he can't forgive Lucio is also well-made. He does condemn him to 'whipping and hanging', hardly a Christian attitude to sin and salvation, I agree.

    But in the end, I would say, Shakespeare does invest him with a kind of divine power, rather as he does Prospero. And like Prospero, he forgives everyone – he dispenses grace in Act 5, doesn't he? ...

2 Apply AO1 and AO4 to this (remember that accurate written expression is a requirement of AO1). How well does it score? How interesting do you find it?

3 Turn part of your draft into a final version. Hand it in and take your teacher's advice.

Activity 60

1 Use AO1 and AO4, plus your own experience of writing in Activity 55, to judge the following extract from a creative critical response.

> **Topic:** A programme note for a sixth-form college production of *The Revenger's Tragedy*, bemoaning the fact that it is so rarely performed.

Thomas Middleton (or is it Cyril Tourneur?) has been badly-served in the theatre. Although performed steadily in its own day, *The Revenger's Tragedy* has had a vote of no confidence for the last 300 years. Within living memory, there has been only one production at Stratford in 1967 (it was allocated a miserly eight performances) and a more recent one at the Swan with Tony Sher as Vindice. Both got rave reviews. So why the reluctance – or should that be 'timidity' – on the part of directors and theatre managers?

Partly, it must be the language. 'Knotty', say some. 'Convoluted and opaque,' say others. Actors notoriously find it difficult. Tony Sher describes speaking the verse as 'like spitting diamonds'. Well, it's a kind of compliment. Yet try 'spitting' this:

> Does the silkworm expend her yellow labours
> For thee? for thee doth she undo herself?
> Are lordships sold to maintain ladyships
> For the poor benefit of a bewildering minute?

Has anyone described joyless sex better? It could be taken from yesterday's tabloid stories.

Here we come to the truly baffling thing about the disappearance of *The Revenger's Tragedy* from modern stages. It illuminates our own day and age with a cold, cynical clarity that box-office winners like *Romeo and Juliet* and *Much Ado* simply can't touch. Ours is a world of fractured morality; so is Middleton's: 'Now cuckolds are a-coining, apace, apace, apace'. Ours is a world where 'lordships' are 'sold' on an almost daily basis: look at Cash for Honours and the late-departed, but not lamented, Tony Blair. If ever a play was (awful word) 'relevant' to the twenty-first century, this is it.

2   Look carefully at these examiners' comments on this creative critical response.

- An appropriate choice of topic and format. Allows the candidate to meet AO4.
- A clear sense of purpose and audience. Allows the candidate to meet AO1.
- A style and register suited to the task. Meets both AO1 and AO4 well.
- A coherent piece of writing: well structured and developed. Meets AO1 well.
- An interpretation is offered, recognising contextual factors. Meets AO4 well.
- A point of view is established: a persuasive approach. Meets AO1 well.

Refer back to these observations before you write the final version of your creative critical response and use them as a checklist.

Activity 61

Put yourself in the place of an examiner. Evaluate the extract below from the final version of a creative critical response. Annotate a copy of it to show what you judge to be good and less good about it.

> **Topic:** A review of a production of *She Stoops to Conquer* for the student *emagazine*.

Well, she stooped but she definitely didn't conquer this reviewer. Billed as 'a sparkling comedy of eighteenth-century manners', Goldsmith's satire on sentiment fizzed briefly, spluttered and died well before the interval in the Cotswold College's forgettable production.

A play based on the comic confusions caused by mistaken identity needs to be slick, fast-paced and crisply acted. Yet here the action dragged, particularly in the lengthy exposition where Goldsmith winds up the spring of misunderstanding between Hardcastle and the two travelling toffs, Marlow and Hastings. Little was made of Marlow's crippling bashfulness with Kate, the stooping conqueror of the title. In fact, the two seemed to be on remarkably easy terms from their first meeting, as a result of which the deft humour of their 'asides' was all but lost.

Only an over-the-top pantomime performance from Mark Crossley as Tony Lumpkin, the slow-witted yet mischievous idiot son, captured the bumptious good humour of a comedy that nowadays seems laboured and far too wordy ...

Glossary of key terms

abbreviation [page 43]
the shortened form of a word or phrase

amphibrach [page 29]
three syllables: one unstressed followed by one stressed and rounded off with one unstressed syllable

anti-structure [page 67]
a term to describe a narrative structure that deliberately appears unconstructed and chaotic, apparently without an overall plan

anapaest [page 29]
a type of metre – three syllables: two unstressed followed by one stressed syllable

ballad [page 11]
a poem that tells a story or describes a series of events, originally sung by a strolling minstrel

blank verse [page 29]
a form of unrhymed poetry written in iambic pentameter

caricature [page 75]
an exaggerated or distorted portrait of a character, presented as such for comic or satirical effect

catastrophe [page 150]
the final phase of a tragedy, involving suffering and death

caesura [page 22]
a slight pause that occurs approximately in the middle of a line of metrical verse

character [page 75]
a person in a novel, film, play or other work of fiction and the qualities they possess

characterisation [page 75]
the description of the distinctive qualities that a character possesses

chronological time [page 64]
the arrangement of narrative events in order, beginning with the earliest events and moving forward in time

chronology [page 157]
the order of events in a narrative

connotation [page 69]
the ideas, feelings or associations that a word suggests in addition to its primary, literal meaning

conventions [page 52]
the traditional rules of writing in a particular genre

craft guilds [page 162]
associations of people working in the same trade, central to town life in medieval Europe

crisis [page 146]
the turning point in a narrative or drama which moves the plot in a new direction

dactyl [page 29]
a type of metre – three syllables: one stressed followed by two unstressed syllables

declarative [page 150]
a type of sentence which makes a statement

demonology [page 158]
the study of evil spirits

dénouement [page 146]
the closing sequence of a narrative or drama, in which events are explained or resolved

dialect [page 61]
a form of language with its own terminology, grammar and pronunciation; often regional or ethnic

dialogue [page 61]
a conversation between two or more people

diction [page 33]
the language a writer gives to a character; the choice of words in a literary text, also sometimes called lexis or vocabulary

domestic [page 154]
referring to a story taking place on a small scale, often involving events within a household

ellipsis [page 33]
'leaving out' in Greek, a phrase or sentence where words are missed out but can be inferred from the surrounding context; three dots to show words are missed out or to indicate suspense

end-stopped line [page 20]
a strong grammatical pause(usually punctuated) at the end of a line of poetry

enjambement [page 20]
a line of poetry which is not *end-stopped*, where the sentence continues to the next line without a grammatical pause or stop

envoi [page 16]
a refrain or summary that comes at the end of a sestina or ballade, often four lines long or half the length of a stanza

epic [page 154]
a large-scale narrative or drama, normally about characters from legend or history

epic poem [page 16]
a lengthy narrative poem that is heroic and written in an elevated style

epigram [page 16]
a short, witty saying usually about an event or a person and written in very compressed language

epilogue [page 58]
a passage at the end of a story/play, commenting on or concluding events

episodic structure [page 67]
a form of narrative or drama in which the plot is presented in distinct consecutive stages

exposition [page 132]
the setting of a scene at the start of a narrative or drama

farce [page 123]
an exaggerated comic drama with an improbable plot

figurative language [page 71]
words that are not being used literally in the text, such as in metaphors or similes, often suggesting a comparison between two things

first person narrative [page 56]
a story that relates events from the point of view of one character, using the pronoun 'I'

flashback [page 64]
a narrative device where the story jumps back in time to an earlier event

flash forward [page 64]
a narrative device where the story jumps forward in time to a later event

focaliser [page 58]
a character through whose eyes events in the narrative are predominantly viewed. There can be different focalisers at different points, or the same throughout

foil [page 75]
a character whose key role is to reveal something about the main character, normally through contrast

foot [page 29]
the basic unit of a metre – certain fixed combinations of weakly and strongly stressed syllables into which the line is divided. Types of feet include **iamb** and **trochee**

form [page 11]
the shape of the poem on the page

formality/informality [page 61]
the way people adjust the tone of their language to suit the situation they are in (see also **register**)

found poetry [page 11]
written by selecting words and phrases from a found object such as an advert, road, sign, article etc. No other words are added and, in strict found poetry, the word order is unaltered

frame story [page 67]
a narrative device where a story surrounds another story, for example revealing how the main narrative came to be told

framing device [page 55]
a technique used by a writer to set the main story in the context of another story

free indirect style [page 56]
the term used when the text mixes elements of the third person report of indirect speech with first person direct speech, allowing the author to be free with the phrasing and to create ambiguity or a colloquial feel for literary effect

free verse [page 11]
poetry that does not use traditional rhyme schemes or metrical arrangements

full rhyme [page 25]
see perfect rhyme

future tense [page 67]
the form of a verb typically expressing something that will occur or exist

generic features [page 52]
the distinctive characteristics of a particular genre

generic structure [page 67]
where the genre itself determines the conventional structure/form of the text

genre [page 52]
a type of writing with its own characteristic form and style

ghazal [page 16]
A popular verse form in Urdu, which is increasingly used in English, consisting of at least five couplets; the first couplet has an *aa* structure with subsequent couplets *ba, ca, da,* etc.

half rhyme [page 25]
see **para-rhyme**

haiku [page 13]
originally a Japanese form, a three-lined poem of 17 syllables often capturing a tiny moment in time

heroic couplets [page 16]
rhyming pairs of lines usually in iambic pentameter with ten alternately stressed syllables and a rhyme scheme progressing *aa bb cc* and so on; the strong rhyme scheme and very regular beat made it a popular choice for satirical or epigrammatic poetry in the seventeenth and eighteenth centuries

iamb [page 29]
the syllabic stress pattern of 'soft <u>hard</u>', the commonest metrical foot in English verse

iambic pentameter [page 18]
a poetic rhythm with five beats to the line: di Dum / di Dum / di Dum / di Dum / di Dum / di Dum

iambic tetrameter [page 29]
a line of four iambic feet, the metre used in most ballad forms

iambic trimeter [page 29]
a line of three iambic feet

idiolect [page 82]
the term for an individual's language or speech patterns

idiom [page 71]
a colloquial or slang expression

imagery [page 11]
the use of descriptive language, including figures of speech, that draws a mental picture or conveys a sensation; a comparison to describe something through simile, metaphor or personification

imperative [page 150]
a type of sentence which gives a command or an instruction

innuendo [page 121]
an implied meaning, normally vulgar or insulting

internal rhyme [page 26]
words that rhyme within a line or adjacent lines rather than at the end of the line

irony [page 33]
language that says one thing but means another

Interludes [page 162]
short moral plays performed in Tudor times in country houses and the Inns of Court in London

kinetic, shape or concrete poetry [page 11]
poems with a distinctive shape or pattern on the page, which reflects the topic

limerick [page 16]
a five-lined poem, which usually tells the story of a character from a particular place, and has a distinctive rhythm and an *aabba* rhyme scheme

linked parts [page 67]
a narrative device where parallel or connected narratives come together at key moments, for example to tell the same story from different points of view

lyric [page 11]
a short poem or song written in the first person expressing a particular emotion or sentiment

main plot [page 154]
the principle events in a drama or a narrative

masque [page 162]
a form of court entertainment, particularly associated with early modern Europe and involving acting and singing and elaborate stage design

metaphor [page 11, 33]
a figure of speech in which an object, person or thing is described in terms of another, without using 'as' or 'like', to suggest a comparison or relationship between the two

metre [page 27]
the dominant pattern of stressed and unstressed syllables that give rhythm to a poem

Miltonic sonnet [page 17]
a sonnet form invented by John Milton using the Petrarchan rhyme scheme but omitting the traditional break between the octave and the sestet

mood [page 42]
a predominant emotion, atmosphere or frame of mind in a composition created through a writer's use of tone

monologue [page 134]
a discourse of one speaker, ranging from a person alone speaking to themselves, to one person addressing a large public audience

motif [page 69]
a recurring and distinctive idea running through a text, such as an image or symbol, or a word, phrase or idea

murder mystery [page 123]
a type of fiction dealing with crimes and their detection, and with criminals and their motives; also known as crime fiction, it contains several sub-genres

narrative [page 50]
a construct in which a sequence of events is selected and recounted for an audience, in speech, writing or visual media;
a story

narrative poem [page 16]
A poem that tells a story or describes a series of events

narrative time [page 64]
the time-scale chosen by a writer for a story, not necessarily following real time

narrative voice [page 55]
the style and language in which a story is told, either first person ('I'), second person ('You') or third person ('He/She')

narrator [page 55]
the person telling the story, either the writer or a character in the story

octet [page 18]
in Petrarchan sonnet form, the first eight lines consisting of two quatrains, rhyming *abba abba*

ode [page 16]
a poem that addresses an object, event or element of landscape or a person, sometimes in an elevated style; modern versions of the form can be witty or even irreverent

omniscient third person narrator [page 56]
a third-person narrator, telling a story from the outside and knowing both everything that occurs and the internal workings of all the characters

onomatopoeia [page 33]
a word whose vocal sound imitates its description, eg buzz, pop

oppositions [page 67]
words that are used in contrast to each other for literary effect

over-the-shoulder narration [page 56]
a narrative technique where the writer presents events from the viewpoint, but not in the voice, of a particular character

oxymoron [page 33]
a contrasting word or phrase that contains two elements with opposite meanings

para-rhyme [page 25]
in poetry, occur where the consonant sounds at the end of lines match, rather than the vowel sounds (eg 'flesh/flash' 'yours/years')

parallel/connected narratives [page 67]
a literary device where several different characters or groups of characters are followed alternately

parody [page 72]
a writer's technique for mocking something through comic imitation

past tense [page 67]
the form of a verb expressing something that occurred or existed previously

patron [page 158]
a person who provides financial support to an artist or artistic project

perfect rhyme [page 25]
where the vowel sounds at the end of lines echo each other exactly (eg 'sash/cash' 'imply/defy')

performance poetry [page 11]
written to be performed to a listening audience, it has a distinctive rhythm and can be about a wide range of topics

personification [page 33]
the representation of a quality or idea as a human figure or having human characteristics

philosophical (context) [page 157]
general ideas about prominent in the period in which a writer lives

plot [page 132]
the main sequence of events in a story

point of view [page 56]
the perspective from which a story is told

present tense [page 67]
the form of a verb typically expressing something occurring or existing now

prologue [page 55]
an introductory passage to a story

proscenium arch [page 162]
a type of theatre design – a large archway at or near the front of the stage

protagonist [page 127]
the leading character in a narrative or drama

punctuation [page 71]
the marks used in writing to clarify its structure and meaning

quatrain [page 16]
a stanza comprising of four lines

realistic [page 75]
something that has been created, such as a character in a novel, that seems true to life

Received Pronunciation or **RP** [page 61]
the accent provided as the standard pronunciation of individual words, also recognised as a marker of social status

register [page 82]
a form of language appropriate to a particular situation or context

representative [page 75]
a character who symbolises an idea in a literary text

resolution [page 150]
how a story finishes, finding an ending/solution to the conflict the story sets out

rhythm [page 11]
the pace and pattern of words and sounds in a piece of writing

rhyme [page 11]
when one sound is echoed by another sound exactly the same or very similar

rhyme scheme [page 16]
The pattern of rhymes in a stanza or section of verse, usually expressed by an alphabetical code

stanza [page 16]
one or more lines making up the basic unit of a poem, separated by a space. Often verse is split up into regular stanzas of two (couplet) three (triplet) or four (quatrain) lines

role [page 75]
the part played by a character in a narrative or drama

satirical (satire) [page 121]
the use of various forms of humour, especially irony and sarcasm, to criticise and bring to light human vices or failings, often in the hope of bringing about improvement

second person narrative [page 56]
a writer's technique for presenting a story be addressing the reader as 'you'

sestet [page 18]
a group of six lines; in Petrarchan sonnet form, the final six lines rhyming *cdcd*

sestina [page 16]
a 39-lined poem with six stanzas and a final three-lined envoi (summary), in which the six words in each stanza are repeated in a set pattern but a changing order

setting [page 78]
the time, location and circumstances where a narrative or drama occurs

sibilance [page 33]
repetition of 's' sounds

sight rhymes [page 25]
half rhymes that look on the page like they should be a full rhyme, but the words actually sound differently when spoken (eg 'now/know', 'plough, trough')

simile [page 33]
a comparison between two things that are not usually compared, using the words 'as' or 'like'

soliloquy [page 138]
a speech made by a character alone on stage, normally revealing their private thoughts and feelings

sonnet [page 11]
a 14-lined poem in iambic pentameter, usually following either a Shakespearian or Petrachan form

Spenserian sonnet [page 17]
a sonnet form invented by Edmund Spenser using three quatrains and a couplet, rhymed *abab, bcbc, cdcd, ee*

spondee [page 29]
a type of metre – two stressed syllables in succession

stagecraft [page 146]
the dramatist's skills in presenting a play's action to the audience

stage emblem [page 146]
a picture created on stage to highlight an important idea in a play

Standard English, SE [page 61]
the form of English considered to be the norm and used as the medium for formal writing, such as in education, government and the law.

stereotype [page 75]
a character who fits into a conventional and predictable type

stock characters [page 162]
familiar characters that are drawn from cultural stereotypes and used in particular genres

story [page 50]
an account of what happens (plot) and who it happens to (character)

stream of consciousness [page 56]
a form of first person narration, where the writer reveals the inner workings of the narrator's mind through a raw and unedited outpouring of thought and feeling

structure [page 11]
the way a piece of writing is constructed and organised

sub-genre [page 52]
a type or style of writing belonging within a broader type or style of writing

subplot [page 154]
a secondary sequence of events in a story, often involving supporting characters

symbol [page 69]
something that is used to represent something else. Concrete things are often used to symbolise abstract ideas

synopsis [page 127]
a brief summary of a work of fiction

syntax [page 33]
the arrangement of words in their appropriate form and in the proper order to achieve phrases, clauses or sentences

tag [page 56]
the words a writer uses to introduce direct speech in a narrative

tense [page 67]
the set of forms of a verb typically expressing the time when something is occurring or existing

theme [page 69]
the ideas or issues raised by the story in a narrative or a drama

theological (context) [page 157]
religious ideas prominent in the period in which a writer lives

third person narrative [page 56]
a technique for presenting a story in the writer's voice, referring to the characters as 'he', 'she', and 'they'

thriller [page 123]
a type of novel, play or film designed to excite the audience and usually involving crime or espionage

tone [page 42]
the quality or character of a voice, the way it expresses a feeling

trochee [page 29]
a type of metre – two syllables: one stressed followed by one unstressed syllable

tyrant [page 158]
a cruel and oppressive ruler

unreliable narrator [page 56]
a narrator who has a partial or biased view of the events s/he reports and therefore cannot be trusted by the reader to be objective

utterance [page 61]
a stretch of spoken language by one person

verbal patterning [page 138]
the arrangement of words into a pattern by repetition or other emphasis in order to highlight a key theme

verse form [page 146]
the generic structure of poetry, eg a ballad, blank verse, a sonnet

vice [page 162]
immoral or wicked behaviour, or weakness of character

villanelle [page 16]
a 19-line poem with an aba rhyme scheme and five three-lined and one four-lined stanzas, in which lines from the first stanza are picked up and repeated in the rest of the poem

virtue [page 162]
behaviour of a high moral standard

vocabulary [page 71]
a body of words, used and understood in a particular language or sphere

voice [page 38]
a term in poetry that refers to the speaker or thinker who is expressing a view, the person who is talking to the reader

volta [page 17]
in sonnet form, a turn of thought in the poem which often occurs after the first two quatrains

Published by:
Pearson Education Limited
Edinburgh Gate
Harlow
Essex CM20 2JE

First published 2008
10 9 8 7 6 5 4 3 2 1
ISBN 978-1-84690-248-2

Typeset by HL Studios, Long Handborough, Oxford

Printed in Great Britain by Henry Ling Ltd., at the Dorset Press, Dorchester, Dorset

We are grateful to the following for permission to reproduce copyright material:

AC Black Publishers for an extract from Educating Rita by Willy Russell published by Methuen Drama 2001. Reprinted with permission; Alan Brodie Representation Ltd for an extract from "Teechers" by John Godber copyright © 1987 John Godber. Reprinted with permission of Alan Brodie Representation Ltd, Fairgate House, 78 New Oxford Street, London WC1A 1HB; Alma Books Ltd for the typewriter poem "The Honey Pot Poem" by Alan Riddell from Eclipse: Concrete Poems published by Calder & Boyars 1972. Reprinted with permission of Alma Books Ltd; Anova Books for the poem "Gunpowder Plot" by Vernon Scannell from New and Collected Poems of Vernon Scannell copyright © Anova Books; Anvil Press Poetry for an extract from the poem "The Cliché Kid", and the poems "Disgrace" and "Mean Time" by Carol Ann Duffy from Mean Time by Carol Ann Duffy published by Anvil Press, 1993. New edition in 1998. Reprinted with permission of Anvil Press Poetry; Autonomedia for an extract from Caliban and the Witch by Silvia Frederici, published by Autonomedia. Reprinted with kind permission; The BBC for an extract from the transcript a panel discussion of Shakespeare's Henry V at the National Theatre broadcast on Newsnight Review on BBC2 copyright © The BBC; Bloodaxe Books for the poems "Evans" and "Children's Song" by R.S. Thomas from Selected Poems 1946-1968 published by Bloodaxe Books 1986; "Childhood Still" by Jackie Kay, from Life Mask published by Bloodaxe Books 2005; and "Arrival" by George Szirtes from Reel published by Bloodaxe Books 2004. Reprinted with permission of Bloodaxe Books; Jean Binta Breeze for the poem "Simple tings" by Jean Binta Breeze published by Bloodaxe Books; Cambridge University Press for an extract from Players of Shakespeare 4 by Robert Smallwood, published by Cambridge University Press 1998. Reprinted with permission of Cambridge University Press; Carcanet Press Limited for the poems "Opening the Cage" by Edwin Morgan from Selected Poems published by Carcanet Press 1985 and "Money" by C H Sisson from Collected Poems published by Carcanet Press. Reprinted with permission of Carcanet Press limited; Curtis Brown Group Ltd for the poem "Praise Song for My Mother" by Grace Nichols from The Fat Black Woman's Poems by Grace Nichols, published by Virago 1984. Reprinted with permission of Curtis Brown Group Limited; David Godwin Associates Ltd for the poem "A Martian Sends a Postcard Home" by Craig Raine, from A Martian Sends a Postcard Home 1979. Reprinted with permission of David Godwin Associates on behalf of Craig Raine; The Edna St. Vincent Millay Society for the poem "Oh, Oh, you will be sorry for that word!" by Edna St. Vincent Millay copyright © 1923, 1951 by Edna St. Vincent Millay and Norma Millay Ellis. Reprinted by permission of Elizabeth Barnett, Literary Executor, the Millay Society; Faber and Faber Ltd for an extract from Habeas Corpus by Alan Bennett published by Faber and Faber Ltd copyright © Alan Bennett 1973; and the poems "Poem" by Simon Armitage from Kid published by Faber & Faber 1992 copyright © Simon Armitage; "Afternoons" and "Mr Bleaney" by Philip Larkin from Collected Poems and The Whitsun Weddings published by Faber & Faber 1998, 1964 copyright © The estate of Philip Larkin; an extract from the poem "Prayer before Birth" by Louis MacNeice from The Collected Poems of Louis MacNeice published by Faber & Faber copyright © The estate of Louis MacNeice; "Mirror" by Sylvia Plath from Collected Poems published by Faber & Faber 1981 copyright © The estate of Sylvia Plath; and "Rain" by Edward Thomas from Collected Poems published by Faber & Faber 1978 copyright © The estate of Edward Thomas; Farrar, Straus & Giroux, LLC for the poem "Midsummer, Tobago" by Derek Walcott from Sea Grapes copyright © 1976 by Derek Walcott. Reprinted with permission of Farrar, Straus & Giroux, LLC; The Gallery Press for the poem "Grandfather" by Derek Mahon from Collected Poems 1999, reproduced with kind permission of the author and The Gallery Press, Loughcrew, Oldcastle, County Meath, Ireland; Henry Holt and Company, LLC and The Random House Group for the poem "Stopping by Woods on a Snowy Evening" by Robert Frost from The Poetry of Robert Frost edited by Edward Connery Lathem copyright © 1923, 1969 by Henry Holt and Company. Copyright © 1951 by Robert Frost. Reprinted by permission of Henry Holt and Company, LLC and The Random House Group; James Kirkup for his haiku "In the Village Pond" by James Kirkup from Shooting Stars, 1992 copyright © James Kirkup; New Directions Publishing Corporation for the poem "The Red Wheelbarrow" by William Carlos Williams from Collected Poems 1090-1939, Volume I copyright © 1938 by New Directions Publishing Corp. Reprinted by permission of New Directions Publishing Corp; News International Syndication for the article "The Cheap Laughs" by Rod Liddle published in The Sunday Times August 2007 copyright © NI Syndication Ltd 2007; Nick Hern Books for extracts from Letters to George by Max Stafford-Clark copyright © Max Stafford-Clark 1989; Year of the King by Anthony Shear copyright © 1985; and Theatre Writings by Kenneth Tynan copyright © The Literary Estate of Kenneth Tynan 2007. Reprinted by permission of the publishers, Nick Hern Books: www.nickhernbooks.co.uk; Oxford University Press for excerpts from two definitions from "Shorter Oxford English Dictionary" 1993 and an extract from Fields of Light: An Experiment in Critical Reading by Reuben A. Brower (OUP 1951) copyright © Oxford University Press. Reprinted with permission of Oxford University Press; Pan Macmillan for the poem "Hoard" by Kathleen Jamie from The Treehouse published by Picador 2004 copyright © Pan Macmillan; The Penguin Group Limited for an extract from 'Blackadder Goes Forth' in Blackadder: The Whole Damn Dynasty by Richard Curtis and Ben Elton. (Michael Joseph 1998) Copyright © Richard Curtis and Ben Elton 1989. Reprinted with permission of The Penguin Group Limited; PFD for the poem "Uncle Jed" by Roger McGough from Sporting Relations copyright © Roger McGough 1974, reproduced by permission of PFD www.pfd.co.uk on behalf of Roger McGough; The Random House Group for the poem "The House" by Matthew Sweeney from The Bridal Suite published by Jonathan Cape, reprinted by permission of The Random House Group Ltd; Rod Hall Agency Limited for the poem "Men Talk" by Liz Lochhead from Four Women Poet's edited by Judith Baxter; Royal Shakespeare Company for the synopsis of the production of Anthony and Cleopatra by Royal Shakespeare Company, 1998. Reproduced with permission; Shearsman Books for the poem "A Fish-Hook" by Gael Turnbull from There are words: Collected Poems by Gael Turnbull, reprinted with permission of Shearsman Books, Exeter; Telegraph Media Group Limited for a review of Twelfth Night by Charles Spencer, published in The Telegraph 8 September 2007 copyright © The Telegraph 2007; and West End Whingers for a blog review of Equus by Peter Shaffer www.westendwhingers.net. Reprinted with permission.

In some instances we have been unable to trace the owners of copyright material and we would appreciate any information that would enable us to do so.